I0824342

Alan Wigness and Janella Reiswig of Wig-Wig Cosplay

LEATHER *in cosplay* FROM HIDE TO HERO

TIPS, TOOLS & TECHNIQUES

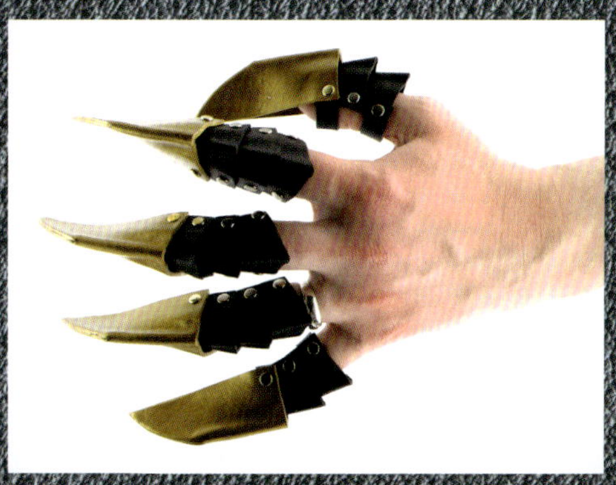

The Huntsman's pouches from *Monster Hunter: World* • Kamura Armor Set's finger armor from *Monster Hunter: Rise* • The Huntsman's knife handle from *Monster Hunter: World*

Publisher: Amy Barrett-Daffin

Creative Director: Gailen Runge

Senior Editor: Roxane Cerda

Cover/Book Designer: April Mostek

Copy Editor: Nordvest LLC

Production Coordinator: Tim Manibusan

Illustrator: Aliza Shalit

Photography Coordinator: Rachel Ackley

Front cover photography by Court Matthies/cremebrulee.cos

Front cover: Jagras Armor and Hunter Rank Armor from *Monster Hunter: World*

Cosplays by Wig-Wig Cosplay

Photography by Charlie M./O2.Supply, unless otherwise noted

Published by FanPowered Press, an imprint of C&T Publishing, Inc., P.O. Box 1456, Lafayette, CA 94549

Library of Congress Cataloging-in-Publication Data is available upon request.

Printed in China

10 9 8 7 6 5 4 3 2 1

Hiccup and Astrid from *How to Train Your Dragon 3*
Cosplays by Wig-Wig Cosplay • Photo by Court Matthies/cremebrulee.cos

Dedication

This book is dedicated to our families, who encouraged our artistic hobbies; to our friends, who cheered us on through highs and lows; to our cat, Peppy, who "supurrvised" each costume we made; and most importantly, to each other.

Keep crafting, keep writing, keep being creative.

ACKNOWLEDGMENTS

We finally understand why authors say that the acknowledgments are the hardest part to write. Writing a book is truly a labor of love, and it cannot be done alone. We poured every moment of time and every ounce of effort into this project, all the while supported by a community of our friends and family who understood when holiday gatherings involved sneaking in an hour or two of writing, when game nights were postponed due to a deadline, and when we would disappear for weeks at a time to ensure that this book would reach its fullest potential. Despite the many pages of words we put together for this book, we're stumped on the language to completely express the gratitude we have for those who helped our dream become a reality.

This book required so many tools and materials to get it to the finish line, and we want to say special thanks to the companies that sponsored us. Thank you Tandy Leather (shout-out to the Roseville store!), Weaver Leather, and Famoré! With your generosity, interest, and support, we've been able to bring leatherworking to another community of crafters.

We also wanted to say thank you to our featured cosplayers whose beautiful work is speckled throughout this book! You inspire many with your passion and skill.

Speaking of photos, we have some seriously incredible friends. Court, you pulled together the most amazing photoshoots for us! We are so happy to be able to include your work as you've been a huge part of our cosplay journey! And Charlie, *thank you!* Seriously, you (and Liz) are the glue that kept this all together and kept us sane. With your camera wisdom and willingness to spend your evenings and weekends with us to see our work across the finish line, you made this book happen. We really developed a bond full of inside jokes, lime time, and blizzard conditions. We cannot overstate your contributions to this book or the sheer amount of effort you've put forward for us and our friendship.

For our beta readers, Alicia, Zorian, Matthew, Kirsten, and Robin, your input made this book improve and grow! We appreciate every comment, every laugh or groan at our terrible puns, and every hour you spent for us.

We've been wanting to publish a book for the cosplay community on leather for years, but we didn't know how to start. Life is full of serendipitous moments and fate, and becoming friends with our fellow C&T author, Annye, is a moment that will always be special in our memory. From a listening ear, to introduction emails, to a writing support group, we thank you for urging us to do the thing!

And lastly, to Roxane and C&T Publishing: Thank you for believing in us and the cosplay community. Your support has allowed us to pass on crafting knowledge for generations to come!

Contents

Introduction to Leather 6

A Brief History of Leatherworking 7

When to Incorporate Leather into Your Cosplay 7

The Pros and Cons of Leather 8

Types of Leather 9

Leather Grain and Cuts 10

Tanning Types 11

Finishes and Other Terms 13

Shopping for Leather 15

Patterning and Cutting 17

Tools: Measure Twice, Cut Once 18

Patterning 20

Transferring Your Pattern to Leather 30

Cutting 30

Carving and Tooling 32

Tools: Carves and Curves 33

Carving 34

Tools: You Know, Tooling Tools 39

Tooling 43

Dyeing, Painting, and Sealing 51

Tools: The Artist's Arsenal 52

Dyeing and Painting 54

Tools: Burn, Baby, Burn(ishing)! 67

Conditioning and Burnishing 68

Tools: Seal It, Lock and Key! 72

Sealing 72

Hand Sewing, Gluing, and Hardware 75

Tools: It's "Sew" Fun! 76

Hand Sewing 78

Gluing 93

Tools: Metal Bits Mostly 95

Hardware 97

Extra Techniques 108

Lining, Strengthening, and Doubling Layers 109

Wet Forming 111

Leather Braiding 113

Laced Edging 119

Distressing and Weathering 121

Antiquing 125

Garment Leather 130

Tools: Gadgets for Garments 131

Transferring and Cutting 133

Sewing Garment Leather 136

Adding Hardware to Garment Leather 148

Painting and Sealing Garment Leather 148

Practice Projects 149

Belt 150

Pouch 153

Bracer 156

About the Authors 159

The Huntsman from *Monster Hunter: World*

Cosplay and work-in-progress photos by WigTall of Wig-Wig Cosplay
Photo of the Huntsman by DonDolce Photography

Introduction to LEATHER

Welcome to *Leather in Cosplay, from Hide to Hero!* This crash course in leatherworking is written by cosplayers, for cosplayers. In these pages, you'll find guidance on which tools to buy to get started, technique descriptions, how-tos, and inspiration. Before we dive in, let's spend a little time talking about leather and when and why to use it in cosplay.

Jin Sakai from *Ghost of Tsushima*

Cosplay and work-in-progress photos by undeadtoasty • Photo of Jin Sakai by Fresh Perspectives (Stephen Hallam&Julia Harrison)

A Brief History of Leatherworking

Leatherworking is old. It was old when agriculture and pottery were invented. Tools thought to be leather scrapers have been dated back hundreds of thousands of years. However, the leather they were once used on has long since deteriorated, making it impossible to know exactly how leatherworking evolved in pre-ancient history. Metal leatherworking tools show up in the archaeological record somewhere around 5000 BCE, in the form of a copper awl found in a burial site in Israel. The oldest preserved leather shoe, found in Armenia, is dated to 3500 BCE.

Throughout the Bronze Age and Iron Age, leatherwork was continuously evolving and growing, and that trajectory did not stop even in the medieval or preindustrial eras. Globally, leather was often used for footwear, as well as for clothing, armor, bags, saddles, and other goods. The tanning process (see Tanning Types, page 11), quality, and quantity of leather produced varied between regions and time periods, and more decorated and finely made leather goods became a status symbol in multiple cultures.

Tanning was done manually until industrialization drastically changed leatherworking. The chrome tan tanning method (see Chrome Tan, page 12) was invented in 1858 and quickly became the dominant process due to its speed and cost-efficiency. With more chrome tan leather on the market, production of leather goods like gloves, purses, luggage, and modern-style shoes became easier. Leather once again became an everyday material. Now, leather has to compete with plastics, which have pushed into the spaces previously occupied by leather, with materials like vinyl, polycarbonate, and nylon, which are cheaper to produce. Due to its higher relative price, leather has moved into the artisan and luxury goods space.

EMERGENCE IN COSPLAY

Though leather has always been present in the general fashion market and in costuming (theater, movie, and hobby), it has been fairly uncommon in cosplay. To our delight, this is rapidly changing! As cosplay has grown in popularity, the resources available to cosplayers have multiplied. Conventions are more highly attended, with the majority hosting a form of craftsmanship competition. From these competitions came a push in the competitive space to create more of one's costume from scratch, demonstrating both well-known and niche techniques. So, the presence of leatherworking grew from something mainly used by cosplayers with prior experience from reenactment or other hobbies into a craft learned specifically for cosplay. Leatherworking has joined the host of techniques in a cosplayer's arsenal, and we're hoping this book makes it even more accessible to the community.

When to Incorporate Leather into Your Cosplay

Leather is commonly used for belts, pouches, nonmetal armor, and footwear. Dive into leatherwork by replacing pleather or foam when making some of these items. Many will translate smoothly to leather and be more durable. Just watch out if you decide to make a pair of shoes—they're a step up in difficulty compared to most leather projects. Cordwaining (often mistakenly called cobbling) would be a book on its own!

If you're looking for guidance on where to start, our answer is: belts and pouches. These are common, useful, and straightforward leather projects. Both are utilitarian and allow you to practice several techniques. They can also be used as part of your daily wardrobe or at special events. We've definitely worn cosplay leather projects to weddings and Renaissance festivals! To get you inspired and started, check out the practice projects at the end of the book.

Note: *Many costume designs draw from historical sources, which often include leatherworking. If your character's outfit is inspired by a specific time period or setting, researching how leather was used in that era can help you achieve an authentic look. You might even discover a cool new (old) technique!*

The Pros and Cons of Leather

Leather is a great material, and we love it dearly, but we'd be remiss not to touch on the pros and cons. One of the most important aspects to consider when working with leather is sourcing. Ultimately, leather is an animal product, and an animal had to lose its life to create it. The vast majority of leather is sourced as a by-product of the meat and dairy industries. Because the main financial incentive to raise these animals is for the food they provide, it is likely they would be raised whether or not the leather industry exists. But leather production still plays a part in the animal's total value and the decision to raise them. There's an ethical sliding scale present just as there is with all animal product consumption. How was the animal treated? How sustainable is the farm the animal came from? What about the processing plant and working conditions? The answers to these questions are often fairly opaque, but there are leather businesses centered around ethical sourcing. Seek them out if this is particularly important to you, or consider buying secondhand.

CONS

Cost: Leather is usually more costly than synthetic materials like vinyl. You'll also need at least a few specialized tools to get started.

Durability: Leather is tougher than foam or thermoplastic, which makes it more difficult to cut and handle. Many techniques require the use of brute force or fine dexterity, which can be a barrier for some people.

Unforgiving: Compared to foam and fabric, small mistakes made with leather can be very difficult or impossible to undo.

Environmental impact: While the biodegradability of leather is questionable and opinions differ from research paper to research paper, in practice the tanning process itself leaves a bigger impact than the leather it creates because the chemicals used are harmful when not handled and disposed of properly. Some tanners are more environmentally conscious or subject to regulation than others, but many tanneries (like other industrial plants) operate in countries with weak environmental regulations.

PROS

Authenticity: It's easier to use leather where a character would, instead of making one material look like another, such as manipulating foam or vinyl to mimic leather. As a natural fiber, leather has the additional bonus of breathability, keeping you cooler at those summertime conventions!

Durability: Leather is tougher than foam or thermoplastic and can stand up to the wear and tear of a typical convention. You can confidently walk convention hallways or do some squats! The more you wear your leather, the better it will conform to your body, and multiple wears often creates an authentic patina.

No "sand and prime" cycle: Foam and thermoplastics are fun and can create amazing things, but the repeated cycles of priming and sanding to obtain a smooth finish can be time-consuming and stressful. While sanding is a step in some leatherworking projects, it is not always essential.

Time: We've found that the full process for making an item out of leather is usually faster than using alternative materials, mostly due to less time required for prepping before painting or dyeing.

Resources and techniques: There is an enormous wealth of knowledge available in print and online about leatherworking!

Environmental aid: We're more apt to talk about the harm a material can cause our planet, but if animal hides from the meat industry were not used for leather, they would likely go to waste. Also, leather lasts a *long* time. We find ourselves tossing out foam builds (which are definitely not biodegradable) that have deteriorated or broken apart over time, but our leather pieces last much longer when taken care of and stored properly, even if worn frequently. Because leather lasts, you can find it secondhand and often in a workable condition, ready for another life as a new creation.

Types of LEATHER

Shopping for leather in a store or online can feel like trying to navigate a foreign country. Terms and labels distinguish the different options, but they aren't helpful if you don't know the lingo.

Isobel from *Baldur's Gate 3*

Cosplay and work-in-progress photos by Tacocat Cosplay • Photo by Wild Momo Photography

Leather Grain and Cuts

Our first term is *grain*, which is the side of the hide that was on the outside of the animal. The opposite side is called the *flesh* side, because it faced the animal's flesh. On most leather cuts the flesh side will have loose fibers, making it appear fuzzy.

A hide's thickness varies significantly, and the hide often has marks and mars. Based on these and other factors, the tannery chooses whether and how to separate the hide into layers, called *splitting*, resulting in more than one end product. In many cases, it is split into two pieces before the bottom layer is trimmed to a uniform thickness. Other times, it may only be trimmed and not split, or even split more than once. These different splits have different names when sold. Regardless of whether they were split, pieces of leather that include the grain side of the hide are either full grain or top grain.

Full grain: This is when the grain side has not been sanded or embossed. Full-grain leather is durable because it retains the tough outer layer of the hide. It also retains any marks made on this outer layer. In the fashion industry, hides with very few imperfections are often processed into full-grain products, which has created a conception that full grain means the best quality. While this is sometimes true, the term does not inherently mean that a hide is of high quality. Realistically, full grain is the cheapest way to process a hide, because no extra steps are taken to remove blemishes. Cheaper veg tan hides are often full grain, and they show all their individual imperfections.

Top grain: Used for leather products where the grain side has been sanded and buffed, embossed, or otherwise modified during processing. Top grain is a good choice when you want uniformity or when you need an embossed pattern. Most chrome tan is top grain.

Split or suede: Leather products made with any split that does not include the grain side are simply called *splits*. Some splits are then refinished to a smoothness that resembles top grain. Many others are left with a distinctive fuzzy finish, and are collectively called *suede*. Splits are usually soft and pliable, making great liners and texture additions to a project.

THICKNESS

The thickness, or *weight*, of a piece of leather is expressed either in ounces or in millimeters. Historically, the weight of a square foot of leather offered an understanding of the average thickness. Now, the weight corresponds directly to thickness, with each ounce equalling 1/64″ (0.4mm). Even though technology for leather splitting is more effective, leather still varies a bit in thickness, so it is marked as a range, such as 3–4 oz. As a rule of thumb, thin leather is 2–3 oz., medium thickness leather (sturdier but still thin) is 4–7 oz., and thick leather is 8 oz. or more, which has bulk and toughness.

Weight	Thickness	Common Uses
2–3 oz.	1/62″–3/64″ (0.8–1.2mm)	Appliqués, lining
4–5 oz.	1/16″–5/64″ (1.6–2mm)	Embossing, pouches
6–7 oz.	3/32″–7/64″ (2.4–2.8mm)	Belts, bags, pouches, armor
8 oz. or more	1/8″ (3.2mm) or more	Belts, shoe soles, armor

HIDE CUTS

A leather hide may be cut up in a number of ways before sale. Different parts of the animal will behave in different ways, so it's wise to know where you're cutting from for each piece you make.

Leather along the spine of the animal is the firmest, with the least amount of give and stretch. As you work your way away from the spine, the leather becomes a bit less firm. When you get to the belly portion, you get skin that expanded and contracted much more than the rest of the hide, resulting in stretchier, less consistent behavior. This is especially true for veg tan hides, where belly leather is prone to creasing when bent or shaped.

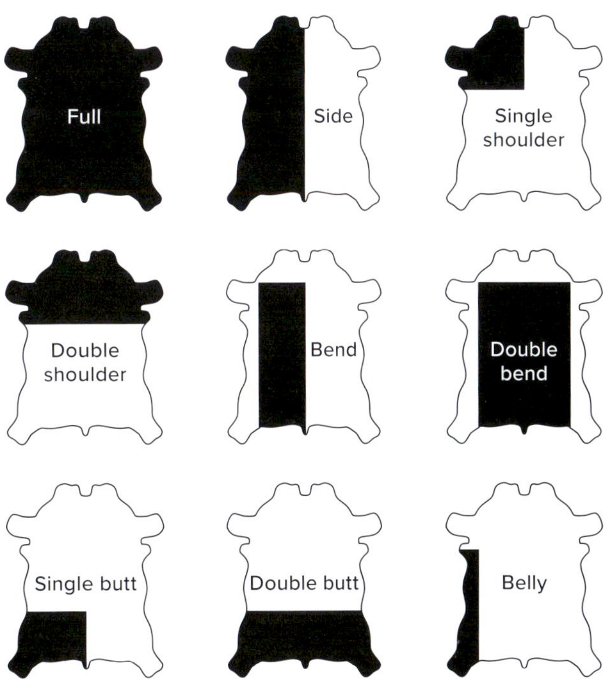

Tanning Types

How a hide is tanned affects its properties and possibilities, so it's almost always part of the name or description of any piece of leather being sold. Chrome tan and vegetable tan are by far the most common commercial tanning methods, so that's where we focus our attention.

Note: *Brain tanning, or smoke tanning, is one other option to consider for specific projects. This method has been used by various peoples throughout history. It results in a soft, supple, and a little bit stretchy end product that is somewhat resistant to water. Brain tanned hides have a natural coloration and generally do not dye. You can use brain tanned leather in place of chrome tan or garment leather when you want a more natural look.*

VEGETABLE TAN (VEG TAN)

We won't go into scientific detail on how it works, but vegetable tanning uses tannins from plants to change the properties of a hide, making it durable and preventing rotting. Veg tan leather was the dominant form of tanning in medieval Europe, so it's often what fanstasy character designers envision when drawing and modeling items such as armor or sheathes.

It's easy to customize veg tan. It can be dyed a variety of colors (see Dyeing and Painting, page 54), and you can carve unique patterns and designs straight into the leather (see Tooling, page 43). On the other hand, it takes multiple steps to go from raw veg tan to a finished product.

Veg tan also needs to be conditioned and/or sealed after being worked. It is prepped for decoration and dye before sale, but it is still vulnerable to oxidation and drying out. Veg tan that is not conditioned or sealed will deteriorate over time.

Vegetable tan

CHROME TAN

Chrome tan tanning uses chromium-based chemicals to alter the hide. This process is much faster and cheaper than veg tanning, and it results in a pliable end product. Chrome tan is the go-to for leather clothing like gloves and jackets, as well as accessories such as wallets and bags. Characters from modern settings are more likely to have chrome tan items, though heavyweight veg tan is still used for sturdier items like belts and gun holsters.

Chrome tan comes pre-dyed and does not need to be sealed (unless you paint or add additional dye colors to it), which allows you to finish your project with fewer steps. It can be purchased pre-textured or with an embossed pattern, but similar to searching for the right fabric for a project, you may need to hunt around to get chrome tan that matches your needs.

Garment or Fashion Leather

Garment leather is a term used to refer to a subset of chrome tan leathers. While there's no technical definition, you can consider any chrome tan that can be sewn on a domestic sewing machine to be garment leather. Because it is easily sewn, it's a very useful cosplay material, which we cover in detail in Garment Leather (page 130).

Lamb is a common garment leather. It comes in a wide variety of colors due to its popularity and is extremely soft. It can be less durable than other forms of garment leather due to its thinness.

Deer is also on the softer side and boasts a good amount of stretch. This makes it useful as a glove leather when retaining dexterity is important.

Goat is another easily found garment leather. It's considered a well-balanced leather with strength and softness. Goat leather is popular in bookbinding.

Pig leather is another durable garment leather, which is a bit tougher than goat but less soft or supple. It has a pebble-like texture, which gives it a different look when compared to other garment leathers.

Finishes and Other Terms

When shopping for leather, you'll see a wide range of terminology, and different carriers label their products in completely different ways. It can be pretty overwhelming not knowing what each means or does. Here we'll highlight a few established terms to help you sort through it all.

Aniline: A family of dyes that penetrate the leather rather than coat it. Aniline dyeing highlights flaws and mars, so it's often used on hides with fewer marks. Semi-aniline has been covered in a protective layer after being aniline dyed. Aniline dyes are most often used on furniture leather, but they may be used on other types of leather, whether marked as aniline or not.

Embossed: Both veg tan and chrome tan leathers might be embossed, meaning that a pattern has been pressed into the leather before sale. This could be anything from a basket weave to a faux alligator skin finish.

Exotics: The term *exotics* is used to refer to less typical leather products. The exact definition varies, but this category is where you'll find things like stingray and crocodile leather.

Note: *There are a couple other animals that, though not exotic, are less common. The first is water buffalo, which is a robust leather sporting a unique grain pattern. The second is kangaroo, which is notable for its combination of strength, light weight, and pliability. It's fairly expensive in the United States, though.*

Dimitri from *Fire Emblem: Three Houses*
Cosplay by Zavage Cosplay • Photo by Jacqueline Zhou/Yin Photography

Fur-on: Fur-on refers to any hide that has been tanned without removing the fur from the grain side.

Grade: Veg tan is often graded by the distributor for tooling quality and lack of marks on the hide. Grading is not universal, so each grading scale should be treated separately. For us, the grade is often irrelevant because we'll be adding weathering!

Milled: Milled leather is any leather that has gone through the milling process, designed to prevent it from stiffening, resulting in a soft and supple end product.

Napa or nappa: These terms are used for a chrome tan hide, generally full grain to retain relative toughness, designed and tanned to be extremely soft and pliable. It is thin and often sourced from younger animals such as calves, lambs, or kids.

Nubuck: Nubuck is a top-grain leather that has been finished to have a slight nap or fuzz, similar to velvet. It's used to add texture while retaining the strength of the grain.

Oil tanned and pull-up: These products have been treated with oil (oil tanned), wax (pull-up), or in many cases both to purposefully create lighter and darker areas on the hide. This intentional patina gives these leathers a vintage or aged look, even on new items.

Printed: Printed hides have patterns painted on them before sale. You might find floral patterns, zebra stripes, or even glitter prints.

Rawhide: Rawhide is hide that has been treated and dried, but not actually tanned. It is thin, light, and tough. Working with rawhide is a different process than working with tanned leather, so do your research if you want to try using it.

Sheepskin or shearling: Sheepskin is leather from a sheep, tanned to still have the wool attached. Shearling is technically the lambskin version, but the two terms have become interchangeable over time.

Shell cordovan and patent: These are two types of leather with glossy finishes specifically designed for footwear.

Another component of a product name you might encounter when shopping for leather is the color. Sometimes the color name is obvious, other times the color might be a cool, Old West-inspired moniker for a specific shade of brown.

Shopping for Leather

In many ways, leather shopping is like fabric shopping. There are a number of online options, but there is always a chance for some variance between what a product seems like in photos and how it is in reality. This is especially true for leather because each hide is sourced from a different animal with its own unique characteristics.

For this reason, we prefer to head to a retail outlet whenever possible, so we can see and touch what we're buying before purchasing. Some smaller businesses are warehouse-based but allow scheduled visits for in-person shopping. If you happen to live near or in a large city with a textile district, you'll find a number of leather outlets catering to the fashion industry, which carry a good variety of leather; these are some of the best sources for garment leather. The most prolific leather retail chain in North America is Tandy Leather, with locations in many major cities across the United States and Canada.

Websites: *As of the writing of this book, here are a few starting points for sourcing leather online (at least for North Americans). Each of these examples also has one or more retail outlet in the United States. Visit if you're nearby.*

- *Global Leathers & Leather Skins, leatherskins.com, retail location in New York.*
- *Rocky Mountain Leather Supply, rmleathersupply.com, retail location in Utah.*
- *Springfield Leather Company, springfieldleather.com, retail location in Missouri.*
- *Tandy Leather, tandyleather.com, tandyleather.ca, and tandyleather.eu, retail locations in the United States, Canada, and Spain.*
- *The Leather Guy, theleatherguy.org, warehouse location in Minnesota.*
- *Weaver Leather Supply, weaverleathersupply.com, retail location in Ohio.*

NAVIGATING THE STORE

There are three common ways for leather to be displayed: hung, stacked, or rolled. When leather is hung, it's quite easy to inspect the hide. Feel free to touch and check the product. When leather is stacked, you may need to dig through the stack to find what you want. Here again, feel free to go through the pile and find a hide you like. When leather is rolled, you should ask to inspect before unrolling the product. Most places are fine with you unrolling whatever you like, but some prefer you make selections before you start unrolling everything or cutting twine, or they may want to have employees unroll it for you.

Hung | Stacked | Rolled

If you're at a location that sells tools, dyes, hardware, and other accessories, these products will usually be clearly marked and labeled, making it easy to find what you're looking for. For guidance on what products to buy initially, look for the "Essentials" headers within the technique chapters. In those sections, we'll outline the starting point for tools and materials needed for different leatherworking steps.

Patterning and CUTTING

Those of you who have experience working with foam will find this chapter familiar because foam and leather are neighbors in terms of rigidity and malleability. If you have no foam experience, don't fret! This chapter walks you through patterning, which is the initial design process in figuring out what shapes and pieces you'll need to complete your project. It also guides you through your options when cutting your leather, focusing on tools and methods. It's the first hands-on leatherworking chapter. Let's dive in!

Note: *The following five chapters guide you through the process of working with the majority of leathers, but working with garment leather is a much different process. If you're working with garment leather for your project, skip ahead to Garment Leather (page 130).*

Loki from the *Marvel Universe*, inspired by concept art by Aleksibriclot
Cosplay by Silhouette Cosplay • Photos by Sennedjem Cosplay

Tools: Measure Twice, Cut Once

True to the old adage, measuring and measuring again will be your strength when it comes to prepping for your project. We won't try to fool anyone—leather can be expensive. So, let's go over what tools you can use to master your measurements and cut with confidence.

ESSENTIALS

Fabric measuring tape: The best way to measure 3-D objects or curves.

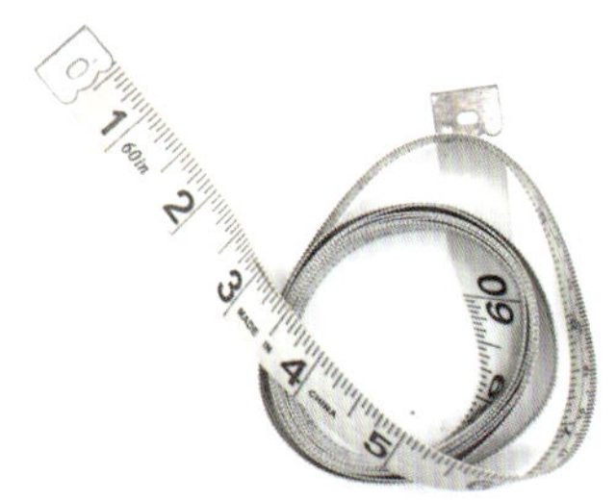

Ruler or straightedge: Useful for measuring, marking, and cutting straight lines.

Writing tool: Pencil, pen, or other option; you'll need something to write and draw patterns with.

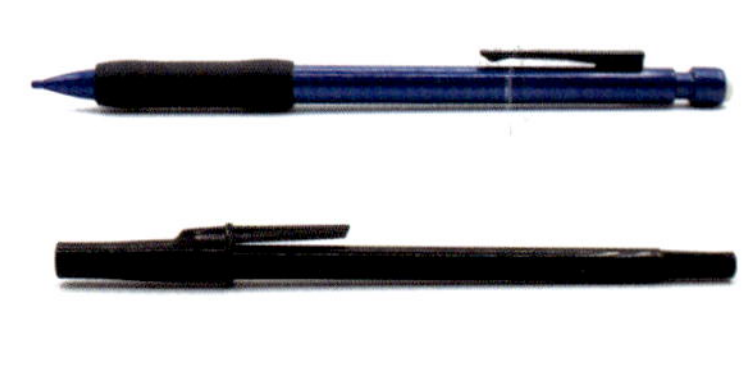

Scissors: To cut your pattern out of paper.

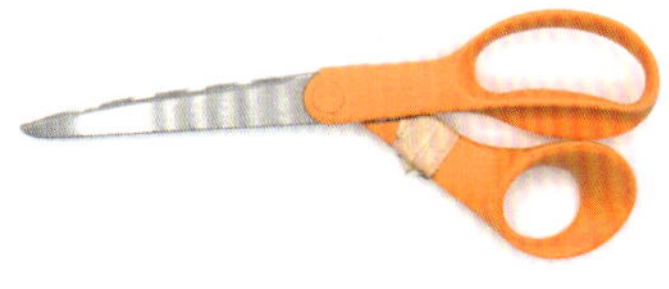

Marking tool: We strongly recommend water-soluble marking pens for drawing your cut lines on leather. Other ink-based marking tools may work, but some inks leave permanent lines that can be visible even after dyeing.

Utility knife (box cutter): Our preferred tool for cutting.

Leather shears: Popular tool for cutting leather. Technically, you don't need both these and a utility knife—you just need one good cutting tool.

Tape: For taping your paper patterns together.

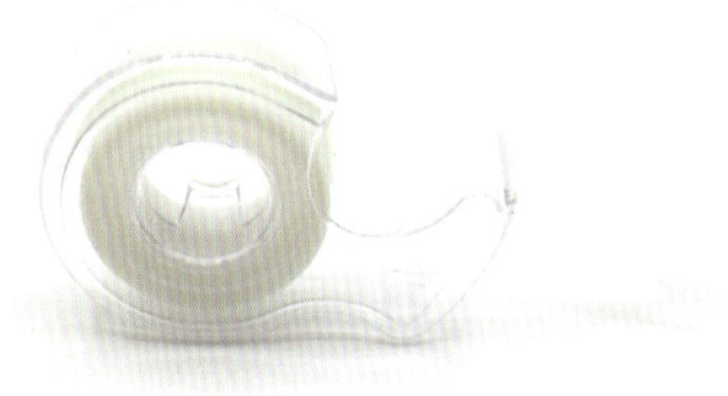

OPTIONAL

Homemade leather ruler: Used to measure around curves and account for leather thickness. You'll find the optional Mini Project: Make a Leather Ruler (page 21) later in this chapter. We recommend making one!

Craft paper/contractor paper: Good paper choice for paper patterning, though you can try it with printer or notebook paper first.

Note: *We like using craft paper/contractor paper because it emulates the bend of veg tan leather and is a heavier paper. It also comes in huge rolls. Efficient and cost-effective: a cosplayer's dream!*

Cling wrap: Used in the duct tape pattern making method.

Duct tape: Used in the duct tape pattern making method.

Permanent marker: Our recommended marker for the duct tape pattern making method.

Painter's tape: Helpful for taping down cling wrap without leaving residue.

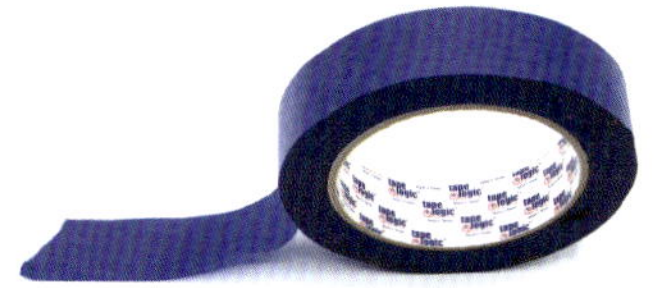

French curve: Helpful for drawing curved lines on self-drafted patterns.

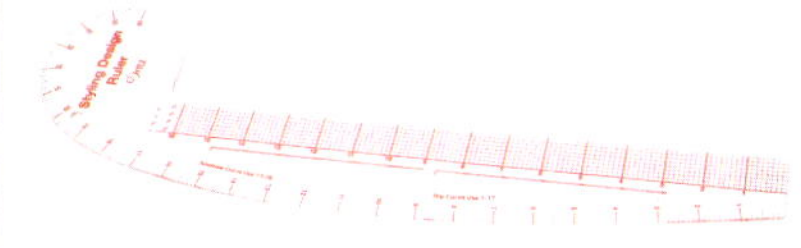

Seam gauge: Helpful as a quick way to add or subtract a specific amount from an edge or point on self-drafted patterns.

Strap cutter: Speeds up the process of cutting multiple belts and straps. Also helps with ensuring consistent cuts.

Rotary cutter: Used to assist with cutting long, straight lines in thin to medium-weight leather.

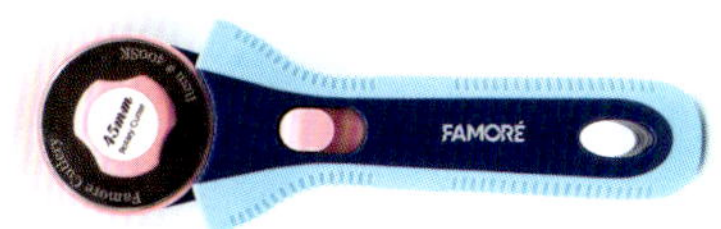

Craft knife: Good for making smaller, more detailed cuts.

Specialty leather knives: A number of knives are specifically designed for leather cutting, such as skiving knives and round head knives. These knives are pretty cool and effective, but they're expensive and not required. Take a look at them if you get really into leatherworking!

A rounded blade reduces contact surface, making cutting easier.

A straight blade helps with precision and even cuts.

Straight snips: A more expensive shears-style option, which we've found cuts more cleanly. We personally use these quite often on thin and medium-weight veg tan.

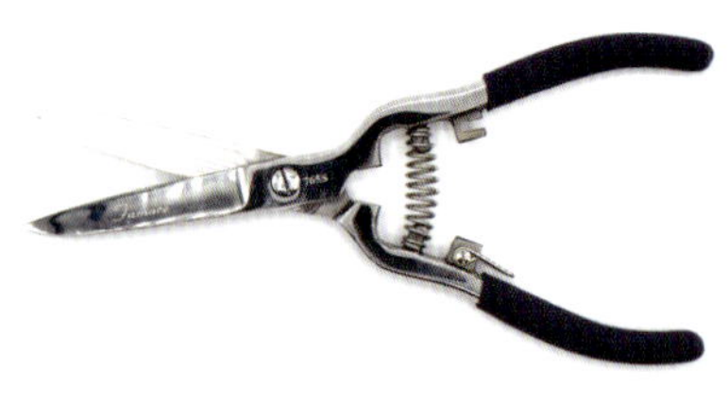

Patterning

Making a pattern is the first step in any leather project and arguably the most important. After all, if the project doesn't fit or the straps turn out to be too short, it can cause rework, or in the worst-case scenario: scrapping the whole piece. As mentioned, leather can be expensive, so we like to spend ample time in the patterning phase to ensure we're not wasting material later. Just as with sewing, making a mock-up or two can save you strife and money in the end.

TIP

If you're going to be water-shaping your leather with water hotter than room temperature, it will shrink the leather, which will need to be accounted for in the pattern. Read Wet Forming (page 111) to determine how much you need to adjust.

Original design of Fire Lord Zuko from *Avatar: The Last Airbender*
Cosplay and photo by Sanit Klamchanuan

HOW MUCH EXTRA TO ADD

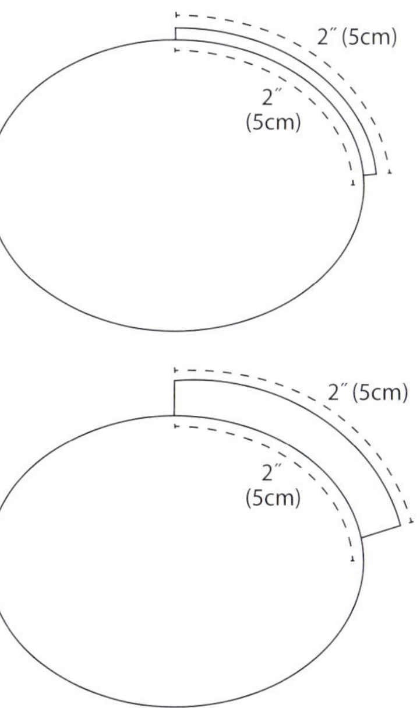

When measuring around a curve, the thickness of the leather will determine whether you need to add to your initial measurement. This is because paper or duct tape patterns are built at the base of a curve, but when a rigid material with thickness is pulled over a curve, the outside edge must follow a longer curve than the original measurement, which in turn compresses the inner edge while the outer edge travels a farther distance. This results in the cut piece not reaching around the originally measured distance of the curve and ending up too short.

Leather isn't a super-thick material, so the amount you need to add usually isn't much. For example, Alan's wrist measures 7″ (17.7cm) using a tape measure.

When he wraps it with medium-weight leather, he needs 7⅜″ (18.7cm) of leather. Often, if you just add a bit extra to measurements with curves you'll come out okay. However, if the piece needs to come out exact or you'd rather skip the guesswork, you can instead make a leather ruler and use it to get a precise measurement.

MINI PROJECT: MAKE A LEATHER RULER

Measuring around a curve can be more guesswork than some people are comfortable with. Here's another helpful tool—that you can make!—that will win back confidence in your measuring time and time again. We present: the leather ruler! Much like foam crafters recommend making a foam ruler to help account for the thickness of foam, we recommend making yourself a leather ruler in the leather thickness you plan to use on your project so you can quickly measure curves.

1. Take the leather you're using for your project and cut a strip, approximately ½″–⅝″ (13–16mm) wide and 20″ (50cm) long. We chose this length because it encompasses many small and large projects that you may find yourself making, but you can easily make shorter or longer rulers. If you have multiple types of leather for your project, we recommend making a ruler from each, especially if they fall into different leather weight categories.

2. Measure something! We recommend your wrist. Take your leather strip and wrap it around your wrist. Using a water-soluble pen, mark where the leather would meet flush.

3. Put your leather ruler aside and measure your wrist with a fabric measuring tape, noting where the tape meets flush.

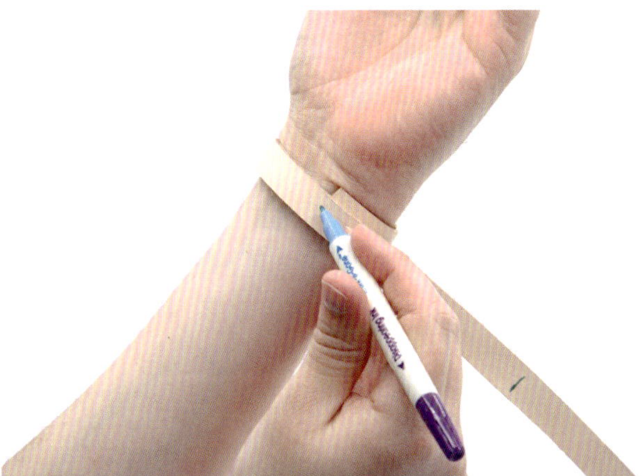

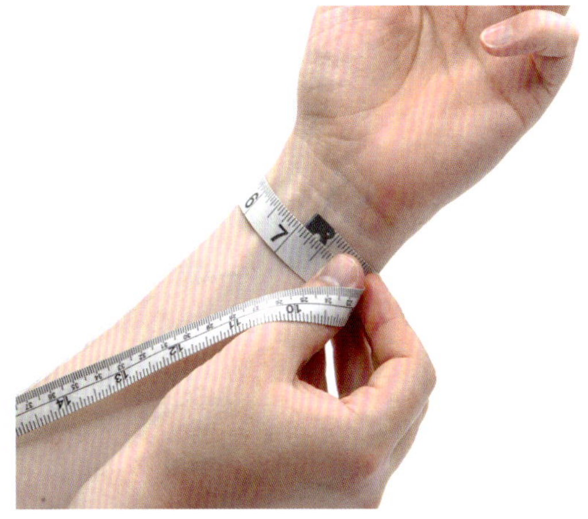

4. Place your measuring tape, noting your measurement, next to your leather ruler. Now compare! The difference may not be much, but it is enough to cause problems for a leather pattern if not taken into account.

There you have it! Your own leather ruler. You'll use this when drafting your own patterns, so keep it close by.

ORGANIZING HACK

If you find yourself misplacing your leather rulers or amassing a few over time, consider punching a small hole with a stitching hole punch (page 76) and looping a cord or piece of yarn through the opening. Now they're neatly together, but you can still separate them if needed for any project you may do! Leaving a note about the weight can also help with future projects.

COMMERCIAL PATTERNS

The prospect of messing up in the patterning step can be daunting, but thankfully there are plenty of commercial leather patterns out there that you can use to bypass a lot of the pressure. Using a commercial pattern as a base is a great way to get your initial shape or structure. For prop items like bags or pouches, you can usually use a commercial pattern as is, with little to no modification. For fitted items like sheaths and holsters or body-fit items like corsets or bracers, you'll have to make some alterations to ensure the pattern works for your or your prop's measurements specifically (see Adjusting Your Pattern, page 28).

Note: *Be sure to read the instructions and suggested type(s) and weight(s) of leather needed for the project, as well as any additional hardware, tools, or supplies you may need to complete the project.*

The downside of commercial patterns is that they may not be close enough to what you're looking for, which happens often in cosplay as we're trying to create very specific fantastical items and outfits. If you're in a situation where you can't find a good starting pattern, you may want to try drafting your own pattern.

SELF-DRAFTED PATTERNS

There may come a time when you run into a leather project where the design does not exist commercially or it can't be made without heavily modifying a commercial pattern. This is when your measuring tools will be called upon to make a self-drafted pattern (a pattern from scratch).

Not Only for the Experienced: *Self-drafted patterns are not locked behind skill level! Depending on what you are making, you might draft your own patterns from scratch or modify existing patterns to achieve the look you want, even on your very first leather project!*

PATTERNING YOUR FIRST DRAFT

There are plenty of ways to make a self-drafted pattern. The following three methods are ones we use to tackle our projects, and we find they allow for great versatility. To walk you through each type, we'll draft a pattern for a basic bracer. Once you're familiar with these patterning methods, feel free to mix and match as needed for your project. No one method is superior, and sometimes they can be better when used together!

Duct Tape Method

In this method, you wrap a part of your body or an existing part of your costume in cling wrap and duct tape to create a layer that you can draw on. You then draw your pattern shapes on the duct tape layer, carefully remove it, and cut out the pattern piece or pieces for more fine-tuning.

Note: *If you're covering a large section of your body (for example, your full torso), a helper may ensure a better fit in hard-to-reach places. Make sure before starting that both you and your helper will be comfortable working in the areas that need to be wrapped.*

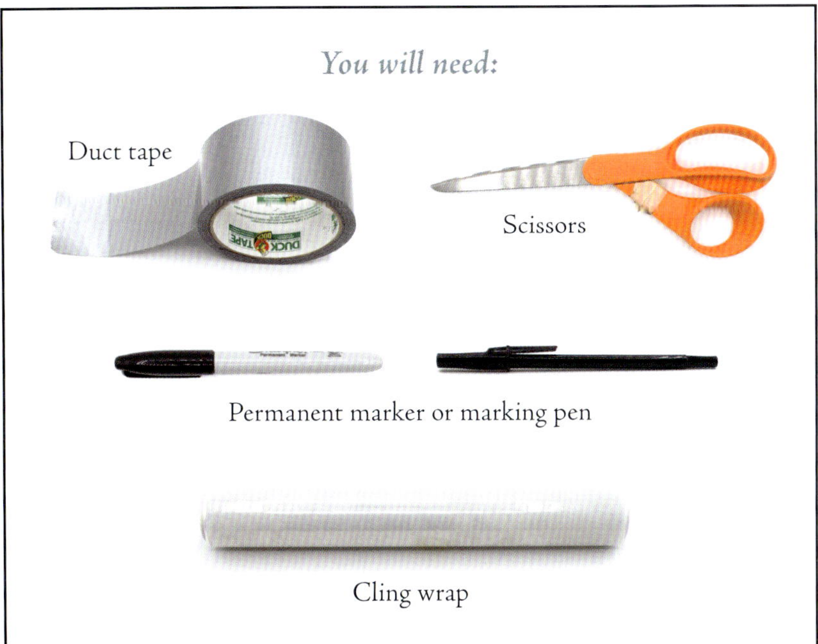

Arya Stark from *Game of Thrones*
Cosplay by SearinCosplay • Photo by Kai Mollerud

1. Begin prepping the area by covering or wrapping the surface with cling wrap. Do not wrap too tightly.

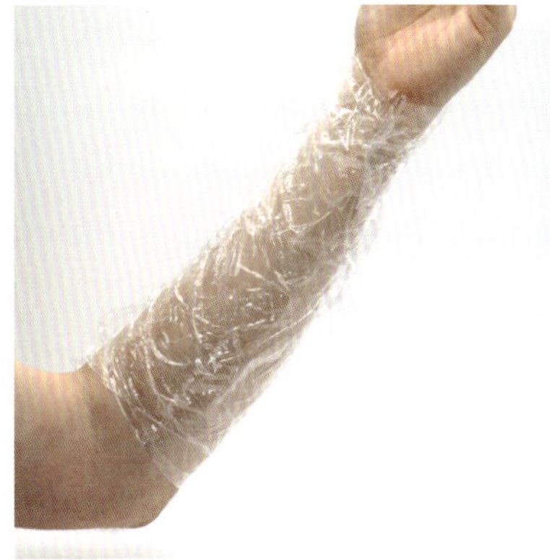

If you're going to be wearing your leather piece over clothing, try to wear either the actual piece of clothing or something similar while you wrap. This ensures that your leather fits over any extra bulk added by your clothing and doesn't bump into other costume pieces and/or restrict your mobility.

PUMP THAT IRON!
Engaged Muscles versus Disengaged: *When patterning your leather, especially on yourself, it is important to remember that your muscles flex, becoming larger or smaller based on what you're doing. Sitting? Your thighs expand. Bending your elbows? Your biceps expand. It is crucial to see if your pattern will work in both engaged and disengaged muscle states.*

TIP

You can use gaffer's tape or painter's tape to secure cling wrap onto items that you aren't fully wrapping and don't want to leave residue on (duct tape can leave some sticky ick behind). We don't want to damage parts of our costume while creating another!

2. Cut strips of duct tape. Make sure your strips are not too long—longer pieces of duct tape quickly become cumbersome to wrap evenly. The amount of tape you need is dependent on how large an area you're covering. It is always better to have more prepared than less. We do not recommend leaving the duct tape on the roll and using it in one continuous strip.

TIP

Duct tape sticking together? Hang it off table edges or a countertop, even a bookshelf or desk will work. However, don't adhere it too well to the surface because you want it to easily unstick when you need the strip.

3. Begin wrapping duct tape pieces over the cling wrap. Be sure to overlap the pieces of duct tape for full coverage. Do not pull the duct tape while wrapping or wrap too tightly as that can cause mismeasuring and warping of the final pattern.

4. Draw your shape outline. On our bracer, we marked the top, bottom, and where we want to split it for lacing.

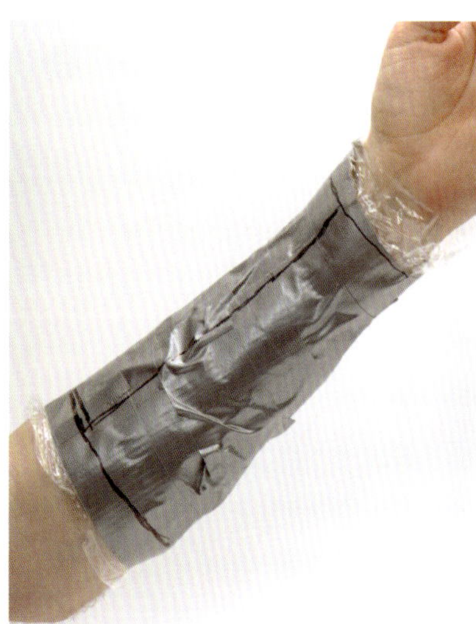

5. Draw registration lines on your pattern. *Registration lines* show where 2 pieces need to meet up again in your final pattern (for example, where the sides of our bracer connect for lacing). To have the best chance at getting these pieces flush again after you cut out your pattern, add perpendicular lines across seams that extend into both pieces. Now, when you cut that seam open, you can line it up again by matching the registration lines together.

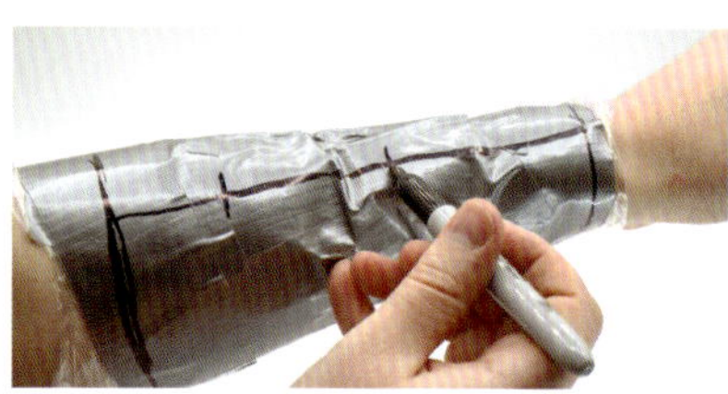

You can mark where you would like belts, snaps, or lacing at this point, or you may do this later directly onto the leather. This is an example of where sometimes the steps of leatherworking can be reordered or condensed depending on the project and your confidence. For more on attachments see Hardware (page 97).

6. Cut your pattern off. This requires **careful** snipping. Do not rush. You could ruin a piece of clothing or part of an existing costume, or harm yourself. So, please snip little by little, making sure to cut only the cling wrap and duct tape.

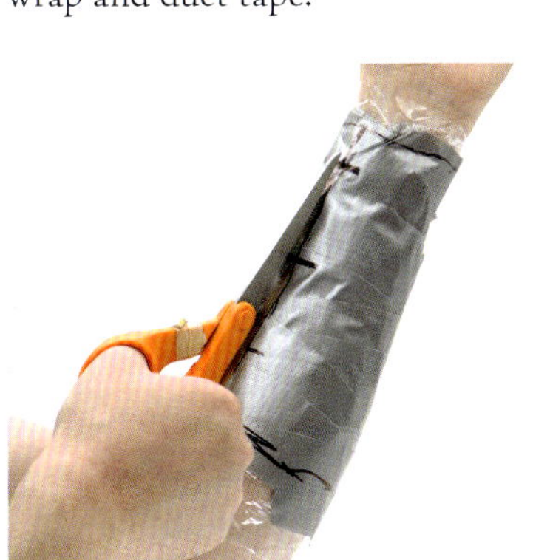

7. Trim away the excess around the edges, and you now have a pattern ... sort of. Check out Adjusting Your Pattern (page 28) to get your pattern from first draft to the finish line.

Paper Method

Similar to the duct tape method, the paper patterning method consists of covering yourself or an item in paper and then drawing your pattern or design on the paper. Because paper has less complex bending ability (meaning it is able to only do a convex bend into a concave bend within limits) and does not have any stretch, it works well to pattern leather pieces. If you'll be using a thicker leather in your finished piece, refer to How Much Extra to Add (page 21) to see how leather thickness will affect your measurements.

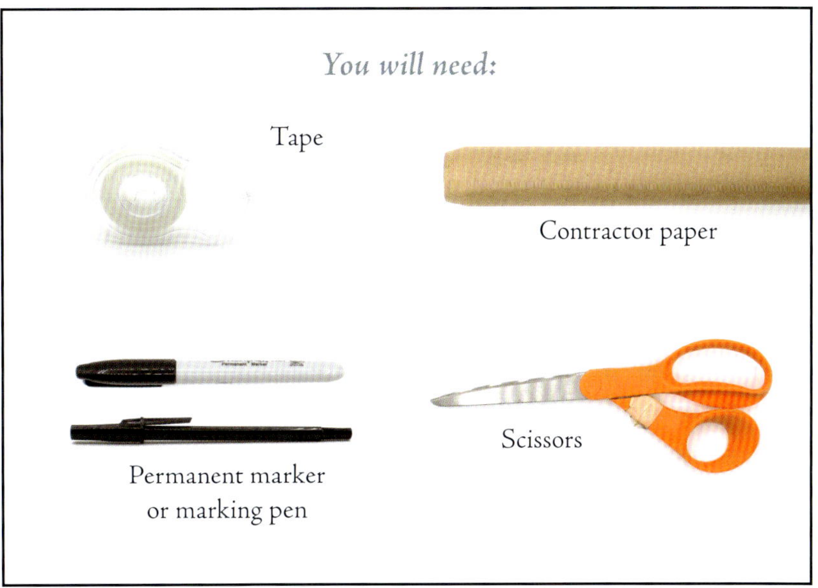

1. Cut a piece of paper and attach it to where you need to pattern. Don't worry if it's not big enough to cover all you need—you can keep adding more pieces and taping them together until you're satisfied. The great thing about paper patterning is that you can add and cut away as you work.

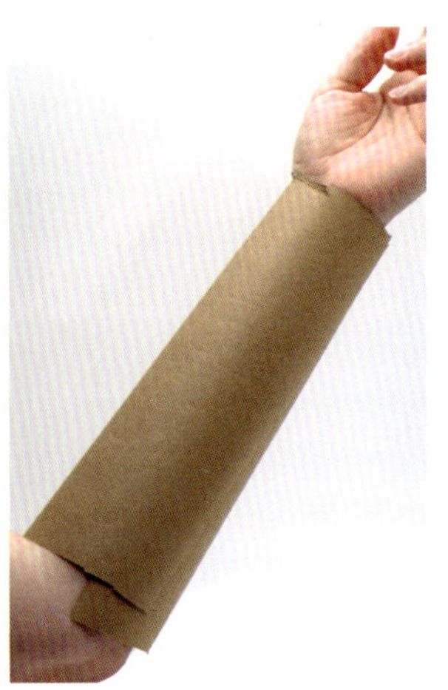

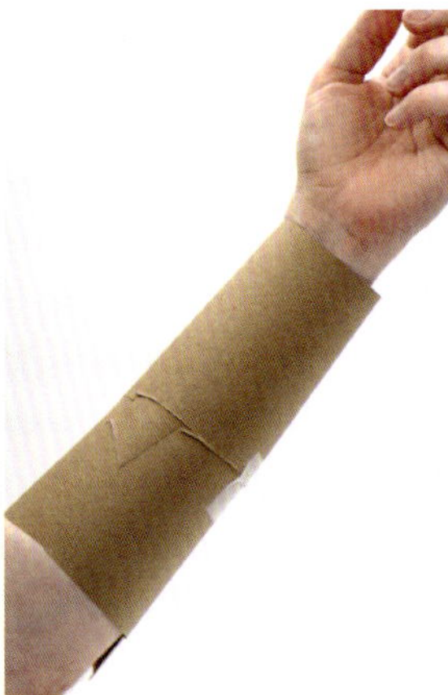

2. Once the area is covered, draw on your pattern, centerline, registration lines, and any hardware or attachments you know you'll need.

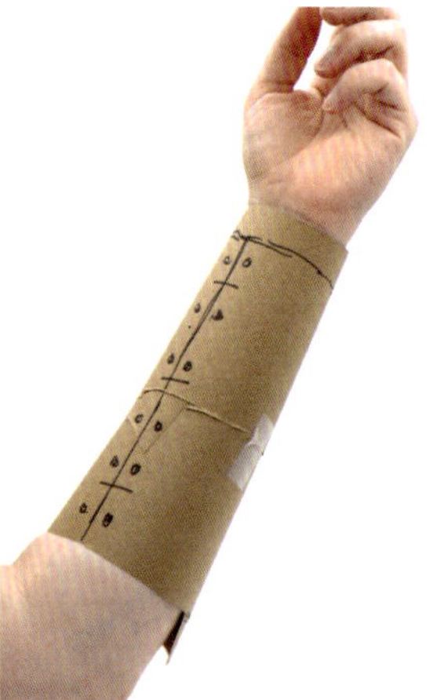

3. Cut your pattern off. This requires **careful** snipping. Do not rush. You could ruin a piece of clothing or part of an existing costume, or harm yourself. So, please snip little by little, making sure to cut only the paper.

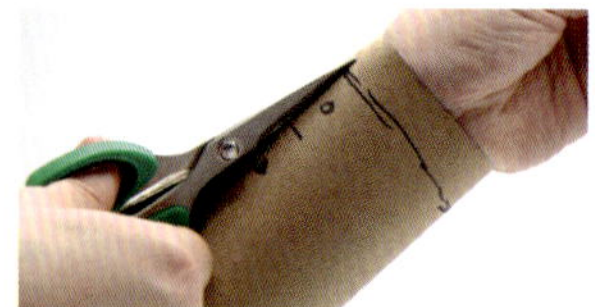

4. Trim the excess paper around the edges to complete your first draft! Move on to Adjusting Your Pattern (page 28) to get that pattern fitted perfectly!

Flat Drafting

Flat drafting is just as the name suggests: a 2-D pattern. So far, we've shown two ways of drafting that result in a 3-D pattern, which will then translate into a 2-D pattern. With flat drafting, you create a 2-D pattern and bypass the initial 3-D mock-up. If you're savvy with a measuring tape and geometry, and you have experience with self-drafting patterns, you may find yourself quite comfortable with flat drafting.

Work Smarter, Not Harder: *Cosplayers are known for our ingenuity in crafting, and we also take steps to reuse when we can! You can flat draft a pattern from previous paper patterns or commercial patterns you may have and work your additions off of that. If you know the base already works, why go through the process again when you can move ahead to the part that makes this project unique?*

1. For this bracer example, you first need to measure the length of the bracer on your forearm. It's important in flat drafting to wear existing pieces of your cosplay or something similar when taking your measurements, especially if these pieces will interact with other parts of the outfit (for example, lower-arm armor next to elbow armor, which is, in turn, next to upper-arm armor) or if your underlayer is thick, like a quilted gambeson. You want to retain as much mobility and comfort as possible.

To measure the length of the bracer (measurement **A,**) take your measuring tape or ruler and measure from wherever the top of the bracer needs to be to just before your wrist (move your wrist around to make sure your ending point isn't interfering with mobility).

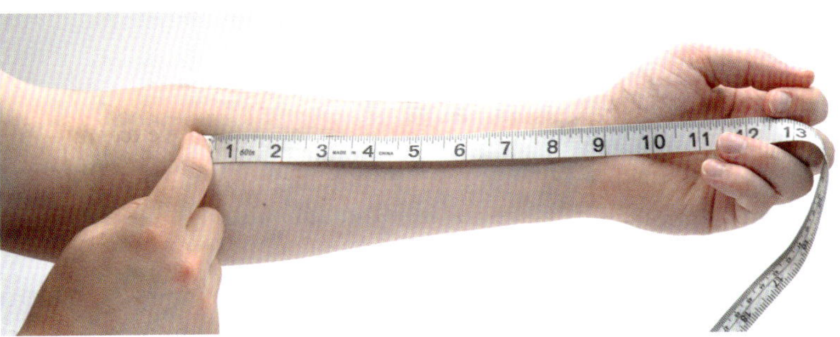

2. Now, with your measuring tape, measure the circumference of your wrist where you placed the bottom of the bracer (measurement **B.**) If you're using a thicker leather, refer back to How Much Extra to Add (page 21) to see how leather thickness will affect your measurements.

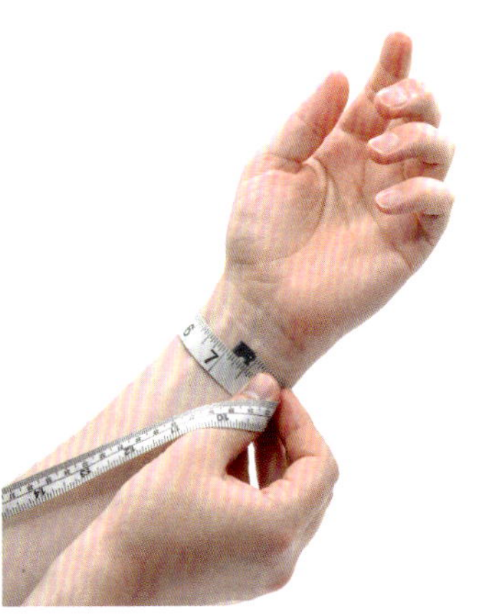

3. Next, using measurement **A,** go to the top of your bracer and measure the circumference of your arm (measurement **C.**) Be sure to flex your arm for this measurement so that your forearm is at its largest.

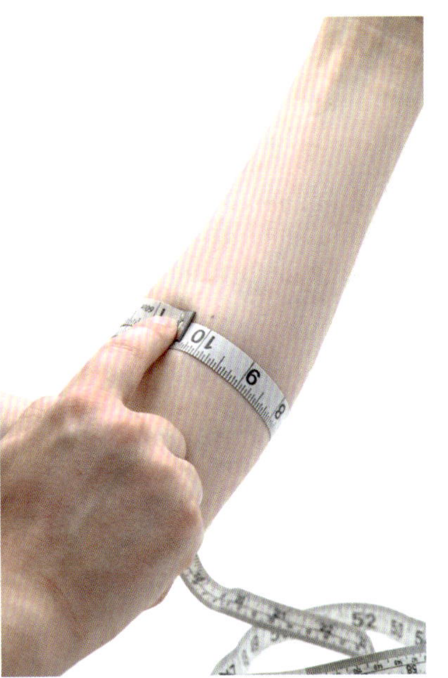

4. In the middle of a piece of paper draw a line with your ruler using measurement **A.** You'll be adding in measurements **B** and **C** off of this line, so be sure to leave space on each side of your measurement **A** line.

5. Using measurement **B,** draw a line from left to right, centered on the bottom of the measurement **A** line. Repeat this for measurement **C**, but draw the line centered on the top of your measurement **A** line.

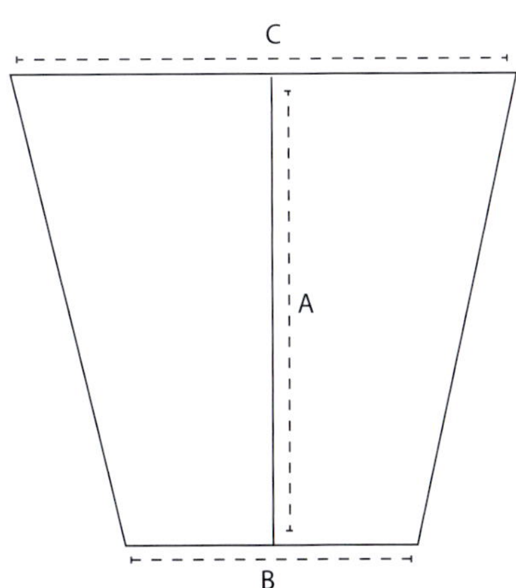

6. Take your ruler and connect the ends of the measurement **B** line with the measurement **C** line. You now have a bracer pattern! From here, go ahead and cut it out. Your first draft is ready for the next section, Adjusting Your Pattern (page 28).

And I'm Free ... Free-Handin'

Sometimes in cosplay you come across shapes that are too wacky or organic to draft using a ruler. That's when you can enlist the skills of freehand drawing the design. If you choose to engage your inner artist, take the time to *true up* your lines after sketching. Hand-drawn lines can get a little wavy, so it is always good practice to take a ruler or French curve and fix those pesky wobbles. The process of truing up lines can also translate to working with foam and sewing. A handy skill for your arsenal!

Seeing Double?

If you have a design that you need to be symmetrical on your piece, here is a quick method to mirror it:

1. Draw and cut out half the design.

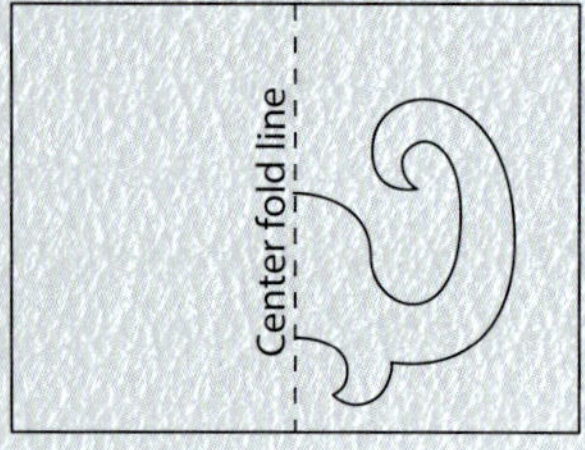

Draw shape

Cut out shape

2. Fold that half over a centerline and trace it on the other side.

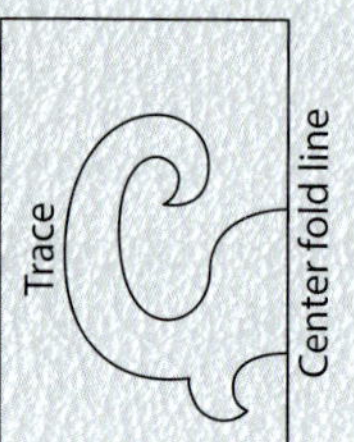

Trace shape

3. Unfold and then cut out the other half.

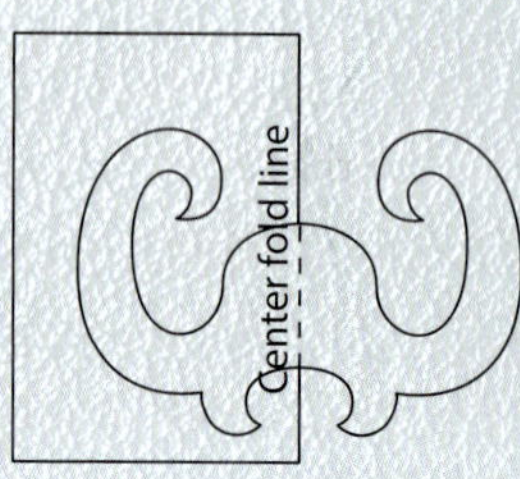

Unfold paper

ADJUSTING YOUR PATTERN

You'll run into many situations where you have a pattern, self-drafted or commercial, and it either isn't complete or needs to be modified to fit your needs. We're big fans of hands-on patterning and mock-ups for adjustments.

Multiple Mock-Ups

This technique is simple but incredibly useful. We make multiple mock-ups for most of our projects.

1. Trace and cut your pattern out of a fresh piece of paper. This may be a commercial pattern that needs to be resized, a first-draft pattern, or a previous mock-up's paper pattern.

2. Try it on!

3. Inspect and note issues and needed alterations. For example, you may have used the flat drafting method above to create a basic bracer. However, you want your bracer to have a different shape at the top of the arm than what you have currently on your mock-up. Make a note with details of the changes you want to make. You may write something like: "Add 4cm here →" or "More curve." Often, we write our notes directly on the pattern paper.

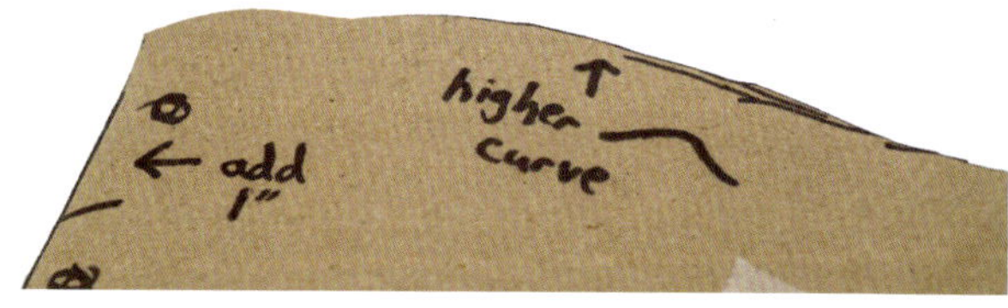

If you didn't add any further alterations, then your pattern is complete and you can move on to Transferring Your Pattern to Leather (page 30)! Otherwise, continue on to the next step.

Note: *We recommend marking on your pattern where you want to place hardware or sew pieces together. Basically, mark for anything covered in Hardware (page 97).*

4. Make the alterations to the paper pattern. If removing material, simply cut it away. If adding material, use tape to add more paper and cut it to the correct shape. Once alterations have been made, return to Step 1. If your paper pattern is still in good shape after alterations, you may be able to skip Step 1 and go straight to Step 2, trying it on again.

FOAM MOCK-UP

If you're not confident in the amount added for thickness or you'd like to ensure perfect sizing and movement in the patterning stage, you can create a foam mock-up. Instead of paper, use craft or EVA foam with roughly the same thickness as your leather to create your mock-up. This allows you to test how the thickness of the leather will affect the pattern and let you move to the cutting step with more confidence.

You can also use foam to test how articulated pieces joined by rivets will move together, which is common in armor covering joints or shoes. You can rivet the foam together or use split pin paper fasteners to quickly join the foam mock-up pieces.

Flattening 3-D Patterns

Sometimes when creating a pattern with the duct tape or paper patterning methods, you'll end up with a 3-D shape that doesn't easily flatten down to create a 2-D pattern. There are a few techniques to turn those 3-D shapes into patterns.

If the 3-D shape can be mostly flattened and has only a small amount of bubbling or crinkling, you may use that pattern as is and wet form your leather to achieve the 3-D shape you need in the final piece (see Wet Forming, page 111).

For large curves or difficult shapes, a seam or dart can be used to create a flattened pattern. As an example, we'll use a small shoulder pauldron. Here, we've made a duct tape pattern in the shape that we ultimately want on the shoulder, but the tape doesn't flatten down into a nice 2-D piece.

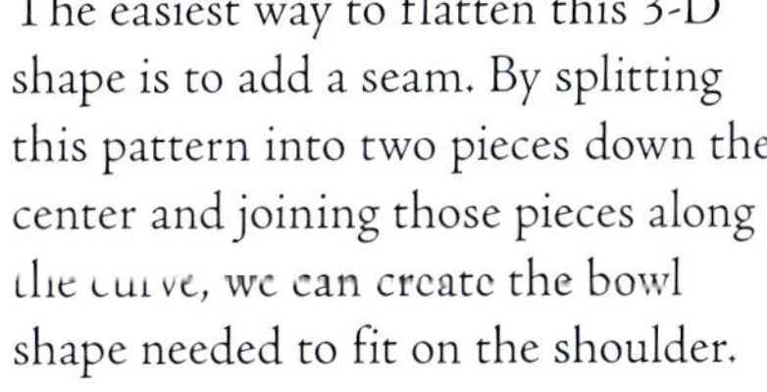

The easiest way to flatten this 3-D shape is to add a seam. By splitting this pattern into two pieces down the center and joining those pieces along the curve, we can create the bowl shape needed to fit on the shoulder.

But what if you only want to have one piece of leather instead of multiple smaller ones, or you don't like how the seam looks? In this case, we use a *dart*, which is a cut in the pattern that will allow the pattern to spread and flatten. For this example, we placed the tip of the dart at the apex of the curve and then cut the pattern open to the edge. In sewing, this is called the *slash-and-spread method*. Once sewn back together, the bowl will regain its three-dimensional shape.

Transferring Your Pattern to Leather

The grain side of leather, especially veg tan, can be susceptible to color and marks, which will stubbornly refuse to be removed, or it may seem like they were removed only to reappear during the dyeing process (this especially applies to air-soluble pens). Because of this, trace your pattern pieces onto the flesh side of the leather. We use water-soluble ink, because it's easy to remove afterward and we've yet to find it reappear like a ghostly message during the dyeing or sealing process.

Always check the grain side before cutting as there could be damage, brands, or wrinkles on the front side of the piece. Depending on the project, you may not mind a little bit of wear and character, but in any case, you want to know what the grain side looks like before you cut. Also, make sure that the part of the leather that you're going to be cutting from has the thickness that you want. Unlike foam or thermoplastic, leather is an organic material, and it's normal for the thickness to vary from one part of the hide to another.

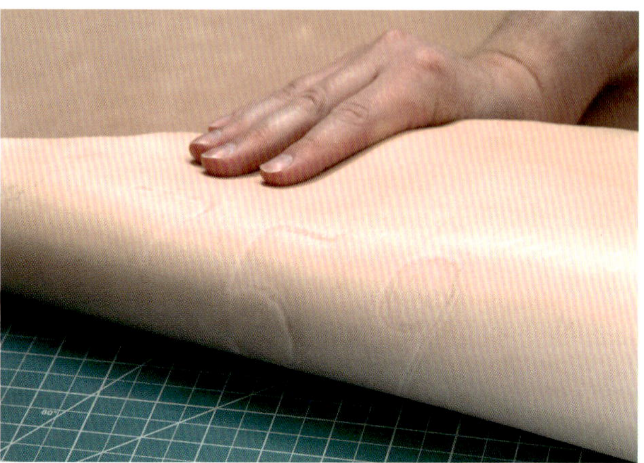

Cutting

How do you cut leather? Just as there are many types of leather, there are varied ways of cutting leather depending on the weight. Let's discuss options, but remember: Safety first!

KNIVES AND SHEARS AND BLADES, OH MY!

Leather is a tough material. One of the primary goals of the tanning process is to increase its durability. To cut through leather effectively, you'll need a sharp tool. Regardless of which type you use, make sure you frequently sharpen or change out the blade to ensure clean cuts. Take extra care before each cut to ensure you're not in the path of the blade, especially when using a brand-new or newly sharpened blade, which may cut more quickly than expected.

In our case, the tool we use the most for cutting all weights of leather is a simple utility knife (also known as a box cutter). For this tool, make sure the piece you're cutting is lying on a flat surface. A cutting mat should also be used, to both protect the surface underneath and reduce wear on the utility knife blade.

Make multiple passes if needed. Don't feel like you have to cut through the leather in one pass. Carefully cutting with less force on the first pass can result in a more accurate trace of the shape, and make it easier to cut through in following passes.

TIP

When you have a long, straight line to cut, line up your utility knife or a rotary blade with a metal ruler to keep your cut from wavering.

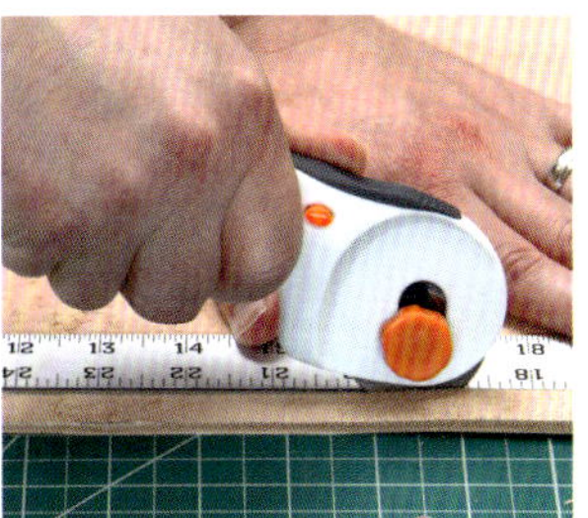

The Ever-Efficient Strap Cutter

If you find yourself cutting a lot of belts and straps, check out the strap cutter (page 19). To use it, loosen the top screw and use the ruler printed on the tool to set the strap width before tightening the screw again. Then set the tool flat against the side of the leather and feed the leather between the two arms holding the blade. As you pull the tool along the edge of the leather, the blade will cut a line at the width you set. Note that the leather edge must be straight before using the strap cutter, or it will create another cut with all the same inconsistencies.

Another common cutting tool is a pair of leather shears. These shears usually have shorter blades and bigger handles in order to move the fulcrum further toward the cutting edge and cut with more force. Cutting leather will dull shears quickly, so they'll need frequent sharpening for best effect. Even when sharp, shears are more effective on thinner leather because thicker leather requires a lot more squeezing force and will dull them and tire out your hands! For thicker leather, we recommend using a utility knife.

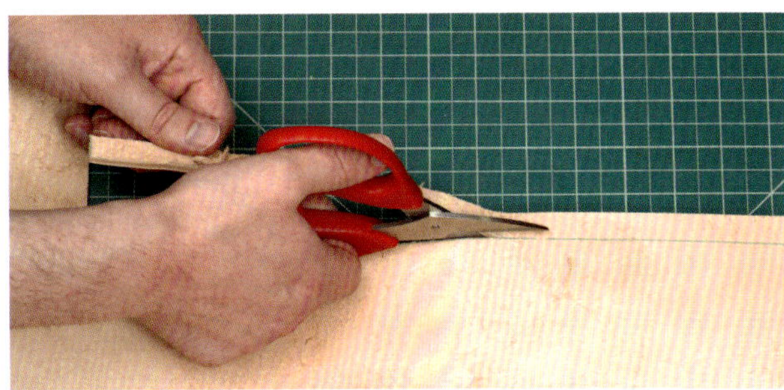

TIP

If you have many pairs of fabric shears, some older than others and maybe not as sharp, you can switch those over to being leather cutting shears. We usually wrap a piece of colored tape on the handle to indicate that it is no longer for fabric and try to keep it with our leatherworking tools. When the blade truly becomes dull and is no longer cutting leather with ease, sharpen as needed. Because these shears aren't designed for leather, you'll want to limit their use to thinner weight leathers.

Carving and TOOLING

Just as with other crafts, it's the little details that really make a project look its best. In the carving section, we'll go over a couple important techniques that will help you give your work a more polished look. Then we'll jump into tooling. Tooling leather is a craft of its own within leatherworking, with a massive wealth of guides, videos, and pattern books to dive into. In the tooling section, we'll impart the basics and touch on several of the major techniques, arming you with the knowledge you'll need to get started.

Tools: Carves and Curves

You won't use skiving and edge beveling on every project, but we still recommend picking up the essentials.

ESSENTIALS

Safety skiving knife: All the skiving tool options are equally viable, and in fact we recommend the round knife or Japanese skiving knife in the long term, but for beginners, the safety skiving knife is a good base tool. On the safety skiving knife, the super-sharp blade is housed to reduce the likelihood of cutting yourself, but you should still be careful. Just touching the blade lightly will result in a cut.

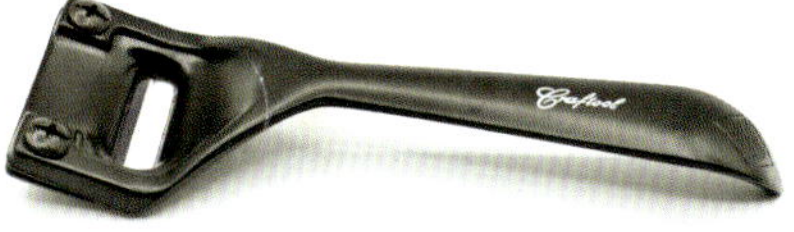

Standard edge beveler: Gives raw cut edges a nice beveled finish. Get one that has a hollow groove, which helps the tool follow the edge of the leather.

OPTIONAL

Japanese round knife: A curved blade that works extremely well for skiving.

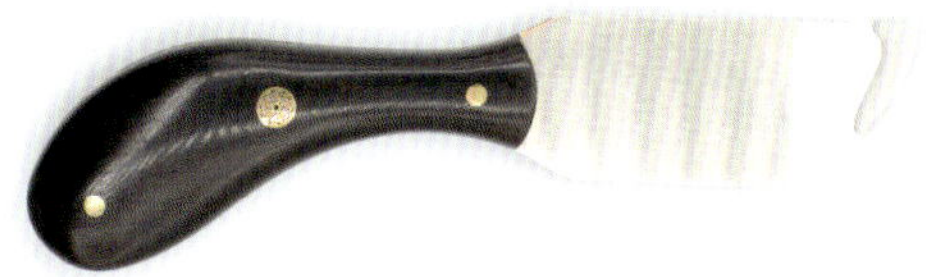

Japanese flat knife: Straight blades designed to give good control while skiving.

Bissonnette: An edge beveler that helps on tight curves.

French edger: An edge beveler with a flat blade like a trough, which is useful for both beveling and skiving.

Carving

Technically, some of the techniques from the Tooling section (page 43) could also be considered carving, but we're going to use *carving* to refer to skiving and edge beveling for ease of reference. Usually, we carve before tooling or dyeing because we want the leather to be dry, and we've not yet introduced moisture to the leather. Leather with moisture is easier to shape and bend, but it's more pliable and difficult to cut cleanly.

SKIVING

Skiving is when you reduce the thickness of your leather where you intend to layer, bend, or fold it. By skiving, you reduce the bulk but not the strength. Unlike tooling, this process is done to the flesh side of the leather. Check out how much skiving reduces bulk in a fold!

Grind It Down: *Skiving is generally done with a blade, but you can also sand away the unneeded bulk. When you have a lot to remove and precision isn't as important, a belt sander can speed up the skiving process. If you take that road, make sure to wear personal protective equipment, because it will generate tons of leather dust.*

Astarion from *Baldur's Gate 3*
Cosplay and photo by Isaiah Blue

Safety Skiving Knife

There are two major types of safety skiving knives. One is flatter with the handle on the sharp side of the razor, so you'll be drawing the tool toward you to skive. It's pretty useful for quickly skiving straps, though we find it a little harder to finely control than other knives, and it is hard to get into small areas due to the safety housing. The other version is more curved and has the handle to the side of the blade. You'll push this tool away from you to slice through the leather. The extra curve helps control the depth of your slice, but you'll have to make multiple, smaller strokes to get the same effect as the pull-toward version.

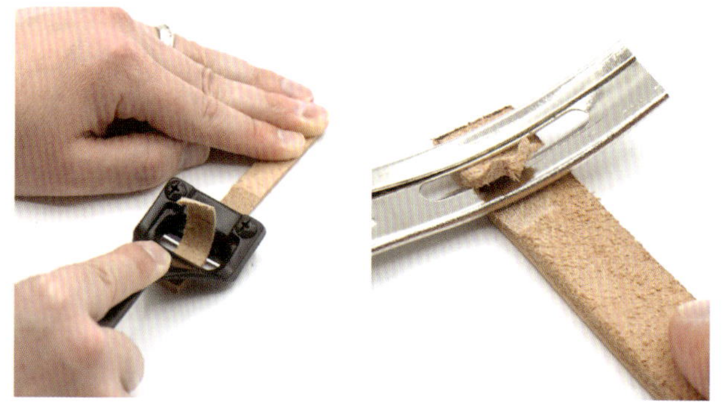

Flat Skiving Knife

With a flat skiving knife, you can achieve a crisp transition between skived and not skived areas. Before you start, mark your back line (where you do not want to skive past) so you can keep a transition point in mind with each placement and pass of the knife. With a flat blade, you'll start by facing the blade to the edge of the leather so when you push forward, you're going toward the edge. Push the blade, slightly angled, to catch the flesh side and slice away from you in the same motion, drawing the knife to the side to complete the cut. You might use more or less of the blade's edge for different-sized slices.

For larger areas or channels, we recommend working from the edge and moving inward, skiving in sections. French edgers (page 33), which also have a flat blade, can be used for skiving channels and smaller areas, though the technique is different.

Round Skiving Knife

With a round skiving knife, the pushing and cutting techniques are the same as the flat knife, but instead you start your slices by placing the top of the blade's curve almost on your transition line where you would like your skiving to start. Some people find that the oblique slicing angle created with a round knife makes the cut easier and gives them more control. If you can test both a flat knife and a round knife, give them a try and compare which feels better for your wrist and provides the best control of cutting pressure. A lot of the old-school leather workers we've met prefer the round knife.

Razor Sharp

The key to skiving is a very sharp blade. If your blade is dull, you risk gouging your leather, and even worse, hurting yourself. You'll be able to tell it's time to sharpen or change out the blade when it begins to take more effort to push through the leather.

For skivers with replaceable blades, just change out the blade.

There are many methods to sharpen knives, and most will work just as well for skiving knives if done correctly, but we'll outline a quick-fix option here:

1. Dampen a sheet of sandpaper of at least 1000 grit.

2. Hold the knife facing away from you, and draw the angled side of the blade back toward you along the sandpaper. Try to match the angle of the blade itself. Repeat a minimum of a dozen times. If the blade is curved, you'll have to twist the knife as you pull to sharpen along the entire curve.

3. Using the grain side of a scrap piece of leather, flip the knife over to the flat side of the blade and draw it back toward you at a low angle. You should not be cutting the leather, just dragging the flat plane of the blade over the grain of the leather. Do this roughly a dozen times. This cleans up the burrs on the flipside that were created by the sandpaper in Step 2. For additional smoothing, add jeweler's rouge (a jewelry polishing compound) to the surface of the leather.

SAVE EVERY BIT!

When skiving, save your cut-off leather. You can use it to create a filling paste by mincing up your skiving scrapes and mixing them with contact cement to reinforce skived seams that need to hold a bend or crease.

Skiving Chrome Tan

Skiving chrome tan is a subject of debate, but in the end, it is doable. This is only recommended for thicker chrome tan hides because thinner chrome tan is quite pliable, making it more susceptible to mistakes with a skiving blade. Keeping your blades sharp will give you best results with chrome tan.

EDGE BEVELING

One way to give your projects a professional feel is by softening the edge from a harsh 90° angle to a chamfered or rounded edge by removing a small amount of leather from both the grain and flesh sides. This is known as *edge beveling, edge work,* or simply *beveling* (not to be confused with the beveling you'll read about in the Tooling section [page 43]). In the context of edge work, beveling removes leather to create different angled planes. To achieve these new looks for your edges, you'll need to use an edge beveling tool.

On this page, we show the difference between a veg tan edge with and without a beveled edge. You can see how the difference is subtle, but the finished look of the item is enhanced by taking this extra step. In our example, we used a 10 oz. (4mm) veg tan hide. We only recommend using edgers on leather 4 oz. (1.6mm) and up. Anything thinner doesn't really show the transformed edge, and beveling both the grain and flesh sides can leave you with nothing or very flimsy fibers to burnish.

Unbeveled (left) and beveled (right)

You usually do not want to edge bevel after dyeing because an edge beveler carves away at the grain side of the leather, and if it's dyed, you may end up cutting away your dyed leather, leaving you with the original veg tan coloring. On the other hand, this can create a cool effect, so play around and see what you like! On pre-dyed leather hides, such as oil-tanned hides, an edge beveler will do just that and give you a two-tone finish.

Unbeveled (left) and beveled (right)

Edge bevelers come in a few different widths, but the overall application is the same between both flat (chamfered) and round profile bevelers. What will change between types is how steep of a bevel you'll create when using the tool and how wide the affected area will be. Note that less expensive edge bevelers may not have a hollow groove to ensure your bevel follows the edge, which makes it much harder to achieve an even grounding and clean bevel.

Standard Edge Beveler

The most common beveling tool, sometimes called the Western or standard edger, is fairly straightforward and will result in either a rounded or chamfered edge, depending on which type you choose. To use, place on the edge of the grain side of your leather so you can see the peak of the 90° corner in the middle of the beveling tool's cloven groover. In order to do this, you won't be aligned straight with your leather, but your hand and tool will be at an outward angle and you'll be pushing inward toward the leather.

With steady pressure, push forward along the edge. You'll create a thin "noodle" of leather as you do so. Continue pushing until you meet the end of your edge. If the noodle doesn't break off when you finish your pass, trim it off with a scissor. Repeat this process on the flesh side of your leather. If you notice that you pushed lighter in some places along your pass, you can go back and even out your bevel, but do so with caution—cutting deeper may create a wavy edge.

BEST BEVEL IN THE WEST

By beveling both the grain and flesh sides of your leather's edge, you'll have less chance of your leather mushrooming when you use an edge burnisher (see Burnishing, page 69). Mushrooming is when the leather edge folds over and creates a little overhanging ridge, like a mushroom cap.

Tighter curves or detailed edges require a smaller beveler head. Using a smaller head also creates a softer angled bevel. You may want to consider a bissonnette edger if your curves are tight turns.

BEVELING CHROME TAN

Chrome tan and other supple leathers are less likely to take an edge bevel with consistency and cleanliness due to their spongy nature, which causes them to compress around the pressure of the blade. Instead of beveling, we've gotten the best results by simply finishing with a nice burnish.

Bissonnette

Instead of the usual single blade, a bissonnette has two blades in an O-shaped opening, so it can be either pushed or pulled along an edge. They really shine when used on interior curves or tight turns. Don't be fooled, though! They also work on straight lines, so you could use the same tool for your whole piece if you want.

French Edger Tool

Use a French edger the same way you would use a standard edge beveler. Place it along the edge at a slight angle, lining up the point of the edge with the middle of the trough, and push with consistent pressure until you get to the end of your edge. These come in several sizes, which dictates how wide an area will be carved away.

You can also use a French edger for skiving (page 34). It can carve away a precise channel of leather to assist with folding or bending due to the flat broad blade in the middle of the trough. When used on the flesh side of the leather, it can be used to skive away thickness for folding corners or for getting into a smaller area when a regular skiver or round knife can't be precise or can't reach.

You can use this tool on the flesh side of all types of leather, even garment grades, which will help with thickness when sewing. Just be sure that you have a sharp blade and don't push too hard, or you may gouge a hole in your leather.

DON'T BE DULL

If your flat profile edger is growing dull (you'll be able to tell because it won't make clean passes and will take more effort to push forward), you can use jeweler's rouge on the backside of a veg tan scrap and pull your tool toward you for a few passes in a technique called stropping. This will sharpen the blade and give you neat cuts.

If your round profile edger is growing dull, sharpening can be a bit trickier. Begin by beveling a piece of veg tan with your dull edger as best you can, or use a sharper edger of the same size and type. Then, put some jeweler's rouge on the edge, and bevel it over again, this time pulling toward you for a few passes.

Tools: You Know, Tooling Tools

The metal tools used for tooling are often referred to as leather stamping tools. There are a whole lot of options when it comes to stamping tools. We'll guide you through the foundational tools and then you'll be ready to explore on your own! Gotta tool 'em all!

Tav from *Baldur's Gate 3*

Cosplay and work-in-progress photos by Mermaid Child • Photo by Misti D. Morrison

ESSENTIALS

Mallets and mauls: Whether plastic, rawhide, or stone, you'll need a mallet or maul to tap and strike your stamping tools.

Much Ado About Mallets

The type of mallet you use makes a big difference. No specific type inherently gets you a better result, and they all behave a bit differently, especially when used for tooling. Even though you might already have one at home, don't use a standard metal hammer! It will damage your stamping tools, especially with continued use.

A plastic head mallet has a firm head. Standard plastic head mallets are very light, meaning that all the force of the strike is coming from your muscle power, which can give you a lot of control but also invites more opportunity for human error in your strikes. They're also reasonably priced.

Rawhide mallets have a certain amount of give and don't recoil like a fully firm mallet can. Some people say rawhide gives them a greater sense of control, which makes it easier to use, especially for setting hardware from the Hammered Hardware section (page 98).

Last is a maul, which doesn't come in the traditional hammer shape but looks more like a little club. Most are pretty heavy and have a rounded face instead of a flat hammer face. When working with a maul, you can execute strikes using mainly the weight of the maul itself. This can help with consistency.

It's a good idea to try out different mallet types, because different people tend to gravitate toward different mallets. If you're lucky enough to have a local leather shop, we highly recommend asking to try them all!

Swivel knife: A tool for scoring leather to prepare it for beveling and other tooling techniques.

Beveler: Used to separate designs and establish foreground and background.

Pear shader or thumbprint: A textured or smooth rounded tool that's good for shading.

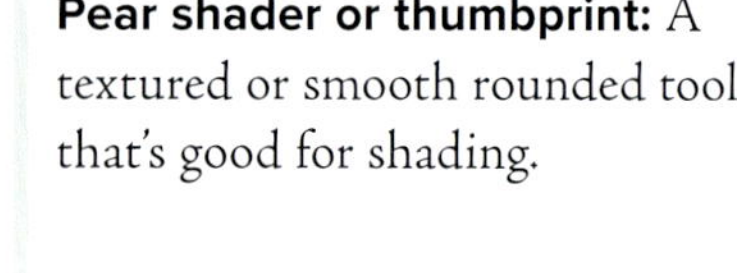

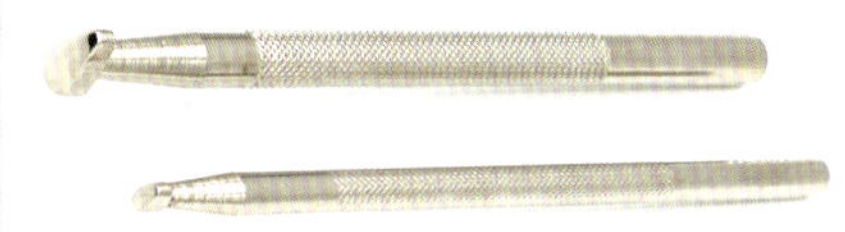

Veiner: A tool with an arc. Useful for a variety of techniques.

Hard surface: You'll need somewhere to work. Only work on a designated work table that can take a little damage.

JUST GET THE KIT

Basic tooling kits are a great value. They usually include a swivel knife and a set of very useful stamping tools at a discount. When you can, don't buy your essentials individually. Save a little money and let the kit choose your first few stamps.

OPTIONAL

Rubber board: Placed under the stone slab to reduce noise and vibration while tooling. Might be helpful with appeasing cranky apartment neighbors or roommates during those long tooling sessions.

Stone slab: A nice, solid surface, usually made of marble or granite, that won't be easily damaged. Try to find a countertop scrap or sample to save money.

Backgrounder: A tool for making nice textured backgrounds.

Textured beveler: A beveler that adds a texture to the background.

Seeder: A tool that makes little circles.

Camouflage tool: A tool that's useful for controlling which areas appear to be in front of other tooling areas.

Border tool set: There are some cool border designs you can pick up and use on your projects.

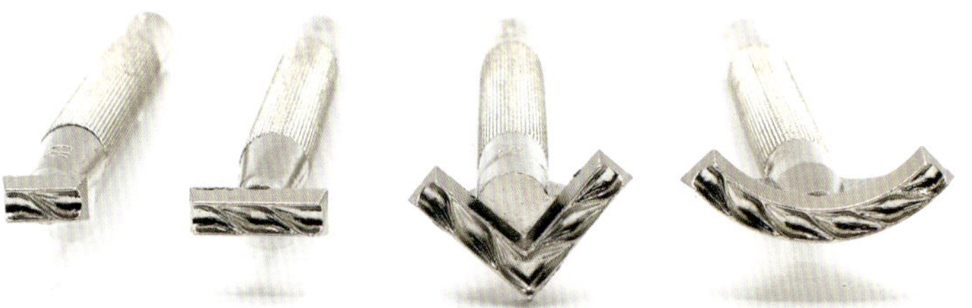

Undercut modeling tool: Easier on the wrist than striking a tool. Can be used for undercuts and bevels (see Beveling with Modeling Tools, page 46).

Modeling spoon: Can be used for smoothing and bevels (see Beveling with Modeling Tools, page 46).

Lifting tool: A tool specifically designed for making undercut lifts.

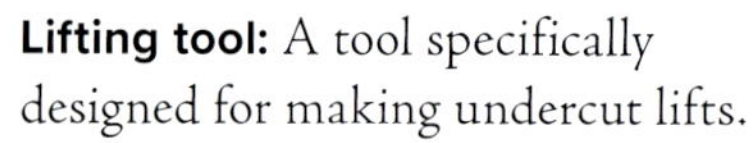

Soft graphite pencil and eraser: For drawing tooling designs directly on the leather.

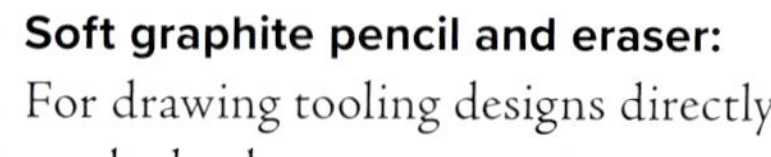

Printer and paper: For printing tooling designs. There are even printable tracing sheets made for printing tooling designs.

Packing tape: For strengthening printed tooling designs.

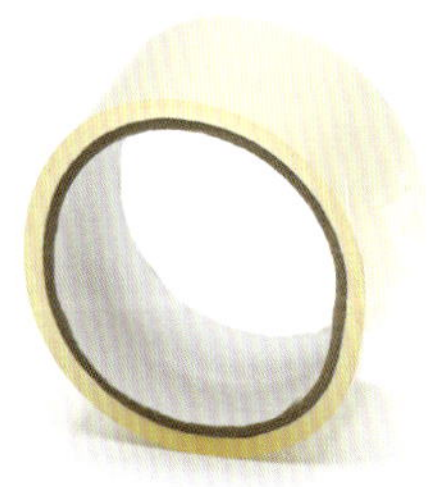

Pen or stylus: Used to push a design outline accurately into the leather. You can really use any handheld tool with a rounded tip.

Other tooling stamps: There are hundreds of stamp designs out there to play with. Try some out!

Tooling

When people think of leatherwork, they often envision tooling. They think of saddles, belts, and holsters with intricate designs pushed directly into the leather and the rustic, beautiful burnished coloration created by the art of tooling. We won't cover everything about tooling in this section, but we'll equip you with a basic understanding and the ability to go out and begin your own personal leather tooling journey. Tooling is not a necessary part of every project, however, so we recommend skimming or skipping this section until you want to really sink your teeth into this technique.

It's worth noting that tooling is a technique for veg tan leather, so our examples use that. Tooling chrome tan is rare due to its pliability and properties acquired in the chrome tanning process.

MOISTURE CONTENT

An essential part of the process is moisture, which loosens and softens the leather, allowing it to be compressed smoothly. Moisture also contributes to the beautiful burnished effect and coloration of a finished piece. You want the veg tan to be receptive to tooling and supple, but with a little bit of firmness. If it's too wet, it will squish around instead of only compressing where you apply force. If it's too dry, it will have less burnish and resist cutting and tooling, making you use more force and have less control. In order to tool effectively, you'll need to evaluate the moisture content before you begin.

Color is an important gauge of ideal moisture levels. The surface of the leather should be just slightly darker than when dry, indicating that the surface has started to dry but there is still moisture in the leather. You'll know your moisture content is correct when the deepest tooling is the darkest and all compressed areas have a nice burnish. It may take some trial and error to be able to accurately assess moisture content by eye or touch.

Left to right: Too dry, ready for tooling, too wet.

CASING

Casing is the act of adding moisture to leather to prepare it for tooling. The two most common methods are quick casing and traditional casing.

Quick Casing

Quick casing is the method we use most often. It works well for small to medium pieces and gets you to tooling faster than traditional casing. To quick case, follow these steps:

1. Set your leather piece flat with the grain side up.

2. Using a sponge or spray bottle, apply a small amount of water to the entire surface.

TIP

If you use a synthetic sponge, rinse it out thoroughly before use. Some are treated with chemicals or soaps that may have an effect on the leather.

3. Let the water soak into the leather.

4. Repeat Steps 2 and 3 a couple more times, until the water takes more than a few seconds to soak in. Do fewer passes on thinner leather, and more passes on thicker leather. The goal is to get the moisture to penetrate most of the way through the thickness of the leather, but not all the way through.

5. Let the leather dry until it is almost back to the original color it was before you added water.

After quick casing, begin tooling the leather. As you work, you may find the leather drying out. Don't be afraid to quick case again, though you should only need one or two passes with the water on any repeat casings because there will already be moisture in the leather.

Traditional Casing

For very large pieces, we recommend using the traditional casing method because it gives you a longer work time and an even moisture application, preventing water staining and inconsistencies that can happen if you quick case in sections instead of the whole piece at once. Follow these steps for traditional casing:

1. Completely submerge the leather in room-temperature water, and leave it until the leather is wet throughout. Opinions vary on exactly how long to leave the leather underwater, but usually it's a bit before or right when bubbles stop forming on the leather's surface.

2. Let the leather dry at room temperature until it is no longer dripping wet but is still thoroughly soaked.

3. Store the leather in a way that will slow the drying process. There are multiple schools of thought here. Some say to wrap it in a breathable material and place it in a cool area or fridge to allow temperature to slow the drying process. Others let the leather dry out close to their desired moisture content and then put it in a plastic bag to greatly slow the drying, or even seal the bag to prevent drying altogether.

4. Leave the leather overnight. The idea here is that after soaking and sitting, the moisture content will be evenly distributed across the entire piece. If possible, don't leave the leather to sit longer than overnight. If you need to leave it for a longer time, consider mixing a little dish soap into your water when you submerge it in Step 1 to help prevent mold from forming. Cold temperatures will also help to prevent mold growth.

5. Pull out the leather piece and check the moisture content. If it's just right, start tooling!

Many users of the traditional casing method recommend tooling your entire project in one sitting without rewetting the leather. This is intended to ensure consistency and crispness in the final product. Usually, this works well, but when working on very large projects, we still quick case (page 43) if the leather begins to dry out during the tooling process. The important thing with any form of casing is to ensure your moisture content stays ideal.

TOOLING DESIGNS

Many people draw their tooling designs directly on the leather before they start cutting and tooling. Do this with a soft graphite pencil and soft eraser. Don't mark too hard—they're just guidelines you'll want to get rid of later. Using a stencil can also help quite a bit! This is especially useful if you need to make identical pieces or if your design is repeated.

Another popular method is to draw (or print) your tooling design on a sheet of paper. Once you've got your design on paper, follow these steps to make it into a transferable pattern:

1. Cut out the pattern so that there is just a little bit of white space around it.

2. Cut a strip of packing tape a little bit longer than the length of your pattern paper.

3. Place the tape over the paper, making sure you don't have any bubbles or wrinkles. You want the finished product to be flat.

4. Repeat Steps 2 and 3 until the paper is completely covered by tape.

5. Turn the pattern over and cover the other side in the same way.

6. If there are any places where there's tape but no paper, trim them away.

7. To use the pattern you've just made, place it on the leather where you want it to go. Then, using a pointed tool like a ballpoint pen or a point/dotting stylus, trace your pattern, pushing the design into the leather. These pressed lines will serve as your design guide as you tool your project.

BEVELING

Beveling is a foundational tooling technique. It's a simple and effective way to outline an object or pattern and add depth, making it appear to be in front of its surroundings. Beveling, in the tooling context, is pushing and compressing the leather at an angle so that it is more and more compressed up to the edge of the bevel. This creates physical distance in the surface of the leather and visually separates and defines shapes and levels.

The first step in beveling is cutting partway into the grain side of the leather, which establishes a crisp edge of the bevel, as well as its depth. As a general rule, for a pronounced bevel line, you want to cut at least halfway through your leather's thickness. Make sure you apply consistent force to your cutting tool so that the cut depth remains even. You can skip this step if you have a specific reason for needing a lighter or less-defined bevel, but the vast majority of your bevels will probably involve a cut line. If you want your bevel to fade out, you can slowly apply less force as you cut to reduce the bevel's depth and intensity.

USING A SWIVEL KNIFE

We recommend using a swivel knife for bevel cuts. To hold the knife, place your pointer finger in the U-shaped top of the swivel knife; then grip the lower part of the knife with your thumb and middle finger. When placing the swivel knife on the leather, you want to tip the blade toward you, placing only the farther corner of the blade onto the leather. Using only that corner, draw the knife toward yourself slowly to make a cut. If you need a curved line, you can easily swivel the knife blade by rotating your grip to get nice, clean curves.

Once you've cut the edge of your bevel, it's time to use the bevel tool itself. Bevel tools come in many sizes, angles, and levels of quality. In general, make sure the bottom edge of the bevel tool isn't too dull. If it's too rounded, it won't push down along the cut edge and your cut line will still be clearly visible after using the tool. This is undesirable, because you want the cut edge to be the clean line at the end of the bevel.

To use the bevel tool, place the bottom edge flush against your cut line. Don't put the whole bottom surface on the leather. You want only the tip of the tool to touch the leather. In other words, the handle of the tool should be standing straight up from the surface of the leather. Once you've positioned the tool, tap the top of the handle with your mallet. Continue to tap the top of the handle as you draw the bevel tool along the edge of your cut line. You usually need multiple passes to complete your bevel.

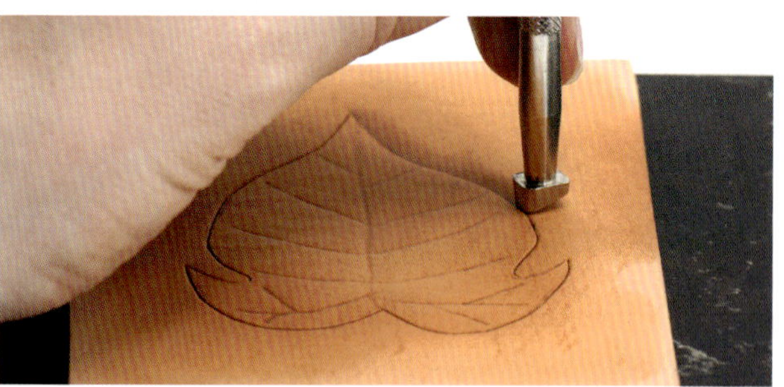

Consistency Is the Key

You'll see the word *consistency* many times throughout this book because one of the primary skills needed for proficient leatherworking is the ability to apply consistent force over a period of time. Many leatherworkers recommend using a heavier mallet and letting gravity maintain the force by dropping the mallet head from a consistent height instead of using your arm to power the strike. Beveling is one of the best ways to practice this, because you get immediate feedback on how consistently you're tapping with your mallet.

Look for two things as you're beveling to gauge your consistency. First, is the edge staying straight? Are your impacts moving the cut edge of the bevel or causing it to become wavy? If they are, you're not holding the tool correctly, you're hitting too hard, or your leather has too much moisture. Second, do you have distinct ridges, almost like you can see each bevel hit? If you do, either you're not applying consistent force to your taps and causing some places to compress more than others, or your leather has too much moisture.

If you find that your leather piece is moving as you tool, you can make a couple of loops out of painter's tape and use it to secure the flesh side to your work surface.

Beveling with Modeling Tools: *Some may call it sacrilege, but a leatherworker we once met talked to us about beveling with an undercut modeling tool, which can help reduce strain on your wrists. This technique is a viable alternative. Instead of striking a bevel tool, you place the point of the undercut modeling tool against the edge, and then draw the tool along the edge while applying pressure. Put more pressure on the tip so that you get the bevel angle you want. Don't try to do too much in one pass. You'll need to go over the edge a few times to get the outcome you want. You can also use a modeling spoon for this technique.*

BACKGROUND AND FOREGROUND

Creating a background and foreground takes advantage of the 3-D nature of leather tooling as an art. Though you have a 3-D surface, it's only a few millimeters thick. You need to make use of coloration combined with small differences in level to give the impression of greater depth.

Beveling is a great way to do this. A deep bevel uses actual distance combined with a strong burnish to show a hard line between an object or pattern and its background. A shallow bevel can be used to more subtly differentiate areas within the foreground or background.

Backgrounding is another common method. Backgrounding is usually done by adding a texture to a section of leather, often a section that has already been separated from the foreground with a bevel. Do this with a backgrounder or texture stamp. As with the bevel tool, ensure that the handle is straight up, and then strike the top with your mallet. Doing this with a backgrounder stamp will push the texture into the leather. Sometimes backgrounder stamps come in pairs, one big and one small, so that you can cover a variety of spaces. Other stamps are rounded out so that you get a stronger impression in the center of the tool. This is useful so that you can move the tool a little, rotate it to add some randomization of the pattern, and tap it again as you work across the area you want to texture. The center of the new mark will impress fully, and the outer edges will help to blend each tap together.

You can also add strong texturing near a bevel, and then fade out the pattern with less force as you move away from the bevel. This allows you to create the illusion of depth in that specific space without having to texture the entirety of a massive area or carry that same background to other parts of the design.

COMMON STAMPS

Once you have a distinct background and foreground, it's time to tool the foreground and give it some detail. There are hundreds of stamps out there, and even more ways to apply them creatively. In this section, we'll talk about a few standard stamps that are often seen in starter toolkits.

Pear shader: The pear shader isn't often used straight down like a bevel or backgrounder. Instead, it has two rounded ends intended to be used at an angle to push in small areas of leather, almost like shading a pencil drawing. These areas will then dye a little differently and lend a bit of texture. It's up to your artistic sense to know when and where to use it, but if you're lost on where to put some shading, a little ways in from a bevel line on the foreground is often a good spot because it accentuates the height of the border of the foreground and helps it pop.

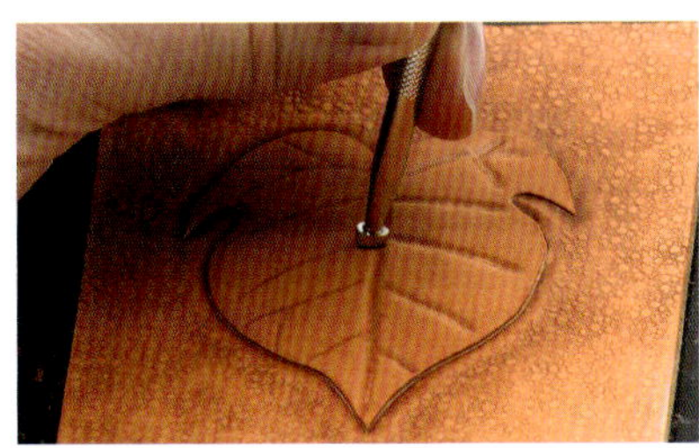

Seeder: Named for its traditional role of mimicking the seeds of a flower or plant, the seeder is a small circle with lines radiating out. While it definitely does a great job tooling seeds, it can also be used as part of a pattern or even as another backgrounding option.

Veiner: Another tool named for its use in floral patterning, the veiner is a highly versatile tool. Think of it as your basic curve generator. It can be stamped flat as decoration or angled to create the fading curves that you'll find on the leaves of floral tooling everywhere. It's also useful as part of a border or repeated pattern.

Camouflage tool: This tool gets its name from its use in interrupting repeated stamping patterns in a way that doesn't look strange and out of place, but gives the impression that the pattern is going underneath something else. Because it's an arc shape, it has a lot of potential design uses.

Repeated Stamping

Repeated stamping is straightforward. Get the stamp into the correct placement on your project, generally with the handle straight up, and strike the top of the handle with your mallet. When stamping, you really want to hit only once if possible, because repeated strikes can muddy the imprint or mess it up entirely if the stamp is at a slightly different angle or placement than it was during the first hit.

A common use for repeated stamps is to create borders. A border stamp or sequence of stamps will be stamped end to end multiple times to create a consistent pattern along the edge of something. Always, always measure before you start stamping a border. There's often no way to do a "half-section," so once you establish your first stamp location, you must proceed only in full stamp lengths. If you don't measure carefully, your ends or corners could end up in awkward, unintended places. If you find yourself in a weird situation, consider using the camouflage tool to make your border appear to go under something else.

Note: *The veiner and camouflage stamps work well for making basic borders, and because they have curvature, they can be used to put borders on curves as well!*

Geometric repeated stamp patterns are really neat, but just like borders, they need to be measured carefully before beginning. We also recommend starting in the middle of an area when you're applying a geometric pattern and making your first row before adding rows up and down. That way, small issues with alignment will have less space to compound on one another. For example, if you start at the top and work your way down in rows, you may find that you can't fit a stamp row at the bottom in the space left. By starting in the middle, if you have any extra space, you'll have that space equally on both the top and the bottom edge, and you can use a backgrounding or camouflage tool to texture it and blend out the stamp's edge.

BORDER ... LANDS?

Some border stamps come in sets with short, long, and corner versions of a design. This is great if you need a frame-like appearance. We use these often on book covers and belts. If you don't trust your ruler and a pencil to make a straight enough line to align your stamp's edge for each placement, you can use a stitch groover (with the spoon tip installed) as shown in Stitch Grooving (page 78) to mark guidelines with ease. These tools leave an indent on the leather's surface that you can use as a guideline that won't smudge or wipe away with handling.

When stamping, you're often looking straight down at your work (a bird's-eye view), but this can trick the eye with border stamps like these and lead to uneven borders. If you're struggling to keep a straight line, turn you piece so you're working toward yourself or "looking down the line" while stamping. At this angle, you can see the edge of the tool on the line better than if you're trying to look over the top of it to guarantee placement. As you stamp, make micro adjustments as needed.

Bird's eye view of border stamping

PHYSICAL DEPTH TECHNIQUES

Tooling isn't just about compressing leather. Many projects treat leather more like a flat canvas, but there are other ways to utilize the thickness of the material.

Undercuts

The first example is an undercut. An undercut is simply removing some of the material under the surface of the leather. Most commonly, this is done after a normal bevel, which allows you to get to the material you've exposed at the bottom of the bevel edge. Two different tools are commonly used for undercuts: an undercut modeling tool and a lifting tool.

With an undercut modeling tool, place the pointed end of the tool against the bottom of the bevel edge with the flat end down. Then push the tool into the edge, rotating it slightly along the bevel edge. Work in small sections and don't push too much at once; otherwise, you risk ripping the leather instead of pushing it. This process will lift the top of the bevel edge, but you can also lever the tool up a little to lift it further.

When using a lifting tool, after completing a bevel line, place the tool against the bottom of the bevel edge just as you would a normal bevel tool. Then slightly angle the tool away from the edge and tap the handle end with your mallet. This will push the bottom of the edge down and into the fibers under the top edge of the bevel, pushing it up. Again, take your time to get an even effect and, optionally, gently lever the tool up and down for more lift.

Embossing

Another way to alter the surface of the leather is embossing. *Embossing* is a generic term for creating raised areas on a surface and is sometimes used in reference to tooling in general, but in this case we're talking about a specific technique where you push the surface of the leather from the flesh side to create the raised area. Tooling requires a hard surface underneath the leather, so use this technique after you're finished with your tooling. To accomplish embossing, while the leather is still cased, use your fingers or a modeling tool to push on the back of the leather and raise the desired areas. If you want a less rounded effect, you can simultaneously push down on the grain side while pushing up from the flesh side to create a sharper emboss.

Embossed after using a lifting tool for even more definition!

Dyeing, Painting, and SEALING

Now for the fun part! Well, one of them—all of leatherworking is fun (we're totally not biased)! Get ready for a deep dive on dyes, paints, and sealants as we take a look at water- and solvent-based mixes and application methods.

Malzeno Armor Set from *Monster Hunter Rise: Sunbreak*
Cosplay and work-in-progress photos by May Jean
Photo of Malzeno armor aet by Anthony V./gfxsoulstudios

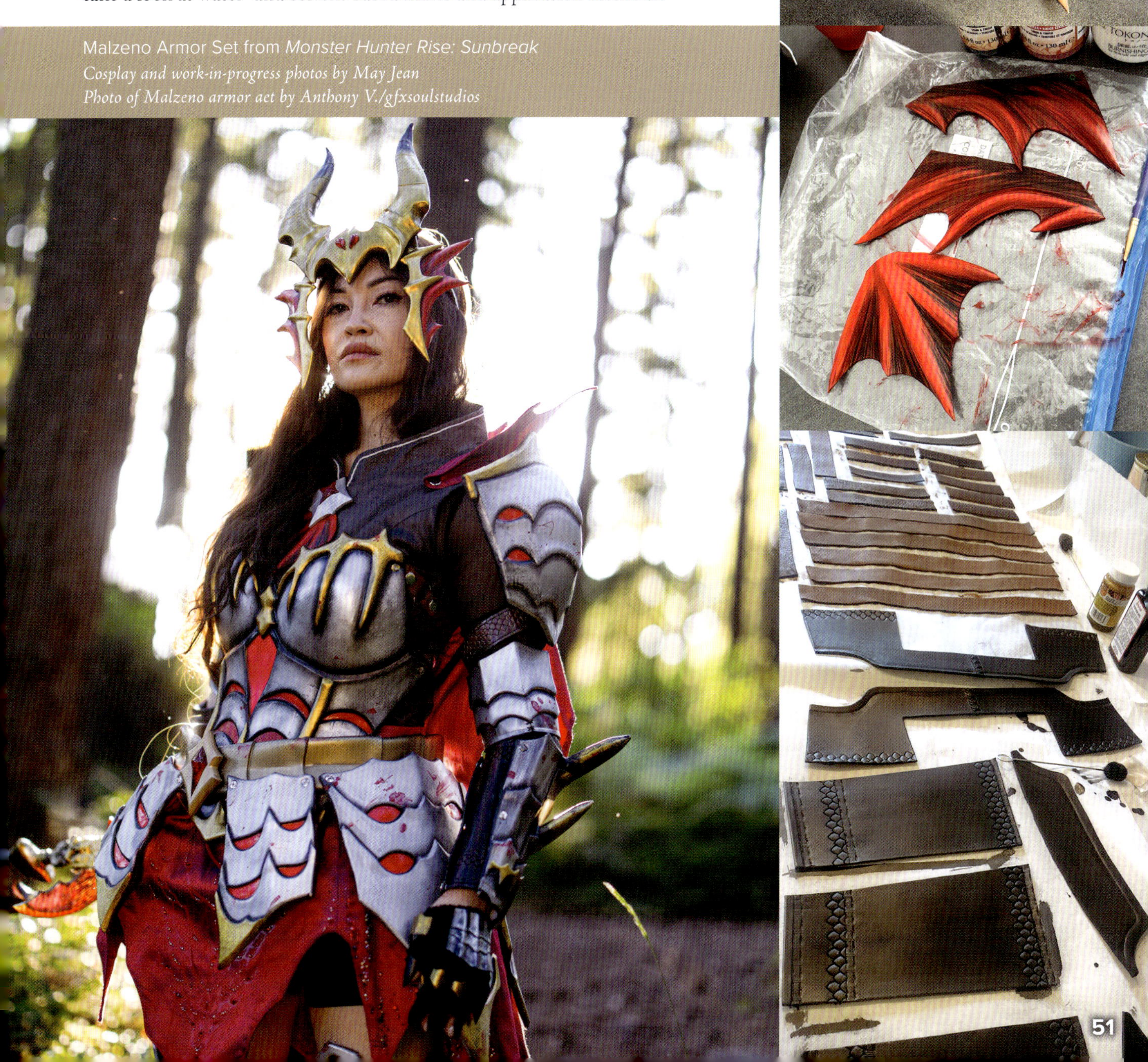

Tools: The Artist's Arsenal

ESSENTIALS

Leather dye: For dyeing leather various colors. Comes in different kinds, most notably solvent- or water-based.

Leather paint: For painting leather various colors. Leather paint is thicker than standard-body acrylics and is premixed with a medium to be flexible.

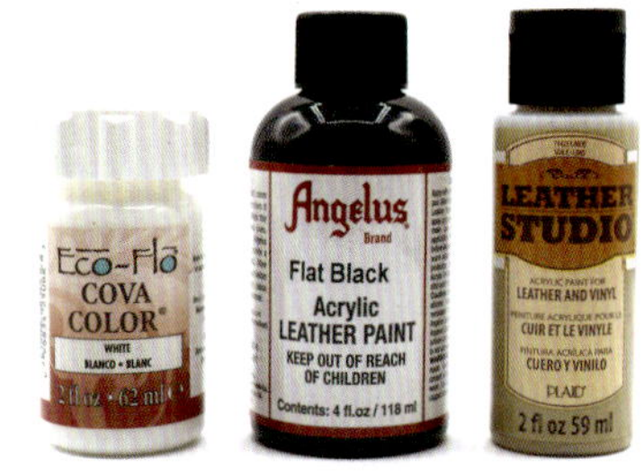

Paint: Acrylic and oil paints work great on leather and come in many varieties. Both craft store acrylics and heavy body acrylics work when mixed with a medium, such as fabric medium, to become flexible.

Paintbrush: Used for both paint and dye applications in small amounts or precise locations.

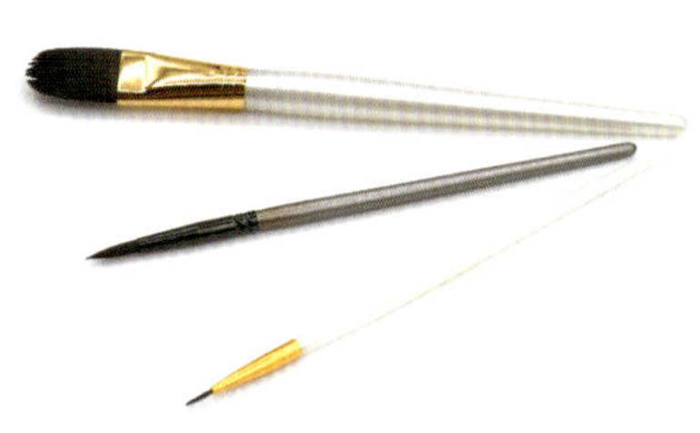

Nitrile or latex gloves: Because leather dyes will also dye your skin, it is best to wear gloves when handling.

Spray bottle: For wetting leather, but not soaking.

Sponge: Used for applying leather dyes and paints. For leather dyes we recommend using kitchen sponges; for paints, makeup sponges.

Everything and the Kitchen Sink: *Although specific tools (called* **wool daubers***) are sold to assist with dyeing leather, we recommend using kitchen sponges for large applications of leather dye. They're cost effective, and we find they make buffing in the dye easier. Any brand works as long as the sponge isn't scratchy. For each color of dye that we plan to use, we use half a sponge. You can also use sponges for applying sealant, so they're quite versatile!*

Fabric rag: Used for buffing and cleaning up excess dye, paint, or sealant.

OPTIONAL

Wool dauber: Used for dyeing leather. Usually has a twisted metal handle and is for one-time use.

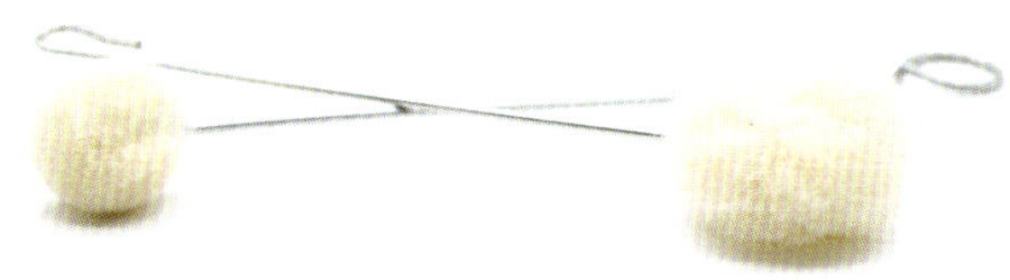

Deglazer: Deglazer is highly flammable and contains toxins. Use it with gloves and personal protective equipment in a well-ventilated area. Read the label carefully before use. It is an acetone-based product that thins and removes layers of dye or chemicals added to the grain side of the leather in the tanning process.

Glass jars: Handy to have if you mix dyes or paints.

Paint pallet: An easy place to mix paints or have several colors ready for your use in small quantities. Also can be used to hold a splash of leather dye if you're using dyes for painting.

Airbrush: Used with either leather dye or paint.

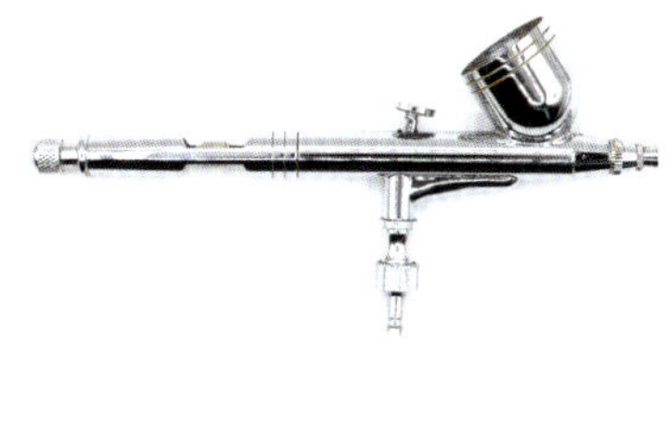

Plastic container: Used when dip-dyeing leather. You want a container that is big enough to fit your project flat along the bottom and deep enough that you can submerge your piece.

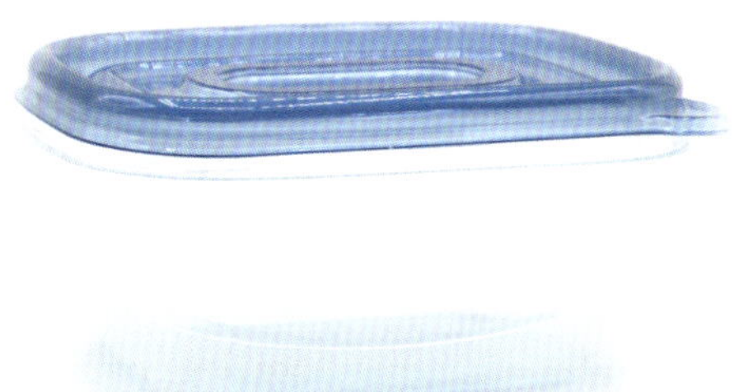

Paint pen: If dyeing or painting the edges of leather, this pen works like a paintbrush would, but it's self-feeding. Fill it up with Edge Kote or paint and follow the instructions to get the liquid flowing to the tip.

Dyeing and Painting

Dyeing leather really brings the project to life. There are so many ways to dye and paint leather. This is truly a part of the process where you can play around with different techniques, borrow from other painting mediums, and invent your own! We'll cover the basic processes and let you in on some fun techniques we've found along the way. Just as in canvas painting, the rules can be mixed, matched, and broken when it comes to art!

Other types of leather usually come pre-dyed or are more likely to have leather paints applied to them to change their appearance, so we'll again be focusing mostly on veg tan this chapter.

TO DYE, OR NOT TO DYE?

If you're wet forming your leather (see Wet Forming, page 111), you should do this prior to dyeing. Wetting the leather enough to be moldable after dyeing can lead to color leaching and cause an inconsistent dye job or cracks in the paint. Some leather is also more prone to wrinkling after wet forming based on which part of the animal it came from. While this can be eased with steam, subjecting your dyes and paints to that much hot moisture can lead to blotching or a change in pigment.

Leather takes dye differently based on the properties of the hide. Each hide comes from a different animal, and no two hides are exactly the same. To get the most consistent dye job, cut your whole project from one hide if possible. Also note placement on the hide and the type of hide you're using. For example, pieces cut from stomach leather dye differently than back leather because stomach leather is naturally softer. Black dye can be an exception to these rules, because it covers most veg tan similarly.

If your project uses hides of different thicknesses or is too large for one hide, do test swatches of dyes and see if you get an even consistency between them. If there is only a slight difference in color, leaving it as is and embracing the variation may work. In the end, having different shades may help your piece look more "real world" and bring your costume farther out of the 2-D realm. If they're far off, consider mixing a darker shade into one of them to reduce the variation.

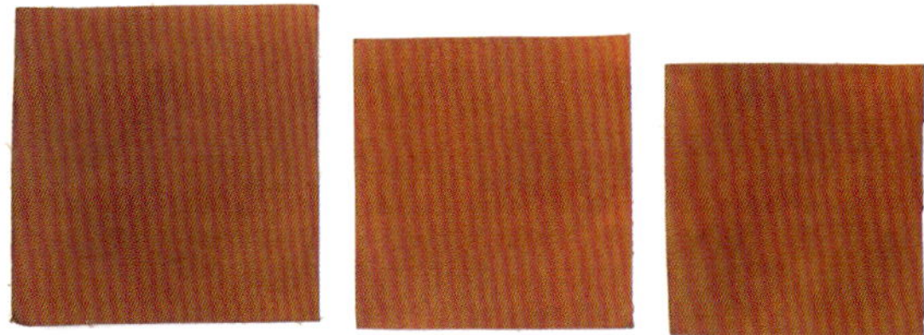

Samples from different hides dyed with two layers of tan Eco-Flo Waterstain. Variation of color is not significant.

Samples from different hides dyed with two layers of turquoise Eco-Flo Waterstain. Colors besides brown and black often show the most variation between hides.

You Are Leather, Too: *When dyeing leather, please wear gloves! Leather dye is specially made to penetrate and dye skin, so it will dye your hands. If you wind up getting some leather dye on your skin, use dish soap and warm water to help with the cleaning process. Please note that leather dye is extremely difficult to get out of clothing. If you're an artist who paints on yourself as much as your project, wear clothes that you don't mind staining with dye.*

WHAT TYPE OF DYE?

There are two main types of dye for leather: solvent- and water-based. Once you begin a project, it is wise to continue with similar-based dyes, paints, and sealants. Mixing solvent- and water-based products can lead to unexpected or sometimes ruinous results. Always read the ingredients and instructions on your bottles and test before applying to your final piece. Be sure to wear gloves and other personal protective equipment any time you're working with dyes.

Solvent-based: These dyes are created with oil, alcohol, or other mediums. They're potent in color and have a faster working time. One downside is the environmental impact of these dyes—they contain more volatile organic compounds (VOCs) than their water-based counterparts and must be used in a well-ventilated area. A popular type of solvent-based dye is Fiebing's oil dye (which is actually alcohol-based but does contain some oils). If you choose to dye your leather with a solvent-based leather dye, you should condition the leather afterward because this kind of dye dries out the hide as the alcohol evaporates. Sealing alcohol-based dyes is also important—these dyes experience color rub-off if not thoroughly sealed. Solvent-based dyes are generally the easiest to use for beginner leatherworkers.

Water-based: Water-based dyes, such as the brand Eco-Flo Waterstain, are thinner and require more layers and longer drying times, but the colors are just as saturated as solvent-based dyes if you take your time. Water-based dyes can be diluted with water, but dilution is not recommended for large applications. Adding water can achieve new colors or techniques (see Watercolor on Leather!, page 65). We enjoy using water-based dyes and find them easier to mix together. Most of the examples of our work are done using Eco-Flo Waterstain.

Here is a comparison of black, brown, and green dye in Fiebing's Pro Dye and Eco-Flo Waterstain. These are all done on veg tan, with a kitchen sponge, after evenly wetting the leather with a spray bottle.

Top: One layer of dye. Bottom: Three layers of dye.

COLORS OF THE RAINBOW

As you start using more dye colors, we recommend making a swatch ring where you write down the color ratios of your mixes, type of dye, and leather thickness. This will assist you when deciding what dyes to use on your future projects. Also, write the date you made the swatch and the topcoat sealant used (if applicable) to gauge how age affects the color.

HOW TO DYE VEG TAN LEATHER

Leather can be dyed indoors, but we recommend having ventilation or a good cross breeze when using solvent-based dyes due to their odor. If you choose to dye your leather outside, set up in a protected area, such as a garage, away from the sun and errant dirt particles. Always read the manufacturer's safety instructions before using any product.

As mentioned in Burnishing (page 69), we've tested burnishing leather prior to and after dyeing on several projects. The difference in overall appearance was miniscule and pre-burnished edges and flesh sides of veg tan took dye just fine. The only exception was when dye was added on top of Tokonole. It did not permeate the leather as easily as leather burnished with gum tragacanth, which is due to the resin compounds in Tokonole.

Once you've decided you're ready to dye your pieces, you need to prepare them. The process is simple but fundamental for achieving an even dye job. (You'll hear this phrase a lot.)

1. Set up your dye station. This doesn't need to be fancy. We use recycled cardboard boxes (something many cosplayers find they have ample amounts of sitting around) or thick paper bags. We set up separate dyeing stations for each color to mitigate any cross contamination. Depending on where we're working, we may put down a painter's tarp or a plastic tablecloth to protect our workstation in case of dye spills.

2. Clean your leather. This can be done using soapy water and a rag. This step isn't always required because leather from suppliers is generally clean, but if you've been tooling your leather (see Tooling, page 43), you may want to clean off any skin oils you've transferred to the piece.

Another way to prep your leather is to lightly sand it. This is useful mostly to get rid of fuzzy leftovers from cutting and removing larger pieces of fuzz on the flesh side. If the edge fuzz and flesh-side fuzz can be trimmed off with a scissor, do that first and then sand your leather with sandpaper, working your way from a medium grit to fine grit (approximately 400–1000).

For stitch holes or hardware holes, you can punch them before or after dyeing. If needed, you can always add dye to them or do touch-ups with a small paintbrush. Whichever you choose, be sure to punch and dye any holes before you seal your leather. If you're dip dyeing your leather, don't punch your stitching or hardware holes until after you dip dye (see Dip Dyeing, page 60).

HYDRATE! DON'T "DYEDRATE"!

When you're using water-based dyes, we strongly caution against dyeing your leather piece without dampening it first. The water, while opening the pores, also acts as an agent to assist with blending of the dye as you work across the piece. If you try to dye dry leather, you'll have stark outlines where the dye was initially placed on the leather and it will have a streaky or splotchy final appearance. Dry dyeing also requires more dye overall, which can lead to dye leakage during or after the sealing process.

When using solvent-based dyes, you can prep with a thin layer of conditioning salve such as neatsfoot oil instead of water if you're concerned about the water reacting with the dye. When in doubt, test it out!

3. *Optional for solvent-based dyes if prepping with a conditioning salve.* Fill your spray bottle with room-temperature water. You don't want icy fridge water or steaming hot water—these will cause shrinking and warping of the leather pores.

4. *Optional for solvent-based dyes if prepping with a conditioning salve.* Spray or mist the whole leather piece evenly, front and back. Doing so ensures that the pores across the entire piece have been exposed to the same amount of water. You want the leather to be darkened in color but not pooling with water, as too much water in the pores makes the dye sit on top, leading to blotchiness.

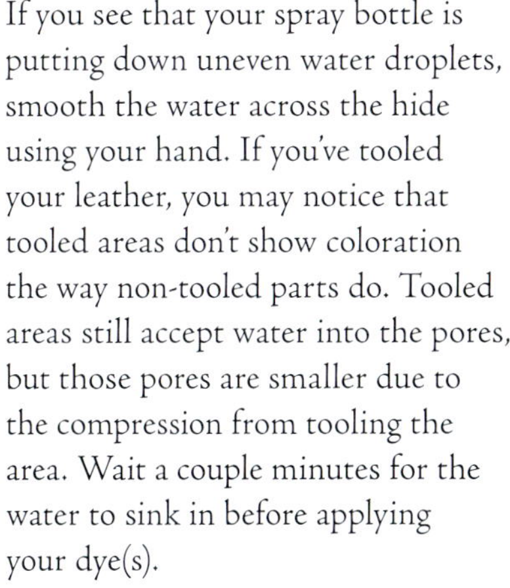

If you see that your spray bottle is putting down uneven water droplets, smooth the water across the hide using your hand. If you've tooled your leather, you may notice that tooled areas don't show coloration the way non-tooled parts do. Tooled areas still accept water into the pores, but those pores are smaller due to the compression from tooling the area. Wait a couple minutes for the water to sink in before applying your dye(s).

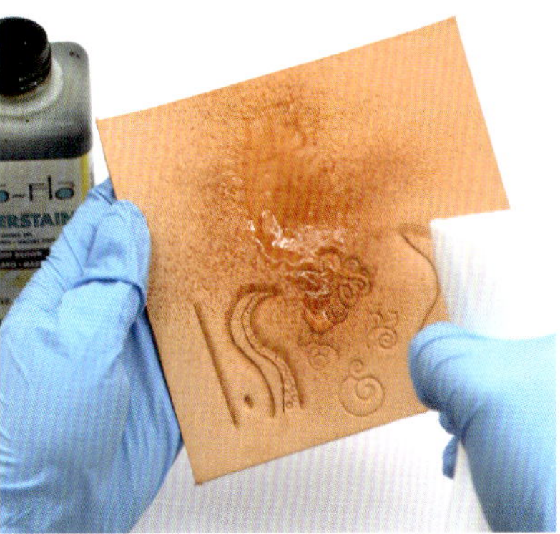

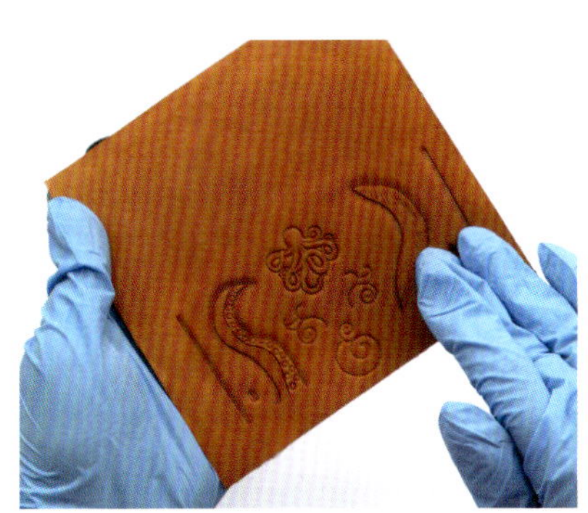

5. Lightly mist the sponge with water, and then add dye to the sponge. If you're using a synthetic sponge, rinse it out thoroughly before use. Some are treated with chemicals or soaps that may have an effect on the leather.

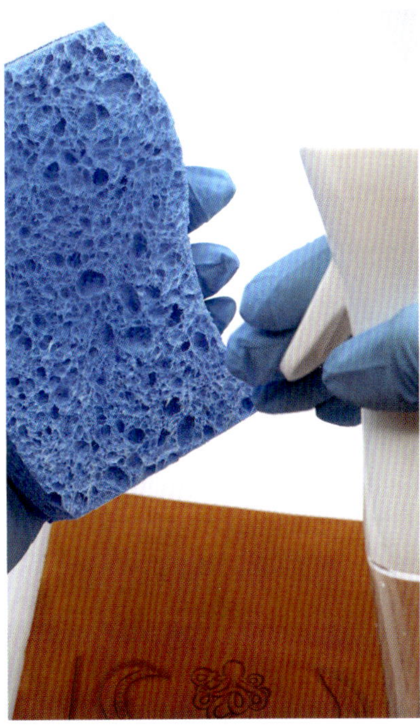

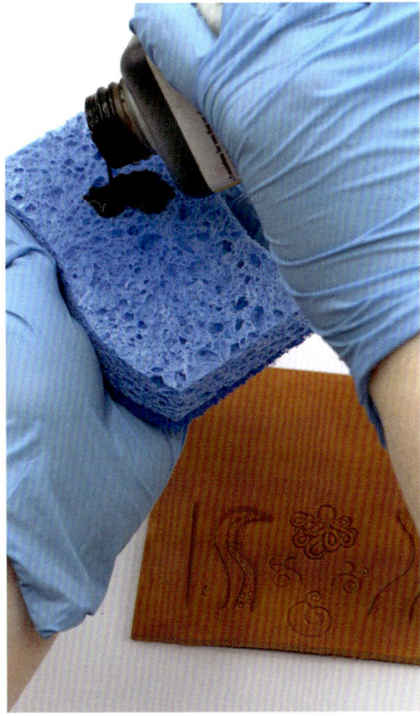

6. For our examples, we're using Eco-Flo Waterstain to dye our project, but the application process is the same with solvent-based dyes. Once you have dye on your sponge, start moving it in circular buffing motions on the grain side of the leather, applying some downward pressure. It is important not to use sweeping lines, which may be tempting if you're doing a belt or strap. To create a seamless base coat, you need to buff out all application lines, which is easiest to do in circles.

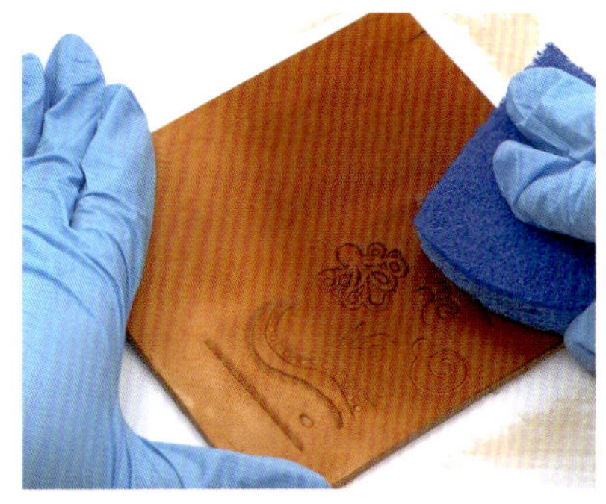

USING A WOOL DAUBER

If you choose to use a wool dauber, the process is similar except instead of applying the dye straight onto your sponge, put your dye in a small cup or glass and dip the dauber end in the dye. Apply the dye in circular motions, or you can choose to move side to side and then up and down if your piece is small enough. Work quickly to avoid streaking.

Fiebing's dye mid-application with wool dauber

7. Special care needs to be taken to get dye into tooled areas because the compressed leather takes dye less easily than non-compressed leather. To get even coloration, apply more pressure on tooled areas and make sure you have a good amount of dye on your sponge or dauber. If it is still resisting color, take a paintbrush and apply dye directly to the tooled area; then buff gently to blend out any hard lines. Sometimes we like to paint a darker dye or add metallics into our beveled areas or stamps to create even more depth.

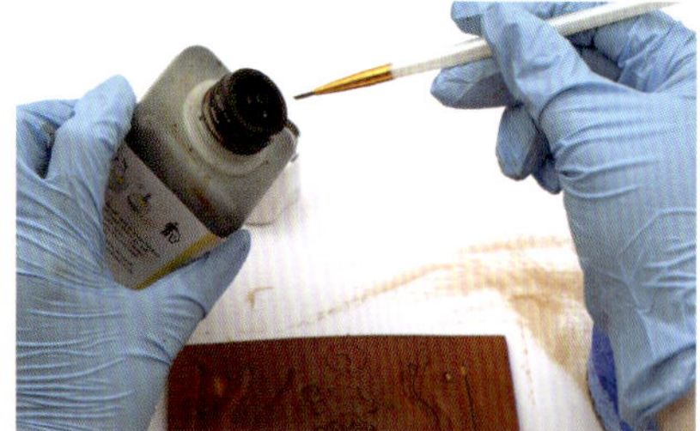

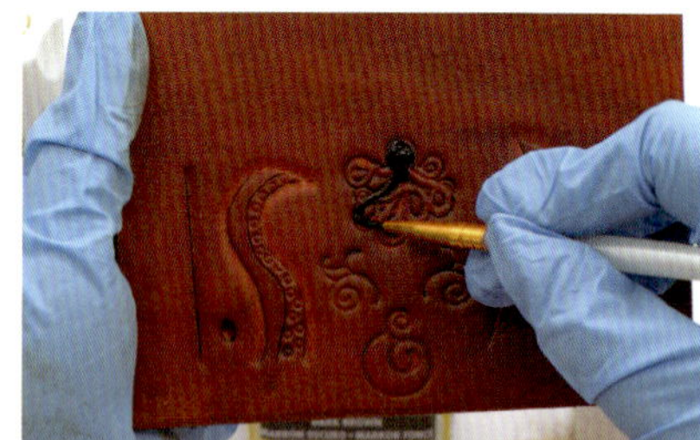

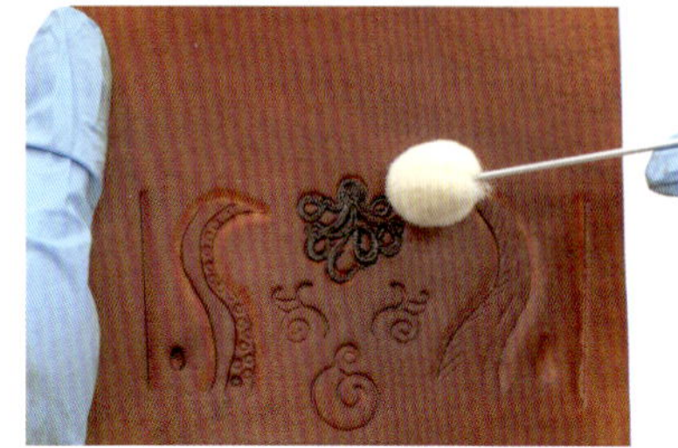

SHINE LIKE SILVER AND GOLD

If you're using pearl, silver, or gold water-based dyes, be sure to apply them on top of a base color. These dyes do not stain leather to a lustrous finish by themselves as a paint would. For silver, we suggest adding on top of gray or black. Gold can be added to tan, yellow, or orange for fun variations. You can also mix your metallics directly with other dyes. Experiment with ratios and log your favorites for future projects!

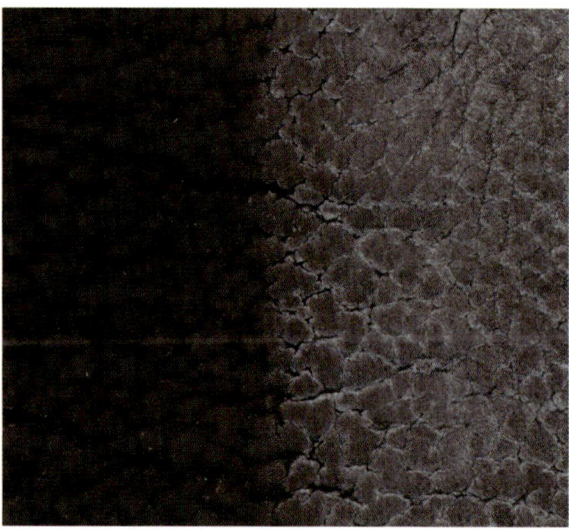

8. While dyeing the grain side of your veg tan, be sure to also dye the edges for a clean finish. For the edges, a quick pass may leave dye dripping to the front and back, so it is important to go back and blend that in before the dye dries. If the back (flesh side) will be seen, dye that, too!

EDGY COLOR CHOICE

If you want your edges to be a different color than the grain side of your veg tan or thicker chrome tan, take extra care when applying the edge dye. You can use a paintbrush, a refillable dye pen, or an extra-small dauber. There are also products in the leatherworking world that are specially made for edge coating (see Edge Kote, page 68).

The flesh side of leather will absorb more dye than the grain side. If your flesh side has a large amount of fuzz left on it, consider burnishing (page 69), sanding, or trimming down the fuzz for better dye application. After sanding or burnishing, it should be fairly smooth. One or two fuzzies is nothing to sweat over!

Here's a secret we have for dyeing the flesh side: After working in circles and covering the piece with dye, work down your piece in straight passes **in one direction only.** This helps slick down the fuzz and creates a smooth back once dried. It is important later to do your sealant layer in this same direction so you don't pull up any errant fuzz.

9. As your dye runs out, add more to the sponge and continue Steps 6–8 until you've evenly covered your piece or dye area. Note that rewetting leather after it has dye on it may lead to discoloration and an uneven dye job.

Most leather dyes require multiple layers to reach the desired saturation. Wait for the leather to dry before adding another layer of dye. While drying, the leather will feel cold and tacky. When dry, it may feel more rigid. This is okay because you'll add conditioner to the leather to regain flexibility after you've finished the dyeing process.

10. Repeat dyeing and drying cycles (Steps 6 and 9) until you've reached the desired color. You can also begin weathering your leather with dyes (page 123).

Acetone and isopropyl alcohol can remove some dye, but we don't recommend using them because they harden the leather where they're applied.

TOO MUCH DYE?

Deglazer can assist but not perfectly fix having applied too much dye. **Deglazer is highly flammable and toxic!** *Use only in a well-ventilated area while wearing personal protective equipment. Always test first on an inconspicuous spot or scrap.*

While there isn't a way to return dyed leather to what we call "original veg tan blond," deglazer can strip off layers of colors to lighten existing dye jobs. Deglazer can also assist with taking off topcoats on finished projects that need to be re-dyed or refinished. When used on chrome tan, we've seen it take off the topcoat and allow for darkening of a chrome tan hide's base color with leather dyes.

ALTERNATIVE DYEING TECHNIQUES

So far, we've shared the most common and beginner-friendly version of dyeing. Like every step of leatherwork, time and technology have evolved this into a vast topic. The dyeing techniques that we cover in the next sections may require specific dye types or tools, but we bring these up as options because many cosplayers may already own these tools and have experience using them in another craft.

Dip Dyeing

To dip dye leather, you need a container that fits your leather piece fully flat along the bottom and enough dye to submerge your piece. Dip your leather for approximately 5–10 seconds in one even dunk; then remove it from the dye bath. Repeat if darker coloring is needed. This method is fast if you have repetitive pieces that are small and need to be a solid color. We do not recommend this for large pieces because there is room for error in the dye consistency over a bigger area, the amount of dye needed can be expensive, and the container itself could also be expensive.

Note that leather can only hold so much dye, and the rest will leak out or rub off. Soaking for longer does not necessarily mean darker in the end, and it could wind up ruining your piece. Leather with too much dye in it can show effects such as a spongy texture on the grain side and may continue to rub off color after being dried and sealed.

DON'T "DIP" INTO YOUR SAVINGS

Because the cost of dip dyeing can quickly add up, search for containers or trays at thrift stores and try to purchase larger dye bottles when sales are happening. We personally have large bottles of brown and black as those are common colors across many costuming and general leathercraft items.

Another thrifty hack if you're dip dyeing using an alcohol-based dye, such as Feibing's Pro Dye, is to mix it with denatured alcohol. Add the denatured alcohol in a two parts alcohol to one part dye ratio. If you want to dilute the color even more, increase the amount of denatured alcohol. When the piece dries, the scent fades, and many leather conditioners and balms have scents like coconut or shea butter that will make your work smell delightful again.

If you're dip dyeing your leather pieces, hold off on punching any stitch or hardware holes until after you've dyed it. If you expose more surface area by making holes, more dye sinks into the exposed fibers when the leather is dipped, causing discolored/darkened rings around the holes. Add any holes after the piece is dry and done being dipped. Color them by using a small paintbrush dipped in dye, buffing out any excess dye that bleeds over to the grain or flesh side with a sponge or rag.

Airbrushing

Many cosplayers may already have an airbrush in their arsenal of tools, which gives them another option for dye application. Dye is recommended to be airbrushed at around 15 pounds per square inch (PSI), which is much lower than the standard PSI for painting. Unlike dip dyeing or regular leather dyeing, this process must be done outdoors. The particles that airborne leather dye emit are toxic and plentiful, so be sure to wear personal protective equipment.

Safety warning! Eco-Flo Waterstain should not be sprayed through an airbrush—it is toxic if ingested. Although water-based, it contains chemicals that are skin irritants and harmful if inhaled.

This dye method is mostly chosen for its speed, but it does not penetrate the leather as deeply as force-applied or full-soak methods. Airbrushing on leather dye essentially makes the dye like a paint and coats the top of the grain. If the leather ever cracks or is cut, the color seen underneath is that of the undyed veg tan.

Marble Dyeing

Marble dyeing may remind crafters of tie-dye, ice melt dyeing, or even hydro dip dyeing. Its random marbling texture makes unique creations with added depth, and it is a fairly cost-effective technique when it comes to materials.

To marble dye, you need to have a foaming shaving cream (no specific brand), cling wrap, and an alcohol-based leather dye. In our example, we used Eco-Flow Waterstain dyes.

1. Cover your workstation with a piece of cling wrap.

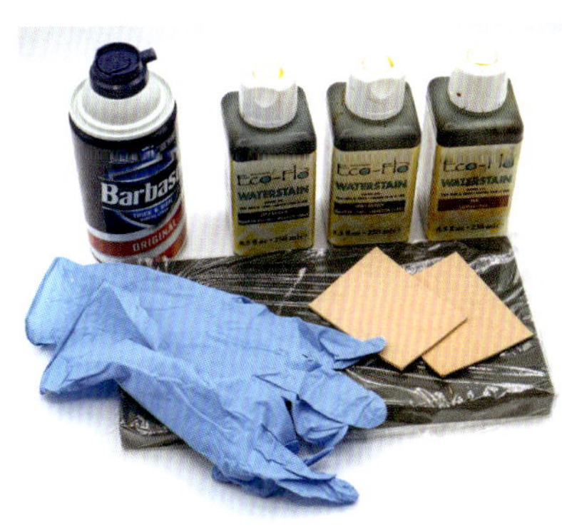

2. Create a bed of shaving cream slightly larger than your leather piece.

3. Randomly add drops of leather dye and swirl them around with a wooden stirring stick, the back of a paintbrush, or a gloved finger. Add more color and continue to mix until you have reached your desired look.

4. Put your dry veg tan piece, grain side down, onto the shaving cream and press down from the center, working your way to the edges.

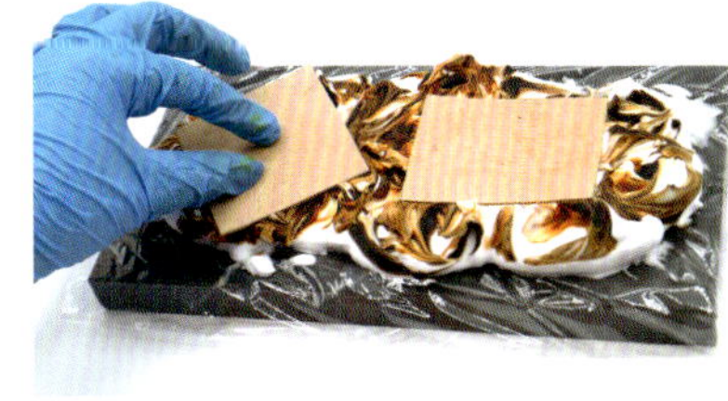

5. Wait 10–20 seconds; then pick up your leather piece and wipe off the shaving cream with a rag or paper towel.

Once your marbling dye job has dried, you can paint on more dye or add acrylic paints. You can also move straight to sealing.

Left: Final results. Right: Other marbling examples.

Chrome Tan

Chrome tan hides come in pre-dyed colors and have had chemical treatments to make the dye stick and not rub off. If you're determined to change the color of your chrome tan, note that you won't be able to change it much (for example, you can go from blue to darker blue, orange to red orange). The exception is if you just blot out the color with black.

Deglazer is helpful during color alteration because it takes off part of the chemical topcoat, causing the hide to be more exposed. Dye as you would a veg tan hide and check out how to seal it (see Sealing, page 72). Overall, we recommend not going through the hassle of re-dyeing chrome tan but understand that it may be necessary to get that perfect shade for the outfit you're re-creating.

When you're ready to dye the edges of your chrome tan, see Edge Kote (page 68) for more insight on how to get a finished look on chrome tan.

Suede

Dyeing suede can be tricky because many regular leather dyes are not designed to dye suede. Make sure you purchase a suede-specific leather dye and carefully read the application instructions.

Prep your suede by cleaning it with a soft-bristle brush or removing stains with a suede-grade soap. If you do need to get your suede wet to clean it, let it fully dry and brush up the pile again before beginning your dye process. If you have hardware on your suede already, cover it with painter's tape.

Due to its texture, the pile of suede can be easily flattened and lose its softness during the dyeing process. When dyeing suede, use a soft brush or dense sponge to apply the dye—hard bristles claw at the suede and could alter the texture or rip a hole in your suede piece. Work in forward-to-back, side-to-side motions. By brushing your suede, you make sure that the dye is evenly distributed on the pile.

Once the dye begins to dry, using a suede brush or a soft-bristle horse brush, brush the pile back up to regain that telltale texture. Now you're almost done! Take a rag and buff the suede. This pulls out any excess dye. Move on to sealing your piece using specific suede-grade sealants.

King Arthur from *Fate/Grand Order*
Cosplay by Autumn's Cosplay • Photos by PSICORP Media

PAINTING LEATHER

When painting leather, you're truly treating it like a canvas, which allows you to use many techniques and tools from traditional painting. If you've painted on foam or thermoplastic before, you may find yourself quite comfortable with this process.

Paint, unlike dye, does not sink into the fibers of the hide but sits on top, allowing for more control of color blocking and blending. Also, traditional color mixing theory can be applied, whereas with dyes, mixing is not always successful under these rules.

Here are a few things to keep in mind when it comes to painting leather:

Flexibility: Use a flexible paint or leather-specific paint for pieces that may bend or flex; otherwise, the paint will crack and flake off.

Friction: Because paint sits on top of the hide, it can be rubbed off in high-friction areas such as gloves or boot armor. Be sure to add extra sealant, or be aware that you may need to maintain these pieces more often.

When to wet form: As with dyeing, wet form your leather prior to painting.

Color consistency: Unlike dyeing, when painting leather, it matters less where on the hide you're painting or whether your pieces come from different cuts of leather (for example, shoulder versus stomach). Overall, paint has fewer variables when it comes to application, which allows for better color matching across pieces.

Fair weather ... ing? Paints can be used to weather your leather pieces. See Weathering with Dyes and Paints (page 123) for ideas and applications.

Whether you choose to use acrylic- or oil-based paints, always ensure that your leather is clean before you start painting. You don't need to wet your leather before painting; in fact, you want to avoid water in this step. If you wipe down your leather with water to clean it, wait until it's fully dry before painting.

You can use standard painting tools to apply paints on leather. Brushes in several sizes are valuable as you make your masterpiece, but don't forget about sponges when looking to add texture or covering large areas without brushstrokes (makeup sponges work great for this!). If you choose to use oil-based paints, be sure to wear gloves, have a specific set of brushes for oil-based paints, and clean them with the proper cleaning solvents.

Acrylic-Based Paints

Acrylic-based paints are the most friendly, versatile type of paints for leatherworking, and they have short drying times. You can paint on dyed or undyed veg tan. However, be sure to read your paint bottle instructions and ingredients to ensure the paint and dye are compatible. The oil and water adage still rings true here. If you're painting on dyed veg tan, be sure you paint before you've sealed the dye. If you've already sealed it, some paints may not apply evenly on top of leather sealant or may react adversely to it, by bubbling or cracking.

PAINTING OUTSIDE THE LINES

If you make a mistake while painting on leather with acrylic-based paints, you may be able to clean it up, whereas cleaning leather dye or oil-based paints is quite difficult. This is because most acrylic-based paints or leather paints are made with a water-based formula. Soap and warm water is the most effective cleaner for acrylic-based paints, but use caution if you're cleaning already dyed leather—it may strip or discolor the dye in that area. If you're unsure, always test a swatch or a spot that is not noticeable. Dark-colored paints, or light-colored paints on a dark hide, may leave some staining or discoloring where paint was once applied, so still try to paint with a careful hand. Applying painter's tape when using acrylics is another way to keep a project tidy from errant paint.

When painting with acrylic-based paints, it's important to apply in thin coats, working carefully to avoid brushstrokes. If you have a full-bodied paint, you can thin down the paint with water, but don't make it too thin! If your paint becomes too thin, the excess water can cause color distortion or seeping. If you're painting on an area you expect to flex a little, or if your acrylics are cracking or dry in a hard shell-like layer, you can mix in a small amount of fabric medium to add elasticity to the paint.

Craft Store Colors: *Full-bodied paints give the best coverage and saturation, but never write off the humble craft store acrylics! They may take more layers, but their colors are just as effective. We love to mix and match on our projects, using both expensive and cost-effective paints, paired with hand painting or airbrushing. If you're using craft store paints, be sure to shake well before use!*

Oil-Based Paints

Oil-based paints introduce extra difficulties, such as drying time, air temperature, and humidity level, and they're just less user-friendly overall. We caution newer painters to research and practice with oil paints before deciding to use them on a project and always do a test. If working with oil paints, it's easier to paint on undyed veg tan than dyed. This is due to the oils from the paint penetrating into the fibers of the leather as the paint dries and causing discoloration. Oil paint can be treated like a halfway mark between leather dye and acrylic paint: It doesn't sink in as deeply as leather dye, but it does sink more deeply than acrylic paint.

Leather Paint

Leather paint is designed for application to leather hides. It is made with thicker body acrylic and is strongly pigmented, meaning a little goes a long way. Sold in all sizes of bottles, you can get a variety of colors, even metallics (which we love!). Using leather paints is similar to working with standard acrylic-based paints when it comes to brushing on, but it doesn't need to be thinned with water because the out-of-the-bottle consistency is formulated for best application. Avoid mixing leather-specific paints with general acrylic paints to make colors.

A common brand of leather paint is Angelus. We find the consistency and color mixing to be easy to work with and have had good results hand painting as well as airbrushing. When airbrushing Angelus products, don't thin with water—that breaks apart a bonding agent in the paint. Instead, use a thinner meant for airbrushing.

Painting Suede and Chrome Tan

Painting suede: Suede is usually dyed in large areas, not painted. However, you can still paint suede with leather paint or acrylic paints (not oil), but because it is difficult to apply smoothly and changes the texture, we suggest painting only small details.

Painting chrome tan: Chrome tan can be painted, but due to the tanning process and chemicals, paint doesn't hold well to it. Most paints flake off over time, even if applied after using deglazer on the topcoat of the chrome tan and then sealing afterward. Try this at your own discretion and always do a test!

Bonus: Watercolor on Leather!

Often forgotten in a crafting world dominated by acrylic and oil techniques, watercolors or water-based inks can be used on leather as well. You can use highly pigmented watercolors from art supply stores or you can water down water-based leather dyes and paints to make different opacities and use them as you would watercolors.

It's handy to have a paint palette or multiple small jars for mixing and storing your watercolors while working on a project. Note your mix ratios in case you need to make more! For best results, use watercolor on white pigmented or natural veg tan.

1. Start by making your mixes. You'll need at least a handful of mixes, ranging from a saturated mix to a diluted mix. Also, have a jar of clean water for further diluting as you work.

2. Do not pre-wet your leather. Just as with watercolor on paper, you want to control where and how much water is put down so you can use it to spread the paint or dye into your desired shapes.

3. Apply your most diluted watercolor with a paintbrush and create your shape. Delicate strokes are the name of the game with watercoloring, so don't be too heavy-handed.

4. Now begin adding your less diluted color mix. If you find that your watercolor is too saturated, you can dilute it directly on the project by painting on clean water. However, don't drench your project—that causes bleeding of the color outside of your design.

5. To create soft ombres or transitions, you want to layer your washes of color, starting with a weak mix of paint and moving to a more potent mix of paint, working your way to the darker sections. Pure water helps soften harsh transitions. Note that watercolors dry lighter.

6. Seal with a water-based sealant once the project has fully dried.

Stencils and Decals

When painting on leather, you may want repeating patterns that need to be crisp and equal or designs that might be difficult to freehand. Pull out your die-cutting machine such as a Cricut or Silhouette (or your trusty craft knife and patience) and cut out your design on sticky-back vinyl. Be sure you're using removable vinyl; otherwise, your stencil will stick to the leather and peel up your paint or mar the grain side of the leather when trying to remove it.

If you want your design to be permanent like a decal, use the permanent sticky-back vinyl. We've paired permanent vinyl with antiquing for a raised design with plenty of tiny details. If you find your vinyl is lifting, apply a small amount of leather-specific glue to the back of your decal and to the grain side of the leather. This helps the vinyl stay down and also move with the leather. Because the vinyl is a raised surface on the leather, this makes it susceptible to peeling off. Do not use this technique in high-friction areas.

Tools: Burn, Baby, Burn(ishing)!

ESSENTIALS

Burnishing agent: A compound, usually liquid or gel, that is used to aid the burnishing process. Some agents have sealant properties and come in both water- and acrylic-based mixes.

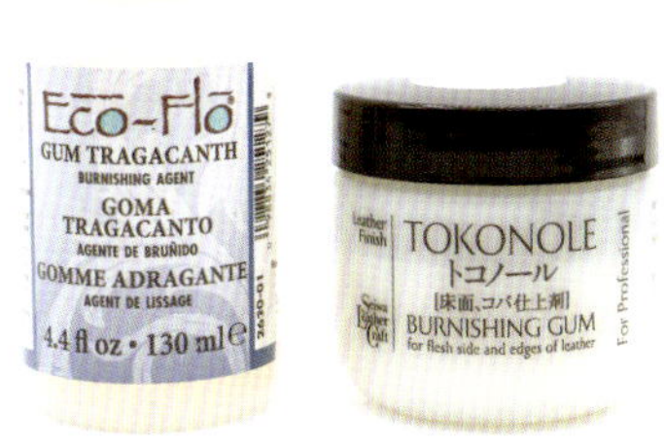

Burnishing tool: A handheld tool that aids in finishing leather edges. Used for burnishing or slicking, these are usually wooden or plastic and come in many shapes with different-size grooves for various leather thicknesses.

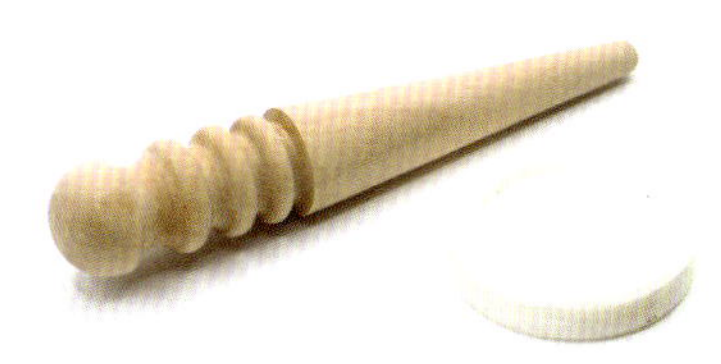

Note: *In the context of finishing edges on leather,* **burnishing** *and* **slicking** *are interchangeable terms. Advertised tool names by leather companies will even flip-flop between the two.*

Buffing rag: A small piece of cloth that is used to create friction and polish a burnishing agent after slicking. They range from cotton to denim but should never be a scratchy fabric that would leave marks. Also used to apply some leather conditioners.

Leather conditioner: Applied to leather projects before sealing to assist with softening and longevity. Also used for upkeep and maintenance. Comes in many varieties.

Sponge: Can be paired with a burnishing agent to apply in large sweeps, such as on the flesh side of hide. Also used to apply leather conditioner if it's a soft sponge.

OPTIONAL

Edge Kote: A specific burnishing agent used to finish edges of leather pieces. The top choice for chrome tan pieces.

Glass slicker: A tool with many uses, from stretching leather to creating a glossy finish on the flesh side of leather when paired with burnishing agents.

Rotary tool: Used with burnishing and buffing bits. Easier on the hands and wrists.

Conditioning and Burnishing

LEATHER CONDITIONING

Before you jump into sealing your leather pieces, it's important to condition them. Throughout the dyeing and/or painting process, you handle and add chemicals to the leather, which causes dehydration of the grain side. To keep it from cracking or rippling with wear, you need to introduce hydrating mixtures known as *leather conditioners* before you do a final topcoat of sealant. However, you need to strike the right balance. Over-oiling leads to "soaked" leather, which is spongy to the touch, and it's hard to recover the leather's natural rigidity after it reaches that point.

Conditioners darken the color of natural, undyed veg tan on a sliding scale by product. The pure oils, such as neatsfoot or mink, give you the darkest outcome once dried. Be sure to test on a scrap piece or hidden part of your project to see if the color is what you want before applying to your whole project. If you're using suede, look for conditioners marked "safe for suede" or "suede-grade."

Applying a conditioner is fairly universal:

1. Use a soft rag or sponge to buff an even, thin layer of conditioner onto the leather.
2. Allow for 1–2 minutes of resting time.
3. Use a clean soft rag or paper towel to remove excess cream or oil, gently buffing as you work.
4. Let your leather dry completely before applying any additional layers. Usually 1 layer does the trick—you don't want to over-oil or over-hydrate your leather.

AU NATURALE

If you want the least amount of change in your undyed veg tan's color, we recommend using a leather cream to condition your leather. In our examples below, we used pure neatsfoot oil, mink oil, and Aussie Leather Conditioner. You can see that, when they're wet, they change the color of the leather quite aggressively. Once wiped off, the color ranges are apparent: Neatsfoot oil brings out the yellows in the natural veg tan color, mink oil brings out the reds in the natural veg tan color, and leather cream makes a neutral to slightly darker change in the color.

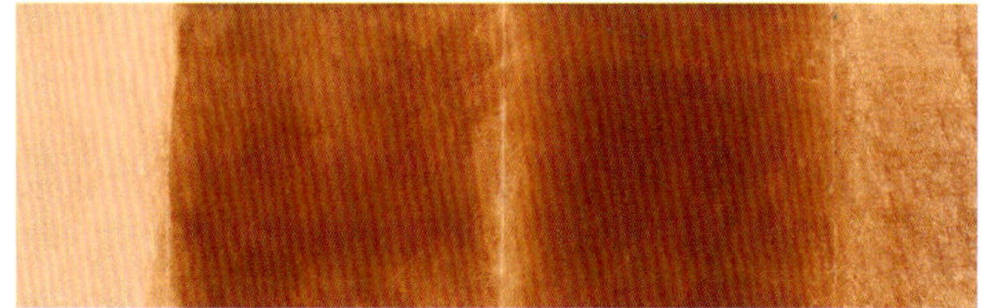

From left to right: None, neatsfoot oil, mink oil, leather cream

Neatsfoot Oil versus Neatsfoot Oil Compound (NOC)

Neatsfoot oil is a by-product of the hooves and shin bones of many animals in the leather industry. It is a natural oil, so it works well on natural fibers when applied in thin layers that are left to dry between applications. It is a leatherworker's go-to conditioner, but use it in moderation! It's easy to over-oil while using neatsfoot oil. A little goes a long way with this product.

Neatsfoot oil compound (NOC) is neatsfoot oil plus other compounds—usually silicone, petroleum jelly, or mineral oil. It is less expensive than pure neatsfoot oil, which, paired with being a mixed compound, has caused a host of rumors to be attached to its use. Some say that it deteriorates natural threads, ruins glue, and makes your leather brittle. The theories on thread and glue are based in truth, but those products deteriorate over time by themselves; NOC may be expediting that process on a small scale. As for making your leather brittle, NOC does contain some pore-sealing additives, which you'll learn in Sealing (page 72) can dry out your leather over time.

Looking at these products through the lens of a cosplayer, both are applicable and appropriate to use. The amount that you're applying is miniscule, and the repeat treatment of your leather costume pieces with neatsfoot or NOC are not as frequent as that of daily-used leather products like boots or saddles. So, give them a test and use whichever you prefer.

SHOWING OFF SOME NEAT(SFOOT) SCRATCHES

A fun technique with neatsfoot oil is using it to bring out the natural wear and tear of aged, undyed leather. If you're interested in showing off those scuffs and scrapes, apply neatsfoot or mink oil to your undyed leather, and watch that patina pop! As an added benefit, these oils ever so slightly change the undertone of your leather's color and even darken it, giving it a natural dye tone, not to mention conditioning your leather in the same step. To finish, continue on to burnishing and sealing.

We mentioned reapplication of leather conditioner a few times in this section, and that's because leather requires some upkeep. Because it was a living product, it was creating its own oils and hydration. Now, as a veg tan hide, it requires you to reintroduce oil and hydration into the pores. However, the frequency is dependent on the type of sealant you choose for your topcoat.

BURNISHING

Getting those super-polished, slick edges is every leatherworker's dream—and nightmare! Like some of the processes in this book, it can be done out of the order we've presented it here. Burnishing can be done before or after the dyeing step. Full transparency, we burnished our edges beforehand on veg tan for over a decade before hearing that it *should* be done after dyeing. Now having done projects both ways, the myth of which is better lives on because we have yet to see a true difference. You can also mix and match, which we'll dig into.

When painting your leather, we suggest burnishing the edges prior to painting because burnishing after may strip away your paint due to friction.

TIP

Burnishing after dyeing does transfer dye to your tools, so clean your tools well to avoid transferring colors between projects. If you use water-based dyes, cleanup is easier—soap and warm water is the solution. Wooden tools may stay stained, so be aware that you might have to have a burnisher for each color family.

Burnishing Edges

Burnishing, or slicking, the edges of your leather is a process that involves patience and consistent pressure (noticing a theme?). Whether your edge is beveled or not, the process remains the same.

If you're using a handheld tool, after you have applied your burnishing agent on the edge fiber, place your slicker on the edge and run it back and forth. Some slickers have a one-size-fits-all approach; others have specific groove sizes or angled grooves to match your thickness and bevel type. Your leather should fit comfortably in the groove, not too tight against the grain and flesh, nor should it be gapping to the point that you can accidentally bend your edge as your burnish.

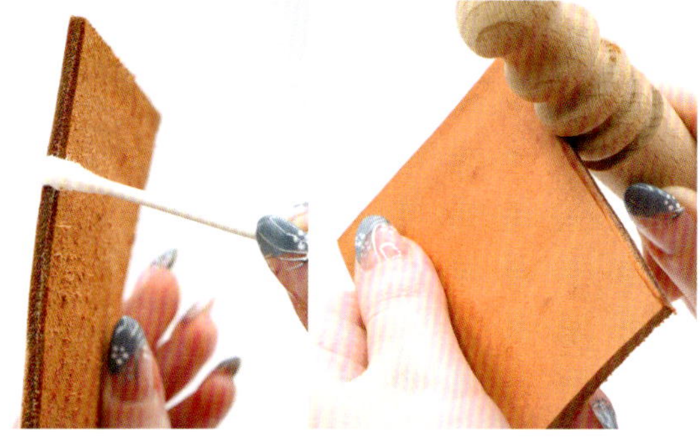

Moving the slicker back and forth on top of the burnishing agent creates friction and begins to push down the fibers, making them glossy in appearance and smooth to the touch. This can take a lot of wrist strength, so we recommend either taking several breaks to stretch and rest your wrists and forearms or investing in a set of burnishing bits for your rotary tool to use on a low setting. Using burnishing bits on high settings may burn your leather or create divots.

After a minute or two, your edge should look glossy and feel super smooth! Repeat for all edges you want to burnish.

Burnishing the Flesh Side

To burnish the flesh side of leather, use a glass slicker because the wide surface area allows you to cover a lot of leather quickly. Apply an even coat of burnishing agent to the flesh side of your leather. You can also sand the backside of your leather if there are large fuzzies to help reduce them and allow for a smoother end result. Once your flesh side is prepared and the agent is applied, push your glass slicker away from you. Repeat this motion until all the fuzzies are pushed down and begin to look glossy. Add burnishing agent as needed, and continue until you reach your desired smoothness.

Burnishing to Combine Layers of Leather

If you've glued two pieces of leather together, you can use slicking to combine the edges into what looks like one edge. The key is to cut and sand the edges to match; this cannot be achieved if the edges aren't lined up.

Moving from lower- to higher-grit sandpaper, notice that your edges now line up but may have fiber fuzz. Apply your burnishing agent and, using a groove that fits the combined pieces, slick back and forth until the divide between the layers begins to disappear. If you notice that your agent is used up and your layers aren't quite molded together, apply another layer of agent and continue slicking. Note that the more layers you add together, the harder slicking them into one edge will be.

Burnishing Agent Options

Burnishing agents come in a variety of bases and types. Each has a place in leatherworking.

Water: Sometimes plain water can be used as a pre-burnisher if you want to hold off and burnish your leather after dyeing but want to slick the edges a little bit for cleaner dye application (an example of this would be if you used an edge beveler). To do this, gently sand the edge with a high-grit sandpaper and then wet it with water using a rag or your finger and run your slicking tool along the edge. The leather will begin to shine a little as friction pushes the fibers together. Once you get to your desired level of pre-burnishing, let your leather dry completely before moving to any next steps.

Gum tragacanth and Tokonole: Gum tragacanth is a water-based burnishing agent with a jelly-like consistency. It is best used with other water-based products. To apply, use a cotton swab, the tip of a rag, or a small wool dauber. If applying before dyeing, take care to not get excess on the grain side of the leather—gum tragacanth also works as a sealant and can resist dye causing an uneven dye job.

If you're wet forming your leather, you may see your burnishing with gum tragacanth wear off. This is due to warm water dissolving some of the mixture and thinning the product. We recommend using gum tragacanth after wet forming or trying other burnishing agents with more acrylic such as Tokonole.

Tokonole is also water-based, but it has more acrylic mixed in. Its consistency is a bit thinner than gum tragacanth, which helps with application, and it comes in clear, brown, and black colors. We prefer the clear.

If you're looking to see which is better, gum tragacanth has been a true and solid choice for most of our projects. Its viscosity, even though it has a learning curve with application, allows it to coat more of the fibers and creates a thicker seal when burnished. We've found Tokonole is great to use with alcohol dyes like Fiebing's products and gives a nice shiny finish. Both produce a nice shine and almost plastic-smooth finish.

SAND ON REPEAT

Cosplayers who work with foam or thermoplastic are very intimate with the "Sand, sand, and sand again" saying. Well, leather is the same! To get beautifully glossy edges on leather that don't show any fibers, you need to burnish, sand, and repeat. If you have dye on your project, this is where you would reapply dye to your edges between sanding and burnishing as color can strip away with each sanding pass. Continue until you have your desired smoothness.

Beeswax: Beeswax is a natural and cost-effective burnishing agent. However, unlike gum tragacanth and Tokonole, beeswax wears off over time, requiring reapplication. Apply by rubbing the wax block along the edge of the leather until there is a little buildup; then burnish with your tool of choice, rubbing back and forth. The beeswax creates a hardened top on the edge fibers and is soft to the touch. When being burnished, friction creates heat, melting the beeswax and causing it to sink into the pores of the leather.

Like other burnishing agents, beeswax creates a water-resistant, not waterproof, barrier on leather. If you have it around and you're in a pinch, beeswax works to burnish your edges, but overall, it's easier to use gum tragacanth or Tokonole.

Edge Kote: Edge Kote is an acrylic-based product that can be painted onto leather edges with a wool dauber, paintbrush, or edge roller pen. It comes in all sorts of colors, so you have the freedom to mix and match for your desired look. It can drip to the grain side and cause problems, though, so apply with a steady hand and/or angle toward the flesh side when painting the edge. That way, if there is any overflow, it is on the back, which is easier to disguise with a darker color or a lining.

On veg tan, paint on carefully after slicking with a burnishing agent. Edge Kote takes one or two layers and dries with an almost rubbery texture—great for sealing in your edges and giving them a little more protection.

Edge Kote is great for chrome tan because you usually aren't using dyes on chrome tan, but you do need to finish the edges of your leather before sealing it up.

Burnishing Chrome Tan: *Because chrome tan isn't as rigid as veg tan, a burnishing tool may warp the edges under the constant back-and-forth motion. A way around that is to use a sturdy cloth made of a utility fabric such as denim or canvas. Use this as you would a burnishing tool and rub along the edge of your treated leather fibers until it looks glossy.*

Another trick that can come in handy for smaller pieces of chrome tan is using a glass slicker instead of wood or plastic. Place your glass slicker down on your workstation, and hold your chrome tan perpendicular on the slicker. Move back and forth to create friction, and check periodically to see if the fibers are fusing into a smooth shine.

Tools: Seal It, Lock and Key!

ESSENTIALS

Leather sealant: Inarguably the most important tool for sealing leather. Sealants come in a variety of types.

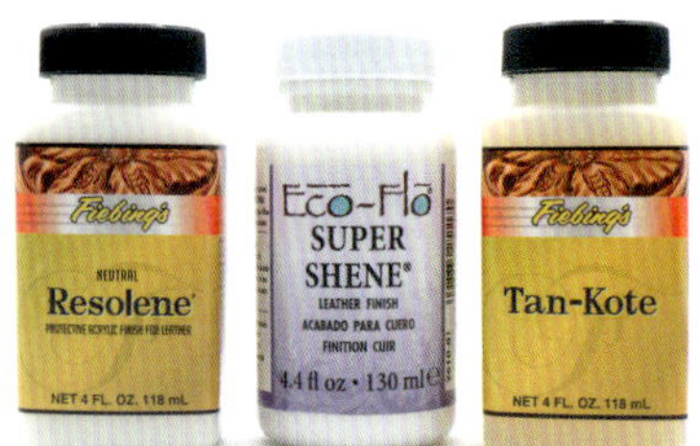

Sponge: Used to apply sealant.

Buffing rag: Used to apply sealant and/or clean off excess sealant.

OPTIONAL

Airbrush: Thin mixture sealants, such as Resolene, can be applied with an airbrush.

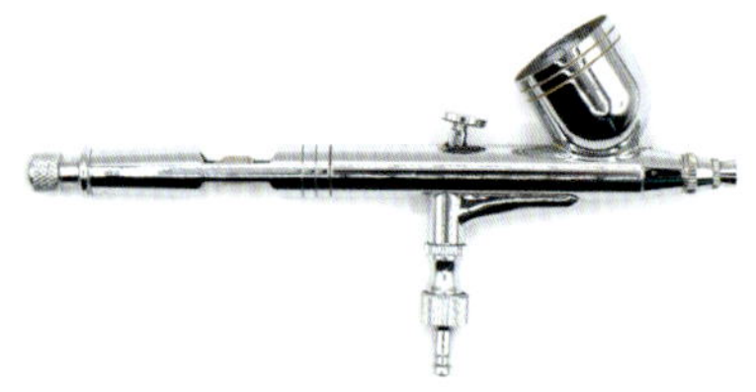

Sealing

Leather is a natural, porous material that can run into many issues if left without a topcoat. We seal leather to:

- Help protect leather from dirt, moisture, and bacteria.
- Strengthen leather against cracking, peeling, and shrinking while enhancing the longevity of the leather.
- Lock in dyes, stains, gels, and paints that would otherwise rub off or fade quickly if left unsealed.
- Provide a professional, finished look to the piece.

Because sealing leather is truly like putting the icing on the cake that is your hard work, it's important to take the time to find the sealant that works best with your project and what you personally need from it. Some solvents don't shine as much or allow for later reconditioning to keep the leather soft. Others stiffen the leather, or give it more waterproofing. What you're making and how you'll use it determine the best sealant group to use.

For the most part, sealants are applied in thin, even layers by buffing the product across the leather's grain and flesh side (as applicable) with a sponge or buffing rag; allowing for drying time; repeating two or three more times to create a good barrier; and finally, shining the piece by buffing again with a clean rag. Applying too much at once or not allowing for proper drying between layers can result in streaking or patchiness. We do not recommend using a wool dauber in this instance because some sealants become tacky and have shorter working times. A wool dauber or fluffy cloth will leave behind fibers.

WATER-BASED SEALANTS

Water-based sealants are the most common sealants in leatherworking and have several variants. Most water-based sealants can be applied straight from the bottle after a thorough shake and do not require thinning with water. These types appear milky and have little resistance when the bottle is tipped for pouring. They can be applied directly to a sponge or rag and buffed across a piece, or even sprayed through an airbrush!

Acrylic

Many labels read "acrylic water-based." These are water-based sealants that have acrylic resin in the mix to create a barrier on top of the leather. They lock in any oils or moisture that have been added previously, but they also don't allow much to get through after they're applied.

Knowing that leather needs conditioning to stay flexible and not shrivel makes an acrylic shield on top seem like a poor choice. How will you condition it? Why even make acrylic sealants? The answer is that sealants with acrylic are durable, and cosplayers love durability! While it's true that you can't condition through an acrylic barrier, cosplayers may never need to recondition their leather pieces as the pieces are not worn daily, nor are they under constant friction (as opposed to something like a horse saddle). Storing leather pieces in a plastic tote indoors is also much different than storing them in a barn. So, all in all, if you're not consistently using or wearing your project, you shouldn't be afraid to use a sealant that has acrylic in it, especially if you conditioned your leather prior to sealing.

You can get these sealants in different finishes, such as matte, satin, or gloss. After buffing, they have more shine to them than the non-acrylic mixture finishes. As an example, we've applied two coats of the different Eco-Flo and Fiebing's finishes to the pieces below. Check out that shine on the Super Shene finish!

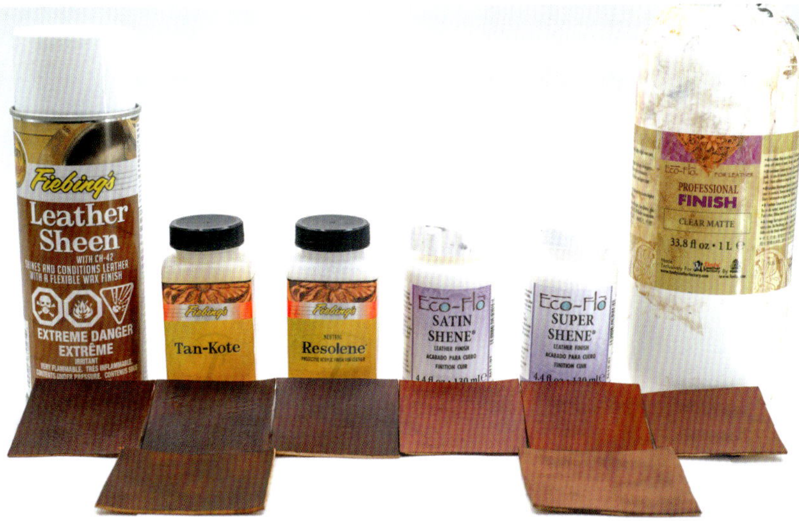

Resolene as a Sealant

Resolene is an extremely common sealant in the leatherworking world, and there are decades of opinions on how to best use it. Because Resolene contains a high concentration of acrylic resin, it seals the pores of the leather and resists oils or conditioners even more than the Eco-Flo line of acrylic water-based sealants. It usually stiffens the leather, sometimes so much that you'll have that telltale "squeak" of leather when wearing pieces sealed with it.

Resolene can be thinned with water to assist with application or with airbrushing. Note that the more water you introduce, the less of a barrier the Resolene creates with each layer. It is not recommended to exceed 30% additional water when thinning.

If your piece is not going to be in a high-friction area, or coming in contact with high levels of moisture on a regular basis, and you want a lustrous shine, Resolene might be for you! We recommend Resolene on items like sheaths, pouches, or helmets. Avoid joint or joint-adjacent pieces such as pauldrons, bracers, or greaves.

We've mainly spoken about veg tan sealing, but you should also seal chrome tan, especially if you've done any deglazing and re-dyeing or painting! Even though it has been treated with harsher chemicals and is water-resistant, it has pores and should be sealed. Some sealants change the texture and finish of the chrome tan's grain side, making it feel more like the smooth and slippery surface of veg tan. To preserve the feel of the chrome tan, we recommend using Tan-Kote.

Wax

If you're looking for a more natural sealant and you don't mind the occasional upkeep of conditioning your leather pieces, sealants containing wax may answer your topcoat needs.

Wax, also being a natural compound, works well when paired with leather. Just as with an acrylic water-based sealant, a wax water-based sealant assists with protecting the leather, but is more like a light windbreaker versus a heavy winter coat. Water, oils, and dirt can still penetrate the leather. However, with a wax sealant, cleaning and reapplication are easy tasks. Leather-approved soaps and cleaning conditioners make removing grime a cinch. Once your piece is spick-and-span, apply a couple of fresh coats of wax sealant. Wax sealants overall create a softer, more natural finish to leather projects, great for making "lived-in" or "well-worn" replications for costuming. Also, in a pinch, you can clean off most of the wax sealant and condition your leather to revitalize it; then reapply your wax sealant.

GOT THIS IN THE BAG-KOTE!

Bag-Kote, a common wax finish, is known for being contradictingly user-friendly and deceivingly tricky at times, leaving behind streaks when applied with a buffing rag. A tip to get rid of those pesky lines is to gently heat your layers with a heat gun (on low heat) or hair dryer after each coat to reduce any streaks. Foam workers may recognize this practice as heat sealing. And just as with foam, wear personal protective equipment. By applying heat, you're melting the wax that is in Bag-Kote's formula, which helps it blend and become shiny. Your leather products will come out looking soft and sleek.

Aerosol

This type of sealant must be used with caution and in a well-ventilated area. Wear personal protective equipment because, as with any aerosol, particles are emitted into the air that can have adverse effects if breathed in. In leatherworking, there are only a few aerosol sealants, and they're sometimes labeled "acrylic wax water-based." This is not to be mistaken for the actual wax water-based sealants discussed earlier. Acrylic wax is an acrylic; it creates a nonporous barrier on your leather and makes your leather less flexible.

If you choose to use an aerosol, like spray-painting, spray from 5″–6″ (13–15cm) away from the leather piece and move across it in sweeps. Do not begin spraying directly on the project—this can cause uneven application. Instead, begin to the side of the project and, while spraying, move across the project. Once covered, allow it to dry. These layers are fairly fine, so we recommend applying three to four coats of aerosol sealant onto your leather to ensure you have built up an even barrier. After applying, use a buffing rag and gently buff the leather to increase the shine.

IS YOUR PAINT RUBBING OFF?

If you experience paint rub off when applying topcoats by hand, try using an aerosol sealant or applying your topcoat with an airbrush. Paint rubbing off is a common issue if the paint was applied too thickly, if the paint is on raised tooling (this is due to your rag or sponge hitting areas and not gliding over, which causes more friction and can lift paint), or if the sealant and the paint are chemically reacting to each other. If you have time and scraps, do a couple tests and see what method of application works best on your chosen paints.

Hand Sewing, Gluing, and HARDWARE

Original Design Suki from *Avatar: The Last Airbender*

Cosplay and work-in-progress photos by Ashley Haapapuro/Sartorial Jutsu Studios • Photo of Suki by Hayley Stein Photography

Tools: It's "Sew" Fun!

ESSENTIALS

Stitching hole punch: A single hole punch for creating round stitching holes.

Stitching chisels: Most common tool for making stitching holes in leather. They come in different styles and sizes.

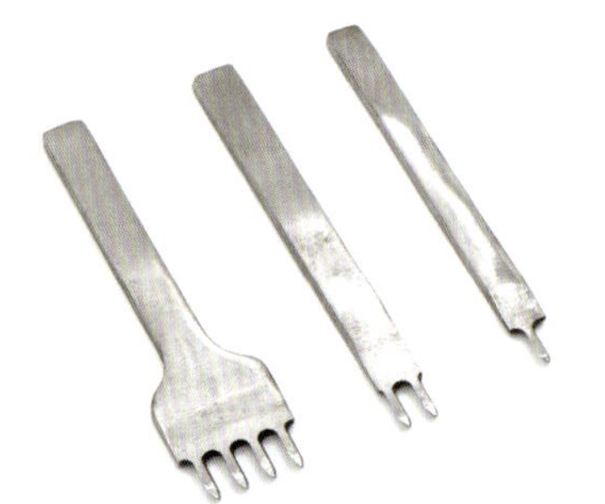

Stitch groover: A tool used to make a measured line from the edge of the leather. Pairs well with stitching chisels.

Waxed thread: Used to sew pieces of leather together. Do not use regular sewing thread in lieu of waxed thread.

Leather needles: These come with either sharp or blunt tips, as well as curved or straight. Some common types are lace, glover's, harness, and curved needles.

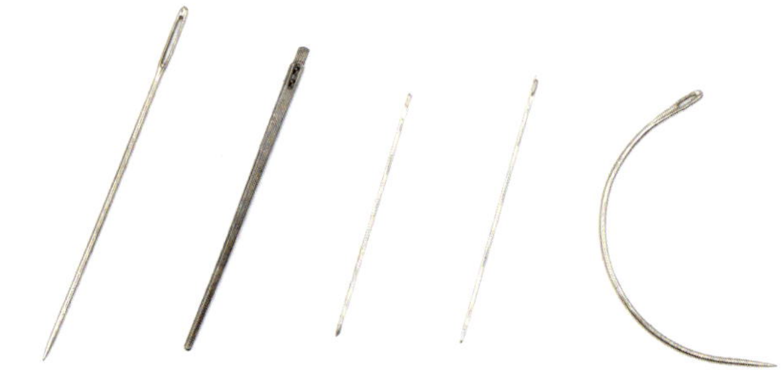

From left to right: Large leather sewing needle, lace needle, glover's needle, harness needle, curved needle

Maul/mallet: Used to hit stitching chisels to make stitching holes and flatten thread after finishing a sewing line.

Lighter: Used to melt polyester thread.

OPTIONAL

Stitching pony: Holds leather pieces while you sew; like a vice grip for leather.

Thimble: Recommended if you're feeling fatigue or hurting yourself by pulling or pushing your leather needles. Thimbles come in many varieties, from standard finger thimbles to the sailor's mit.

Hardware hole punch: Used for making larger holes in leather to accommodate thicker leather lacing.

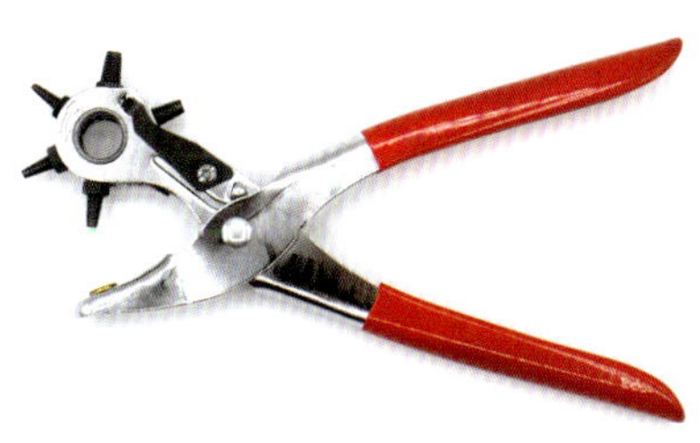

Leather lace: Suede, garment-grade leathers, and rawhide cut into long strips to use for durable or decorative lacing.

Pliers: A hand-saver when pulling through lacing or needles.

Beeswax: Used to re-wax waxed thread. Often used with linen thread to provide extra protection to the fibers against wear and tear of hand sewing.

Pricking irons: As the name implies, these are used to prick the grain side to mark for stitching holes, not puncture through the leather.

Awl: Sharp awls can be used to push through stitching holes that were marked by a pricking iron to create a hole for a needle to pass through. Scratch awls can be used to widen existing sewing holes to assist a needle through.

Sharp awl

Scratch awl

Locking pins: Two-part, reusable pins that help hold projects together as you hand sew.

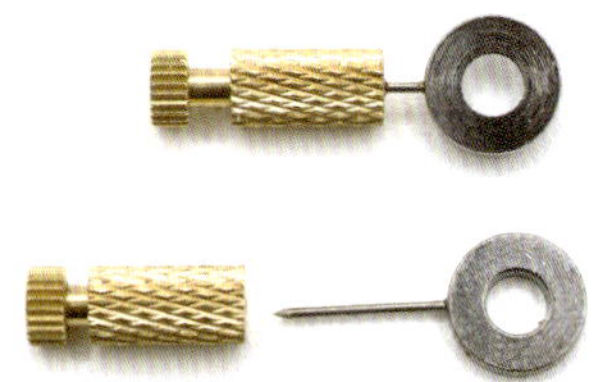

Hand Sewing

Now that you have all your leather pieces dyed, tooled, sealed, and looking great, you need a way to put them all together. You can use glue or hardware (like rivets), or grab a needle and waxed thread for some hand-sewing fun! We focus primarily on veg tan with the occasional tips for chrome tan. Hand sewing for garment leather is covered in Garment Leather (page 130).

STITCH GROOVING

When you look at hand-sewn leather projects, they have the same wonderful consistency and stitch straightness as if a machine were used. This is achieved with the help of a stitch groover. They make a groove using a metal shovel-shaped tip, called a *spoon*, for your stitches to follow. The tool has a guide bar (which looks like an Allen wrench sticking out the side) that can be tightened or loosened to choose how far to put your stitches from the edge of your leather. Make sure the spoon tip is resting with its edge against the leather, not the flat side; otherwise, it won't create a sharp impression when you pull the tool toward you to create your groove.

TIP

You can use a stitch groover instead of a ruler to mark guidelines for edging stamps and even go over it with a swivel knife for a nice straight line to bevel.

With enough pressure, you can create a trough for your thread to sit in when you start stitching. This helps to keep your lines straight and even from the edge and provides a place for your thread to sit so it isn't on top of your leather and more susceptible to friction.

Stitch groovers also come with a cloven tip, called a *cutting tip*, that can be used in the same way as the spoon tip, but it will skive away the top layer of the leather's grain side wherever it's used. You can use this tip with the guide arm or without. We like using it even on edges that aren't going to receive stitching because it adds to a nice, finished look. If you want to add a decorative line, but you don't want to use the cutting tip because it would be too noticeable, use the spoon tip for a softer line.

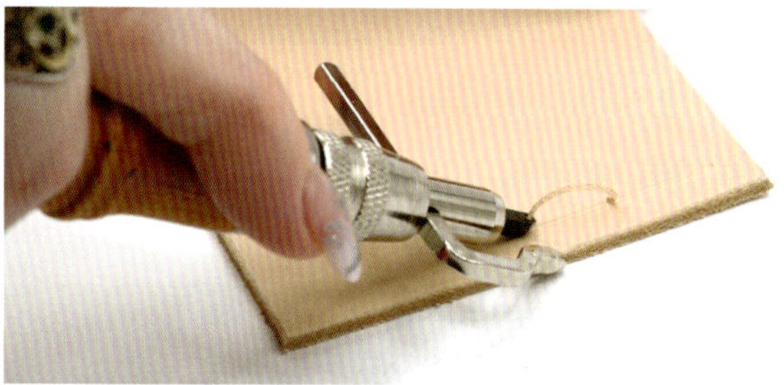

THREW OFF MY GROOVER

If you use both tips frequently, we suggest getting a second groover with one set on the cutting tip and one on the spoon tip. This makes swapping between the two much quicker, and you don't have to remove your guide arm each time, allowing you to keep your measurement in place.

CHISELS, PRICKING IRONS, AND STITCHING HOLE PUNCHES.

Chisels, pricking irons, and stitching hole punches are used for different purposes or aesthetics, but they will all help you in your stitching journey. Chisels are by far the most frequently used, and investing in a good set of chisels will help you create even lines of stitching. A benefit of using chisels is that you aren't removing any leather but simply pushing it to the sides to make room for the needle and thread, leaving the strength of the fibers intact. As the leather relaxes and expands back around the chisel strike, it holds the thread tightly.

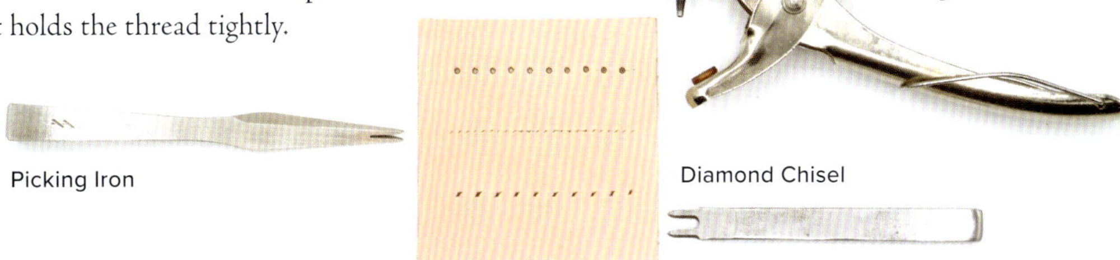

There are a few different kinds of chisels, but the main two are flat and diamond chisels. Flat chisels will give you straight lines, mimicking the stitch of a sewing machine. We like flat chisels for projects where the stitching can't take up too much space and needs to blend in. These work really well for a running stitch or saddle stitch. Diamond chisels are also commonly seen in leatherwork. The teeth points on these chisels are diamond shaped, leaving an angled rectangular hole. Stitching done with these will have a slight slant, which is more noticeable when using thinner threads. It is a finish seen on many high-end leather goods.

You may be wondering why you could ever need both chisels and pricking irons—they look so similar at a quick glance! The difference between these tools is that chisels have a wider, pointed tine meant for piercing the leather, whereas a pricking iron's tines are long but flat on the bottom and are used for just marking the leather, not piercing it. If you're using thin leather, be careful when using pricking irons—you may pierce through with too heavy a mallet strike. The danger of piercing with a pricking iron is that you can bend or break the tines if they come in contact with your work surface. After pricking the surface to mark where your stitching will go, follow with an awl—either a bladed or scratch variety—to complete the hole. This technique is common when trying to do an angled stitch known as a *box stitch*, where you want to sew through the top and middle fibers of the leather but not through the back. This requires precision, or you may rip through the flesh or grain side of your leather. While the box stitch is a staple in the traditional leatherworking world, we haven't found many uses for it in cosplay crafting that can't be accomplished with another, easier, stitch. For this reason, we've chosen to focus on stitches that can be done with chisels and stitching hole punches for this book.

When shopping for chisels and pricking irons, the different measurements equate to the distance between each stitch hole. An easy rule to remember is: The smaller the number, the more stitches you'll get per inch. For example, a 3mm set will give you nine stitch holes per inch, and a 6mm set will give you five stitch holes per inch.

LACING CHISELS

If you want to add decorative lacing to the edge of your project, try lacing chisels. These chisels create a wider hole for sewing lacing. If you're using veg tan cording or a thicker cording, you may still need to punch holes with a stitching hole punch or even a rivet hole punch to make room for the additional material (our recommended strategy for working with lace).

Using Chisels and Pricking Irons

To use a pricking iron or chisel, first prepare them by coating the tines in beeswax. This helps pull them out of the leather more easily as you work. Once ready, place the teeth following your stitch groover line or a marked line. Work with your line placed perpendicular to you so you can see down it when placing your chisel. This helps keep your line straight. Begin with one tooth off the piece or in the corner of your grooved line. We also recommend putting a scrap piece of thicker-weight leather, flesh side up, underneath your leather to make extra sure your tines do not come in contact with your work surface.

If using a pricking iron, gently hit with a mallet once or twice. Remember, you only want to indent, not pierce, the leather. If using a chisel, strike firmly with the chisel two or three times. If your chisel is sharp, it will easily push through the leather. Remove by bracing the leather on either side of the tool and gently rocking it back and forth until it releases.

As you continue, to ensure you're creating a straight line, place one or two teeth of your tool in the previous hole(s) as a guide. Be sure to switch to a tool with fewer prongs when moving around curves or working up to a corner.

Stitching Hole Punch

A stitching hole punch, like a paper punch for leather, differs from a chisel in that it removes fiber to make space for thicker thread, laces, or stitches with more thread passes, such as the corset stitch. Some may argue that cutting holes with a punch weakens the leather if it's done too close to the edges, which is true to some degree, but it won't cause it to rip like a piece of paper. Leather is stronger than we give it credit for! Wider holes allow for different thread types or lacing to be used, expanding the level of creativity, and they can lend a rustic and more graphic feel. One of the downsides of the stitching hole punch is that each hole needs to be measured and punched individually, which may prove to be tricky when you're trying to keep a consistent and even line. One tip is to use a pricking iron (or gently tap a chisel if you don't have a pricking iron) to make markings and save yourself the time it takes to measure each hole with a ruler.

SELECTING THREAD

From left to right: Hemp, nylon, Ritza Tiger polyester, braided polyester, twisted polyester, cotton, linen

When hand sewing leather, purchase thread that is specifically labeled for leatherwork. There are a few types available: cotton, hemp, linen, nylon, and polyester.

Thread for leather hand sewing is made of heavier weights to help it sit snugly in your stitch holes, reducing friction and keeping tension on your stitch lines. It comes with an initial wax coating to help it glide through leather fibers, and it can be re-waxed as you work. Standard sewing thread is prone to snap under the tension needed for leather hand sewing, and it wiggles around in the stitch holes, causing additional abrasion to both the leather and the thread fibers.

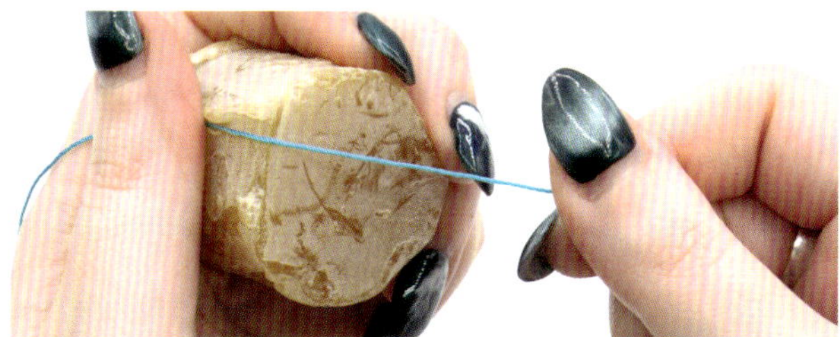

Thread Type	Pros	Cons
Cotton	Natural fiber Soft to the touch Muted but nice coloring	Difficult to source (mostly online Not sold at most chain retailers Expensive
Hemp	Durable Alternative material	Difficult to source (mostly online) Not sold at most chain retailers
Linen*	Natural fiber Soft to the touch Dainty but durable	Expensive Can deteriorate over time (decades)
Nylon	Durable with some elasticity Stiffer than most thread types (chemical bonding materials used) Less shiny than polyester thread Increased UV resistance compared to other thread types	Primarily for leather-specific sewing machines If used for hand sewing, can be too thin for chisel or punch holes Stiffer than most thread types (chemical bonding materials used), which can cause snapping
Polyester*	Beginner friendly Widely sold/most common Budget friendly Durable	Can look bulky on smaller projects Has a shinier, plastic look up close Very saturated color/fake brightness

** Linen and polyester thread get our gold stars for cosplay projects!*

Thread Diameter and Weight

For leather sewing thread, thickness is commonly measured in millimeters (mm). The higher the number, the thicker the thread. Some companies use numerical systems that correspond to measurements and work in a similar way, with #1 being thin; as the number increases, so does the thread diameter.

Tex weight is a form of measurement based on the weight of the thread, not the diameter. Usually seen with leather sewing machine thread (such as nylon thread), it is measured in grams per 1000 meters of thread. For example, if a 1000-meter spool weighs 70 grams, it will have a label of tex 70. Usually, tex weight for leather sewing starts around 60.

Braided versus Twisted

Braided thread is made of lengths of thread braided together in a plait. It is extremely durable and will lay flush to your leather, especially when used in tandem with a stitch groover. Some braided threads are woven around a center strand and have a rounded appearance, which can add a unique look to your final project. It is generally stiffer and wider in diameter, which should be taken into consideration when pairing with a needle and stitching hole size.

Braided Thread

Twisted thread is made of thread lengths that have been twisted tightly around each other or a core strand. This process can give the final thread a "fuzzy," rustic look; it also provides more flexibility. The diameter of this thread type ranges widely, making it generally useful. A downside we've found with twisted thread when compared to braided thread is that when twisted thread snaps or frays, it's faster to come undone because the tension holding the twist has been lost.

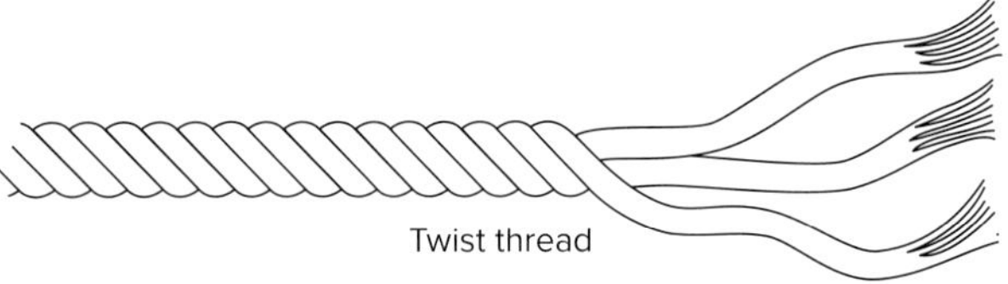

Twist thread

SELECTING LEATHER NEEDLES

Hooray! More numbers! Sewing leather can be like a math puzzle when it comes to figuring out what needle and thread sizes to use based on your project size or the distance between your stitching holes. Outside of a couple rules, these calculations are guidelines, and your final choice is really based on the look you want to achieve for your project.

For leather needles, we keep it simple. There are several different types, but you'll find yourself using either harness needles or curved needles on most projects. Craft stores and some leather supply stores sell needle packs, which can come in handy in a pinch and give you a variety of choices. These packs come with a variety of sharp, triangle-edged needles (glover's needles), curved needles, tapestry/heavy-duty needles, and regular sewing needles (sharp point). The only downside to these packs is that they usually don't include a harness needle.

If you're sewing with rawhide or suede lace, use lacing needles. All the techniques listed in this chapter can be done with lacing, but they'll result in thicker stitches. Lacing needles are threaded in a unique way, shown in Threading a Lacing Needle (page 119).

Harness needles are commonly used in leatherworking due to their blunt tip. When sewing veg tan, we normally pre-punch holes. If, while you're sewing, you're unable to find your next hole, you can wiggle around a blunt-tipped needle to find the hole. With a sharp-tipped needle, you may accidentally pierce the leather and weaken the holes around it or damage your project. Blunt-tipped needles also have less chance of damaging threads already in a stitching hole from a prior pass. And we can't forget to mention that they're less harmful to you if you grab them wrong or poke yourself.

When thinking about needle and thread pairings for your project, be conscious that the eye of the needle and two thread thicknesses need to fit through the stitching hole at the same time. If you find yourself having to tug your needle through the hole or use a plier on every stitch, you may need to try smaller needles or widen your holes with an awl. *Never pull the needle with your teeth!* If you're struggling with one pass through a hole, backstitching could leave you wondering what you've gotten yourself into. To avoid any sewing spiraling, we've included a handy chart to get you started with our advice on needle and thread sizes.

Because polyester and linen thread are our top choices for cosplay projects, we've focused on them in the table below. Needle sizes that are divided by a slash indicate an American and a European size. Sizes with the double zero (00) are based on historic ordering codes from companies. In the end, the needle length and diameter are more important to pay attention to than the numbers labeling them.

Needle Size*	Needle Length × Diameter	Polyester Thread	Linen Thread	Thread Diameter
004	48 × 0.9mm	#5–#20	532–832	<0.6mm
001 002 003	54 × 1.05mm	#1–#5	332–432	<0.9mm
1/0 (18)	57 × 1.09mm	#1	332	>1.0mm
2/0 (17)	60 × 1.42mm	#0		>1–1.2mm
3/0 (16)	62 × 1.63mm	#00		>1.2mm

** Based on John James Saddler's Harness Needles collection*

Threading a Leather Needle

If you're familiar with hand-sewing fabric, threading a leather needle will be second nature! For a long stitching line, start with two arm spans of waxed thread. If you're using a heavily waxed thread, gently tap flat the ends of your thread with a mallet for a sharper, flatter shape that passes more easily through the eye of the needle.

Waxed thread doesn't need to be knotted in the traditional sense, especially because most leather sewing recommends threading both ends of your thread with a needle. If you're using one needle and you don't mind a knot on the backside of your piece, go ahead and tie a knot, doubling it if your thread is thin. If you're using polyester thread, take a lighter and melt the thread tail, pressing it into the fibers of the knot for extra security.

To make a locking knot for your needle, first thread your leather needle, leaving a tail about 5″ (13cm) long.

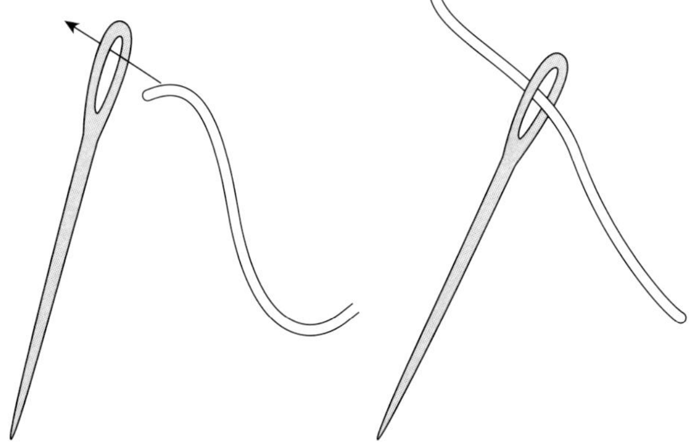

Holding the tail, pierce the tip of the needle through the middle of the thread fibers. Fold the tail back again, and pierce it one more time with the needle.

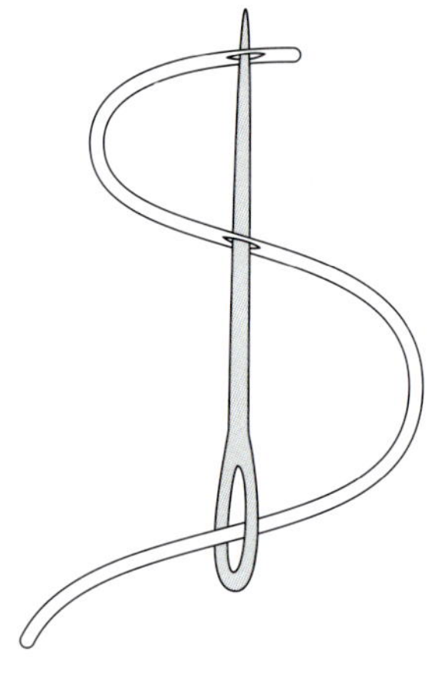

Pull your main thread length to reduce any slack. Now pull down on the tail toward the eye of the needle and your main thread length. You'll see the "loops" push together, move over the eye of the needle, and then lock on the main thread length.

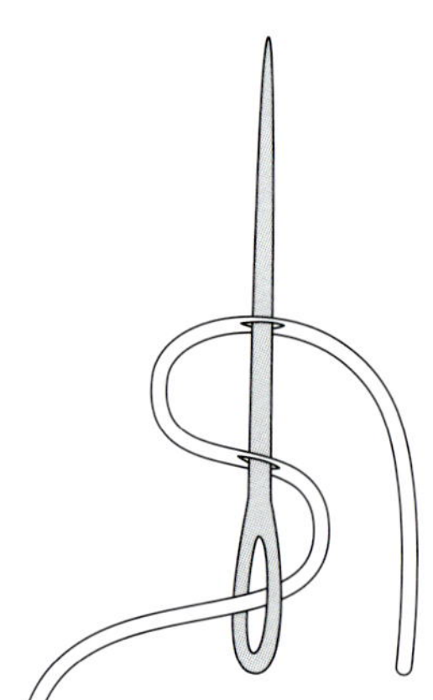

Give a little tug on the main length of thread to tighten your locking knots up against the end of the needle, and you're ready to sew.

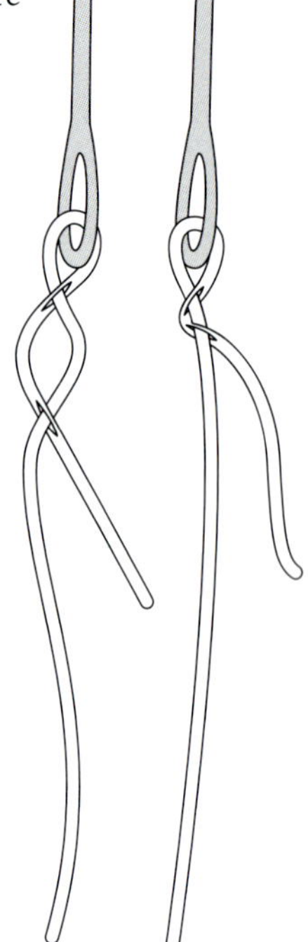

BASIC STITCHES

As with hand-sewing fabric, there are stitches galore in leatherwork! With the basics below, you'll have a solid foundation to change them up, mix and match, and expand your skills.

Stitches for Stacked Leather

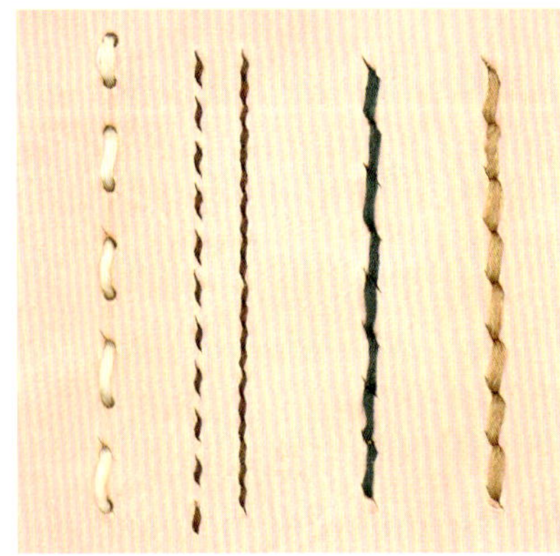

From left to right: Linen thread through stitching hole punches, twisted polyester thread through awl punches marked first with a pricking iron (single running stitch and saddle stitch), Ritza Tiger polyester thread through diamond chisel holes, braided polyester thread through diamond chisel holes.

The Running Stitch Using One Needle

1. Thread your needle and make a locking knot; then tie a regular knot at the other end of your thread.

2. Stitch through the first hole, from flesh side to grain side. Hold tension on your thread to keep the knot flush with the leather.

FANCY KNOT WORK

If you don't have a true back to your project, start by simply threading your needle—don't thread it with a locking knot. Angle your piece so you can see the inside of the first hole and pierce the leather from the inside of the first hole through the edge of the leather. Pull your needle through and unthread it, so you have a small tail of thread extending from the edge of your leather. Rethread from the other end. Proceed with sewing as normal, leaving the tail until you're done with your sewing. On your return pass of the running stitch, you'll seal off your stitching with a glued or melted backstitch. Now take the thread tail and trim it close to the edge of your leather. Seal by melting or by applying a small dab of glue with the tip of an awl.

3. Now go back down through your second stitch hole and back up through the third, weaving back and forth until you reach the end of your stitch line. Your stitch will look like a dashed line on both the front and back of the piece.

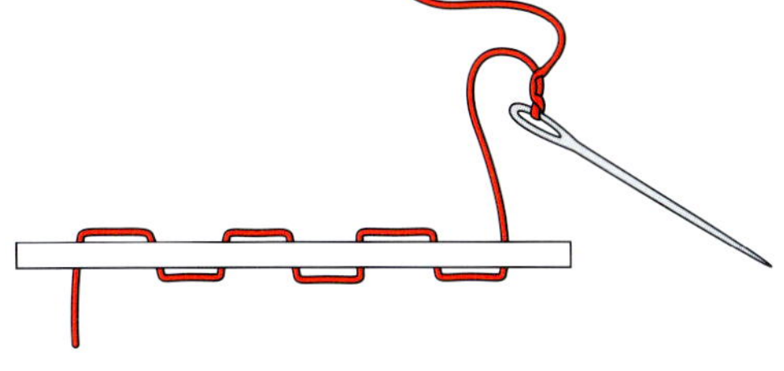

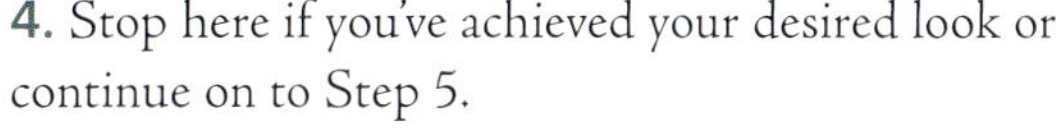

4. Stop here if you've achieved your desired look or continue on to Step 5.

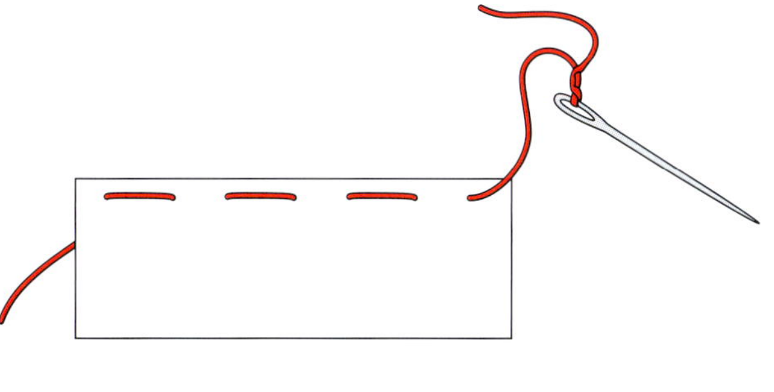

5. A return pass will fill in the spaces between your stitching as you alternate through the holes opposite the way you sewed on the first pass. To begin, at the end of your stitch line, take your needle and feed it through the hole in front of it, moving back along the line you just sewed. Now return through the next hole, repeating the sequence until you reach the original start.

Saddle Stitch (Running Stitch Using Two Needles)

When done with two needles, this is commonly referred to as the *saddle stitch*. This is the most utilized stitch in leatherworking. The reason this stitch is treated as the gold standard for leather hand sewing is because, with each stitch, you're creating a knot, which will prevent unraveling if one thread were to break. It also just looks great and feels really cool to do!

This stitch can either be done starting at the stitch hole closest to you and working away from yourself or vice versa. Use whichever method is most comfortable for you! We also recommend using a stitching pony to lessen strain on your hands and neck. If you don't have one, or if your piece is too bulky, you can use painter's tape or locking pins to help hold pieces together. Whether you use a stitching pony or not, remember to take frequent rests and stretch your muscles to avoid strain or injury.

1. Position your piece perpendicular to your torso so your hands can work freely on the right and left sides of the leather.

2. Cut a wax thread approximately 3 times the length of your stitching line.

3. Thread your needles with a locking knot, one on each end of the waxed thread.

4. Pass 1 needle through the first hole and pull your thread until it is equal lengths on each side of your leather.

5. Holding one needle in each hand, dedicate a hand to always be holding the *leading* needle. This will be the needle that goes through the stitch hole first. The *following* needle will be the one in your other hand and will go through that hole second. During stitching, the needles will move from one side of your piece to the other, but whichever hand you have dedicated to the leading or following role will dictate whether the needle it is holding will go first or second. For example, if you choose your right hand to always be the leading needle, the needle that is in your right hand will always go first. The leading role does not switch sides with the needle passes.

6. Take your leading needle and pass it partway through the next hole.

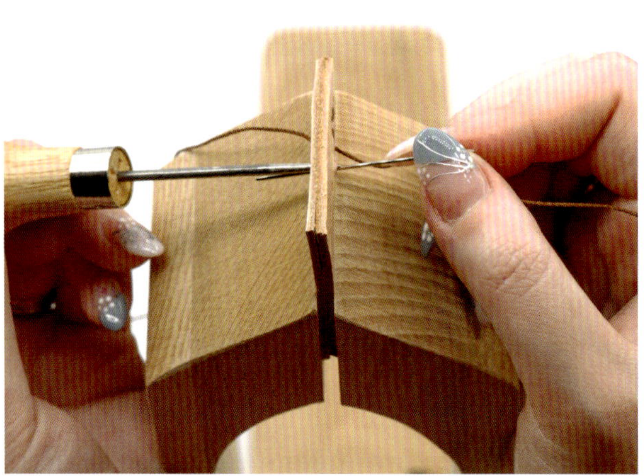

7. With your following needle, put it partway through the same hole from the other direction. Be careful not to catch the thread on either side. If you made your holes with a chisel and are finding it difficult to poke or pass needles through the holes, you can widen them with an awl prior to stitching or during stitching. In our examples, you can see we have an awl handy.

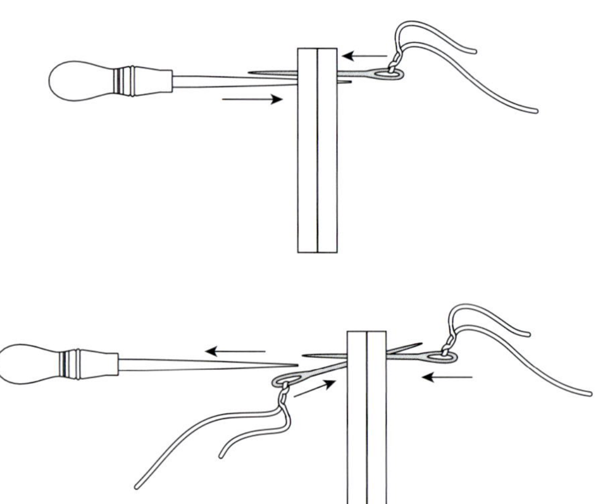

8. Your needles should be pointing in opposite directions out the stitch hole.

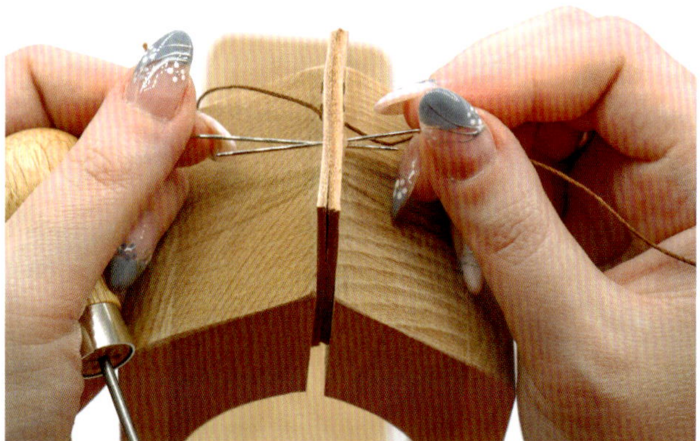

9. Cast the thread slack of the following needle over the leading needle so the needle is in the middle of the loop. When pulled tight, this will make a locking knot and hold your stitch in place.

10. Now pull both needles the rest of the way through the hole. You may need to wiggle one through and then the other.

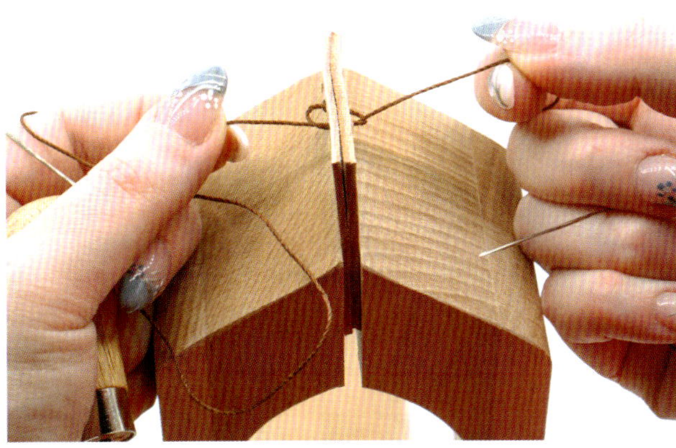

11. Gently pull so the thread becomes taut and the locking knot sets.

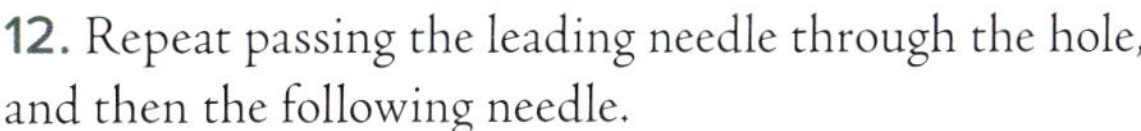

12. Repeat passing the leading needle through the hole, and then the following needle.

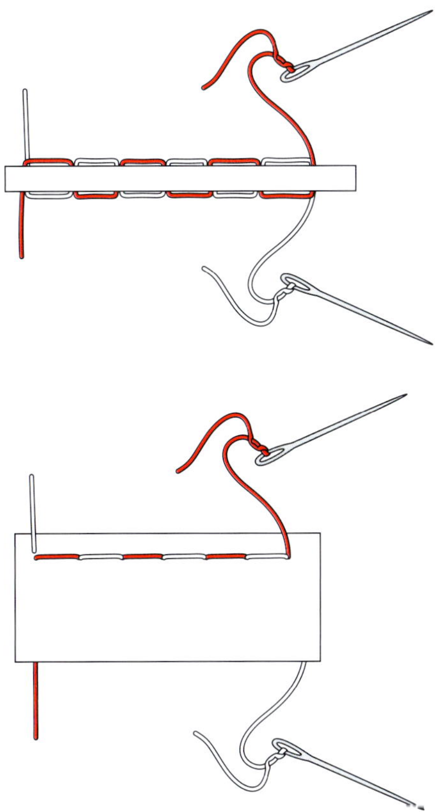

The Gordian Knot

Inevitably, you'll run into a scenario where you misjudged how much thread you needed or you didn't want to work with excessive thread lengths. The best part about the saddle stitch is the knotting of each stitch. So, if you see you're running low on thread, leave your tails, thread up a new needle, and start back a few stitch holes from where you left off. By stitching over your previous threads, you're anchoring the new thread. It's not moving anywhere! Once you've passed the thread tail by a few stitches, feel free to trim off the tails for a clean finish. If you're melting your threads (see Cleaning Up Thread Tails, page 88), wait to do that until you're done stitching.

The Backstitch

Backstitching is exactly as its name states: stitching back the way you came. We use backstitching in hand sewing for the same reason it's used with machine sewing: to hold our threads in place by adding tension and friction in each stitch hole. It's an essential part of each of the stitches shared in this book, but varies whether you're using one or two needles.

To do this with one needle, come out of the last stitch hole of your line, turn your needle around, and go back through the second-to-last hole.

If you're using two needles, pass your needles back through the hole prior to your last one. Backstitch two or three holes before passing only **one needle** through to the other side. Both of your needles should be on the same side now.

Cleaning Up Thread Tails

But what do you do with thread tails? With polyester thread, backstitch at least two or three holes to make sure you have a firm anchor for your stitch line. Now trim your thread close and, using a lighter, melt the end of the thread down. Use a mallet or the bottom of the lighter to press the melted thread into the other threads around it—we don't suggest using your fingers because the thread is hot plastic. Once you've pressed the warm fibers down, let them cool. There you have it! A quick knot using polyester thread.

As a natural fiber, linen will burn instead of melt, so after backstitching, cut your thread close and apply a dab of water-soluble glue or leather sewing glue to the backstitched threads using the tip of an awl or toothpick.

You can add an extra layer of security before trimming your thread tail by encasing it in the middle of a leather piece. After backstitching, place your needle through the next stitch hole, but instead of sewing through as normal, angle your needle so you push through the middle fibers and out the edge. This requires a sharp needle and steady hand. The thinner the leather, the harder this is to accomplish, so use your judgment if you're using 2–3 oz. (0.8–1.2mm) leather. Once you have your thread tail pulled through, trim it level with the edge of the leather. Dab a little glue into the hole and let dry. Gently tap down the stitching with a mallet to press the threads flat against the leather.

Stitches for Side-by-Side Leather Sewing

When sewing two pieces of leather together that will be side by side, two durable and decorative stitches are the corset stitch, also known as the cross stitch, and the baseball stitch. For preparation, one of the most important things when doing a stitch that will join two pieces together is to make sure you've lined up your stitching holes across the edges you're connecting and have the same number of stitching holes. No one wants to have an extra stitch hole or wonky lattice work.

Once you have chiseled or punched your holes, you're ready to join them together.

The Baseball Stitch

A traditional leather stitch commonly seen in the sports world, this stitch achieves a pattern like the seamlines on a baseball, creating a sleek and low-profile design.

1. Prepare a length of waxed thread, thread a needle onto each end, and secure the ends with a locking knot.

2. Taking the thread in your left hand, come up through the first hole on the left side. Repeat for the right and pull your threads even.

3. With your left thread, cross over the left piece of leather and under the right piece, coming up through the second hole on the right side. Take your right needle and cross over the right piece of leather and under the left piece, coming up through the second hole on the left side.

Both your needles are now on the topside of the leather and you've created a chevron of thread, where half of the X is hidden under the leather edges. Gently pull your stitches taut.

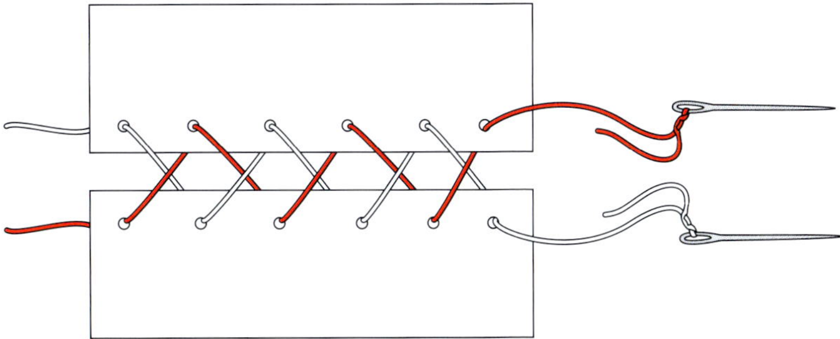

4. Repeat Step 3 until you reach the end of your stitching lines.

5. When you reach the end of your stitching line, cross your needles to the opposite sides and go through the last holes. Do this an additional time for extra strength. Knot the threads together on the backside. Trim or melt your thread tails. If your knot is on top, take a needle or an awl and gently push the knot down between the pieces so it's hidden on the underside.

The Cross/Corset Stitch

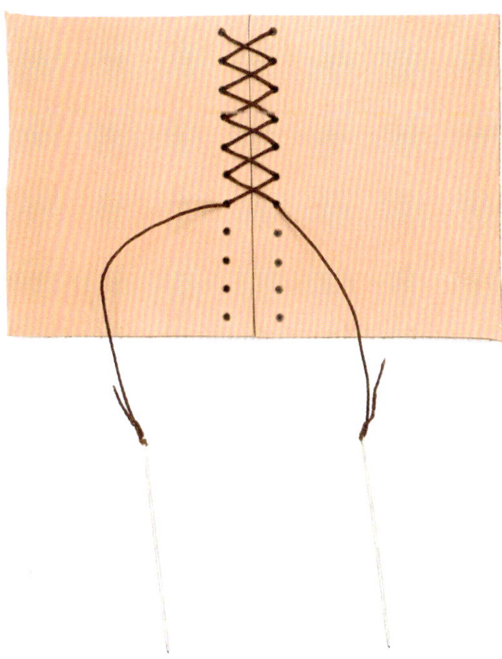

This stitch is similar to the baseball stitch but creates an X pattern on the topside of the leather with a durable crossbar at the base of each X. It looks great both functionally and decoratively. If you're using a thicker thread type, we recommend a punched hole over a chiseled hole.

Note: Your needles will pass from right side to left side frequently in this stitch pattern. To keep directions consistent, we'll refer to the needle that is on the left at any step as the left needle, and we'll do the same for the right needle.

1. To start, make 1 length of thread at least 3–4 times the length of your stitching line. Thread a leather needle with a locking knot on each end of the thread.

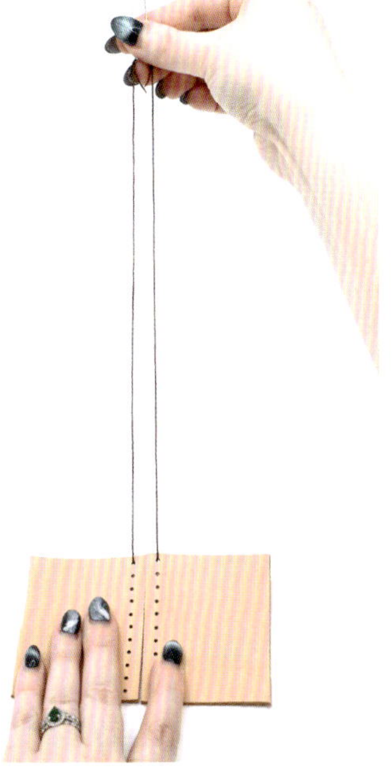

2. Take the needle on your left and put it up through the first stitch hole on the left piece. Repeat with the right needle on the right piece. Pull your needles until the thread lengths are equal on both sides of the leather.

3. With the left needle, cross over to the second hole on the right and stitch down through the hole. Repeat for the right needle, crossing to the left side. Your needles will now be to the back of your project. On the topside, you've created an X of thread.

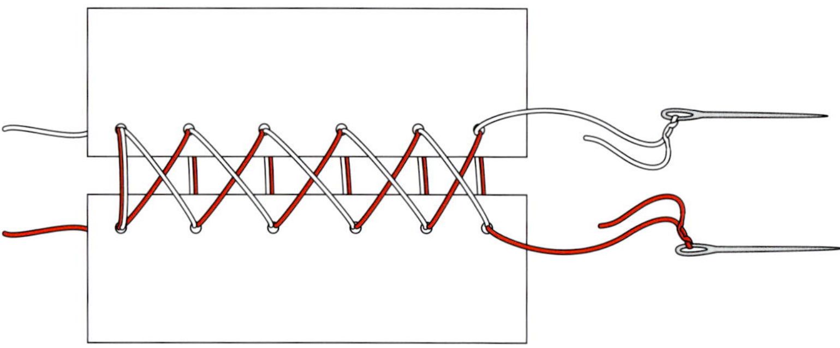

4. Taking the left needle, move laterally to the right side and come back up through the second hole, at the top of your X. Be careful not to sew through the thread already in the stitch hole. Repeat this for the bottom-right needle on the left side. Your needles will now be on top of your project. On the back, you'll have created two parallel bars of thread. Gently tug the threads to tighten up the X.

5. Taking your left needle, cross over to the third hole on your right and stitch down through the hole. Repeat this with the right needle. You've created another X.

6. Repeat Step 4 to create the bars on the backside. With your needles on the topside of your project, repeat Steps 3 and 4 until you reach the end of your sewing line.

7. At the end of your sewing line, insert your needles into the last hole of the opposite piece so your needles are to the backside. Tie off with a knot and then trim or melt it down for a clean finish.

HOLD UNDER PRESSURE

A modified solo corset/cross stitch is a great way to attach straps to other pieces. Instead of sewing two pieces side by side, a single cross/corset stitch on stacked pieces of leather ensures a tight hold.

Thread a single needle with a locking knot, but don't tie a knot at the end. Following the illustration, begin by sewing from the bottom of your piece through hole 1. Leave a tail on the underside long enough to tie a double knot later. Pass your needle over and down through hole 4. Sew up through hole 2 and back down through hole 3. Tie your 2 thread tails together with a double knot. Trim and melt the tails or secure with a dot of water-soluble or leather sewing glue.

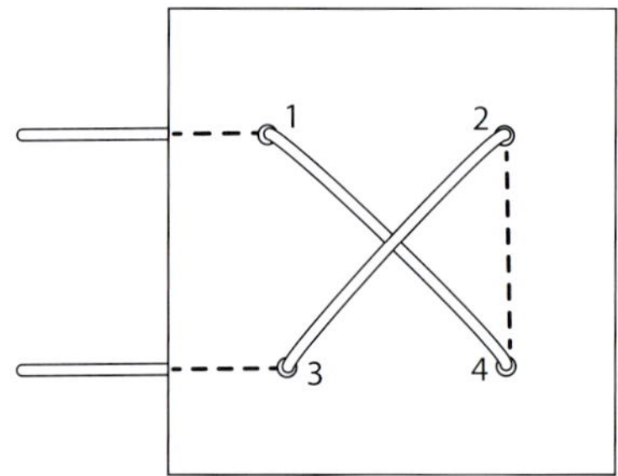

For variation, you can rotate your pattern by 90°.

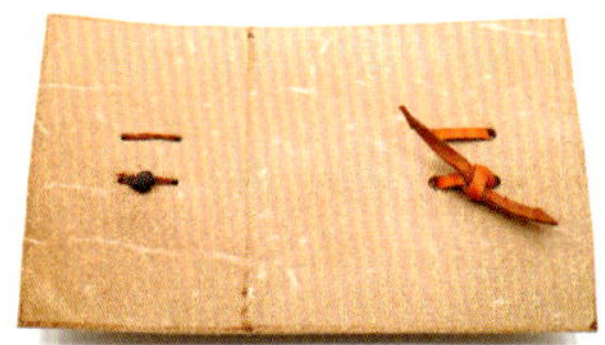

Polyester thread X (left),
kangaroo lace X (right), both rotated

Get a Grip!

In cosplay, all sorts of prop weapons, from knives to staves, have leather-wrapped handles. The corset/cross stitch will be your best friend in adding a lovely leather cover to your prop. This is ideally done with thinner, pliable pieces of leather.

Prep your stitching holes and wrap your leather around the handle you want to cover. It may be hard to keep in place, so we recommend tying some scrap strips of fabric around it or securing it with a piece of hook-and-loop tape. Begin to cross/corset stitch the sides of your leather together, and watch as the gap closes. Keep the tension even so the pieces are nicely aligned.

If you're feeling adventurous or you'd like a different stitch look, you can substitute a baseball stitch for a corset stitch.

Stitches for Angled Leather Sewing

We've covered what to do if your leather is laying flat, but what if your leather is matched up at an angle? Many of the stitches previously covered can be modified to work.

Think Outside the Box (Stitch)!

As mentioned earlier, the traditional box stitch is a complicated stitch that can be mimicked by much easier stitches using fewer tools. One perk about leatherworking is that there are many ways to achieve a desired look. As cosplayers, we're not shy about looking for alternatives or the crafting path less taken. If you want to accomplish a box stitch but you don't want to use the traditional method, try out this "cheat code" version!

This version of the box stitch incorporates a running stitch but on a 90° angle. You can accomplish this by using one or two needles. Using two needles will be faster because it requires only one pass to fill in all stitching holes; it's the method we show here. If you choose to use one needle, you'll need to do a return pass to fill in all your stitch holes.

1. Prep your leather by making your stitch holes, ensuring that they line up across the edges you want to combine.

2. Secure the pieces together at a 90° angle with leather glue and allow to dry.

3. Cut a piece of thread approximately 3 times the length of your sewing line and thread a needle on each end, securing with a locking knot.

4. Start with your needles going from the outside through the first holes on your pieces toward the inside. Pull your thread lengths until you have even lengths on both right and left sides.

5. Cross your needles and sew back up through the first holes. You should have a crossbar on the outside and inside of your piece, and your needles should now be on the outside.

6. To start, take 1 needle and go down the next stitching hole on the same piece of leather. From the backside, cross over to the matching hole on the other piece and sew up through the hole. Your needle should now be back on the topside of the leather, and you're ready to continue the S pattern.

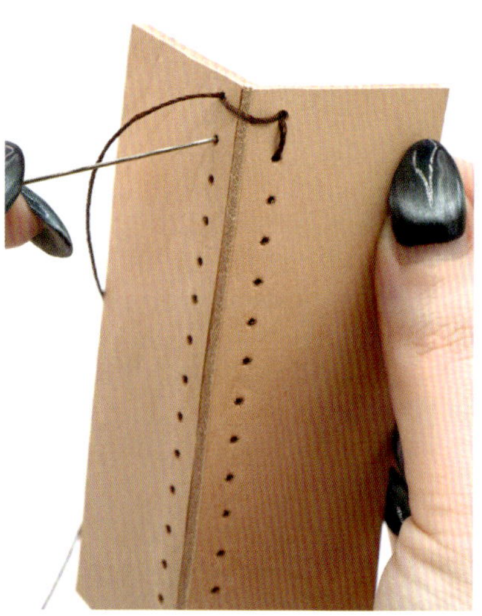

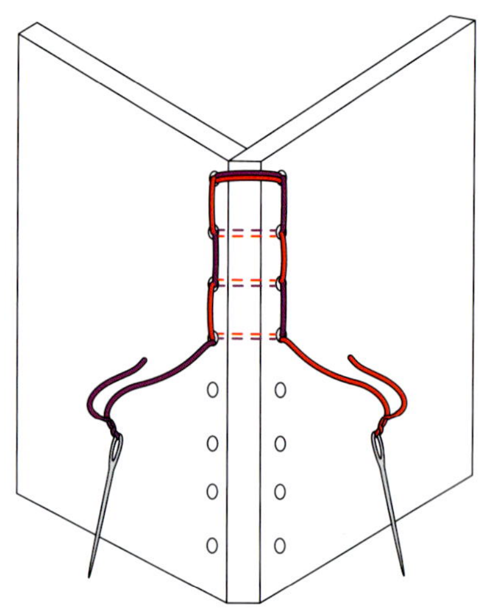

7. Repeat with your other needle. Once you have the pattern down, feel free to work both needles in tandem.

8. Once you reach the end of your stitching line, stitch down through the last holes, cross your needles, and come back up through the opposite side.

9. To tie off, you can either tie your thread tails in a knot to one side and use an awl or stylus to push the knot into a stitching hole, or you can cross your needles and stitch back down through the last holes on the opposite piece once more and tie a knot to one side in the inside. Trim and melt if applicable.

The S pattern shown can be altered to be an X with only a few changes. When your needles are topside, instead of stitching down the next hole on the same side of the piece, cross over to the next hole on the opposite piece. Just make sure you pick a side that will always be the thread to cross on top so you have consistent Xs.

HAND SEWING CHROME TAN

If you're using chrome tan and you see your stitches puckering the leather or stretching your stitching holes, try backing your chrome tan with a thin veg tan. Veg tan is more durable and will take the brunt of the stitch tension. For layering leather, see Lining, Strengthening, and Doubling Layers (page 109).

With all these options to sew pieces of leather together, you can create some truly amazing projects! As you advance your skills, explore more stitches and variations. Try mixing thread colors, adding in lacing or leather braiding (page 113), or even beadwork to decorate your stitches!

Gluing

Though sewing two pieces together holds up better than gluing in the long-term, proper use of glue forms a strong bond that can last years depending on the type of glue.

When gluing with leather adhesive or leather glue, the glue functions somewhat like a tacking stitch. It holds the material in place while you work and then eventually gets reinforced with another attachment method. Even if you're just looking for a temporary hold, you should still use leather-specific glue. For a more permanent bond, you should use contact cement.

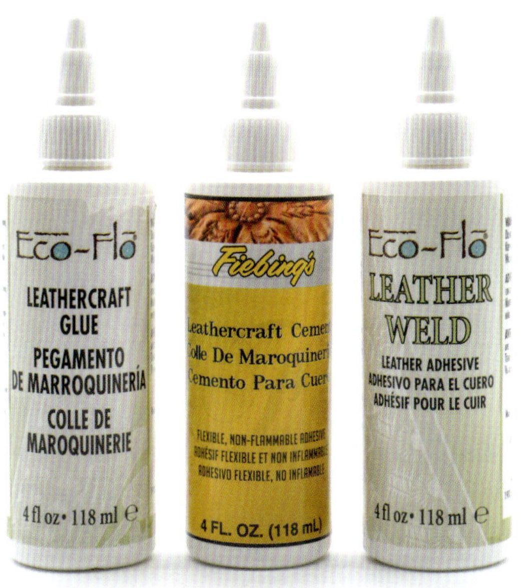

CONTACT CEMENT

Contact cement is the most common permanent glue used for bonding leather to leather. Many types of contact cement are available. One of the major things to look for is whether the cement is water-based. In general, non-water-based types, such as silicone- and neoprene-based, hold longer before deteriorating, often more than five years. However, these cements generate highly harmful fumes when used. Always read the warning labels for your contact cement and follow all safety directions. Water-based cements are more likely to deteriorate before the five-year mark, but they're also less dangerous and harmful to use. You should still read all labels prior to use, though. "Less dangerous" does not mean completely safe, and they should be used with care.

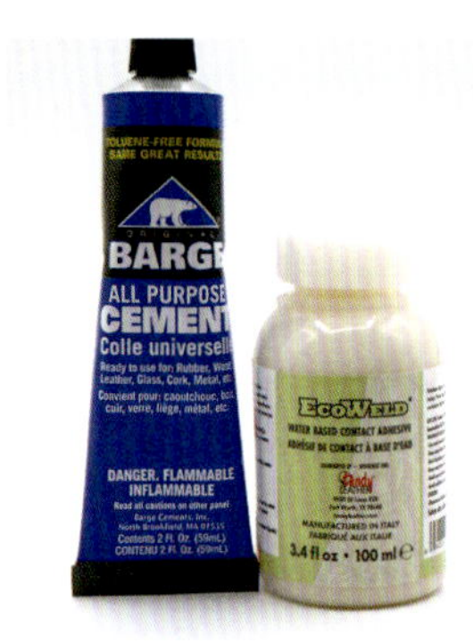

TIP

Most contact cements generate organic vapors, so when you're looking for the proper safety equipment, make sure you have a filter that targets organic vapors. Even armed with this knowledge, always read each individual product's safety information to ensure you're protected.

Contact cement is effective only when applied properly. As usual, you should read the label to understand the correct way to use the product. However, most contact cement varieties can be applied as follows:

1. Evenly but sparingly coat both surfaces to be joined. Full coverage with a thin to medium coat is ideal.

2. Let the glue dry. The adhesives in contact cement are combined with a solvent, which prevents bonding. Applying the glue to the leather allows the solvent to evaporate and leave the adhesive behind. If you push your pieces together before the solvent has evaporated, you'll get weak adhesion because the solvent will still be present.

3. Once the glue is tacky, press your 2 pieces together. The adhesives bond quickly, so make sure you have everything lined up beforehand. It'll be really difficult to unstick and reposition them once you've started.

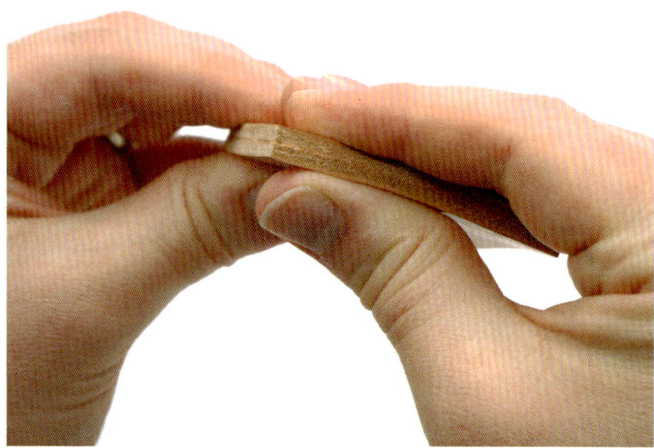

Contact cement can also be used to bond leather to other materials. Stiff and light materials (such as foam or balsa wood) work best. Stretchy or pliable materials like fabrics are hit or miss, but more often a miss. Regardless of what you're cementing to your leather, you probably don't want glue as your attachment method where you have tension or weight. It's just less likely to hold up to wear and tear over time.

Tools: Metal Bits Mostly

ESSENTIALS

Rapid rivets: Basic rivets are a classic way to hold two pieces of leather together.

Rivet setter: A metal cylinder designed to apply force to a rivet correctly and set it.

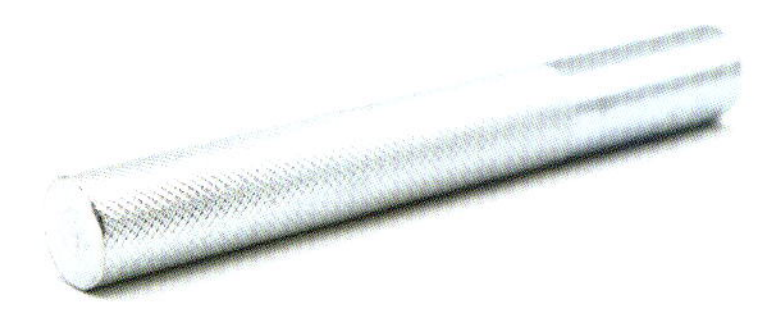

Mallet: For setting your hardware.

Hole punch: Many hardware options require a hole in the leather to install.

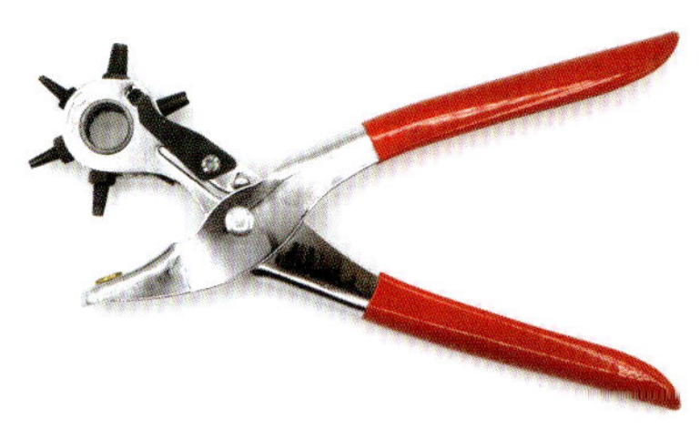

Buckles: To attach and detach belts and straps.

OPTIONAL

Double cap rivets: These rivets have nice-looking caps on both sides, for when both sides of the rivet are visible.

Cap rivet anvil: A little metal bowl to preserve the curve of a cap.

Eyelets: Small rings to line the edges of holes in leather or fabric. Often one piece.

Eyelet setter and anvil: A small setter and anvil with a ring to fit eyelets and preserve their shape.

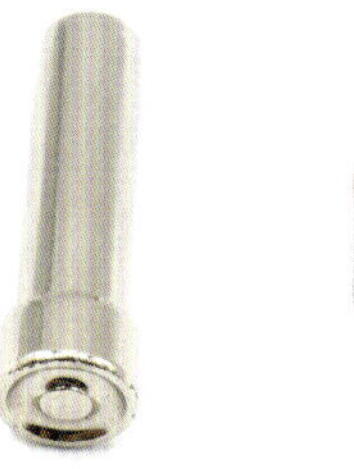

Grommet: A stronger version of an eyelet, creating a larger hole. Often two pieces.

Grommet setter and anvil: Most commonly an anvil with a hole in the center and a ring to fit the grommet, as well as a setter with a similar ring and a spike in the center to roll the post down.

Snaps: Four-part hardware designed for easy attachment and detachment.

Snap setter and anvil: Specifically sized anvil and setter, usually only fitting a single snap style and size.

Zipper: A classic and effective attachment method, particularly for clothing or armor.

Hook-and-loop fastener: An effective and forgiving attachment method, though it does tend to add some bulk.

Oblong punch: A convenient hole punch that makes slots instead of round holes.

Chicago screws: Rivets that screw together, allowing for a less permanent attachment.

Conchos: Decorative pieces with screwed and slotted varieties.

Hardware

What's cooler than leather? The only acceptable answer is leather with metal on it. This section covers how to use hardware for different attachment methods, whether it's attachment between pieces or attachment of the piece onto the body. All of this hardware can also be used for decorative purposes, which is common in anime and video game character designs.

Elizabeth Swann from *Pirates of the Caribbean: At World's End*
Costume and work-in-progress photos by Trine.k.n • Photo by Mai Aggestrup

HAMMERED HARDWARE

Many pieces of hardware are hammered together, forming an extremely durable attachment that, when properly done, is unlikely to fail unless the leather itself deteriorates or rips. This generally involves a front piece, a backing, a setting tool, and an anvil. Most setting tools are unique to a specific type and sometimes size of hardware, so make sure you keep them organized so that you're always using the correct tool. Some anvils are unique, while others consist of a simple flat cylinder of metal with a concave top. The concave surface is intended to preserve the curve of the hardware piece better than setting against a flat surface and prevent the hardware from sliding while being set. Some people use only the basic anvil for certain hardware or when they need to set hardware in a location that's difficult to lay flat, while others use it all the time. While using it, take care to avoid the upper rim of the anvil pushing into your leather piece and making a divot. Using the anvil on a surface with some give, like a pound board or even a little bit of scrap leather, can help to avoid those pesky divots.

Rivets

Rivets are essentially metal pins that, after they're set, hold pieces of leather together. They come in many different styles, sizes, and colors or platings. Most, including rapid and double-cap rivets, are set in the following way:

1. Punch the hole for your rivet. The hole you punch should be as snug against the rivet as possible. You want it just big enough to get the rivet post through it.

2. Push the post through the leather from the back side.

TIP

During this step, check to make sure you've chosen the right post length. Rivets come in many sizes, but the most important measurement is the post length. The actual rivet head can be any size, and some decorative rivets are very large. However, if the post is too short, it won't flatten enough to hold the rivet in place; too long, and the post will shift to an angle so that the ends can be tight against the leather. After pushing the post through the leather, you want 1⁄16"–1⁄8" (2–3mm) of the post to show above the leather when the post backing is snug on the other side.

3. Push the head (often a small cap) onto the rivet post.

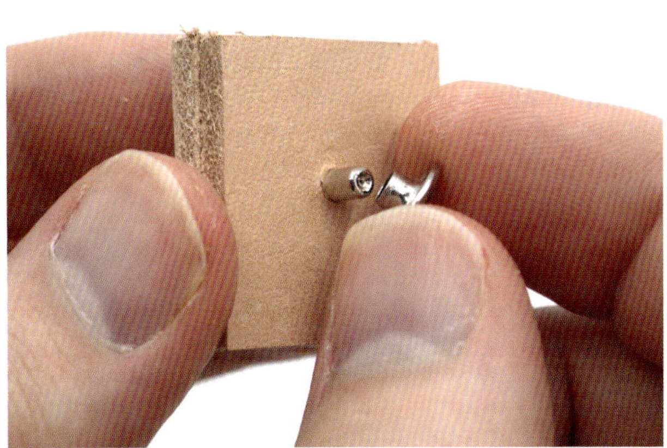

4. Place the post backing of the rivet down on your solid working surface. We recommend a bit of countertop or smooth stone.

TIP

Many rivets are not flat and require the use of a specific anvil to set. Double-cap rivets, for example, use the standard bowl-shaped anvil to allow the head to retain its domed shape. To use a specific anvil, you'll place the head of the rivet down onto the anvil in Step 4, and the setting tool against the post backing in Step 5. If you're applying a breakable decorative rivet, use a rubber board or piece of scrap leather on top of your hard surface to absorb shock and reduce the chances of shattering your decoration.

5. Put your rivet setting tool against your head and strike it with a plastic or rawhide mallet. The tool should be held straight up.

6. Try to apply the force from directly above. If you strike at an angle, your post may not flatten evenly and can shift to the side, resulting in a rivet that can pull out with use and may not sit flat. If the backing doesn't set snug against the leather, strike it again until you get a good set.

Eyelets and Grommets

Next up are eyelets and grommets. These are two different pieces of hardware, each of which creates a protective metal ring around a hole. They're used to make lacing holes more resilient. An eyelet is a single piece that is pushed through the hole and hammered down to grab onto the inside of the material. A grommet comes in two parts that are placed on either side of a hole and then hammered together. Eyelets are often smaller than grommets, but both require a specialized setting tool and anvil to set.

Eyelet setting:

1. Punch the hole for your eyelet. The hole you punch should be just big enough to get the eyelet through.

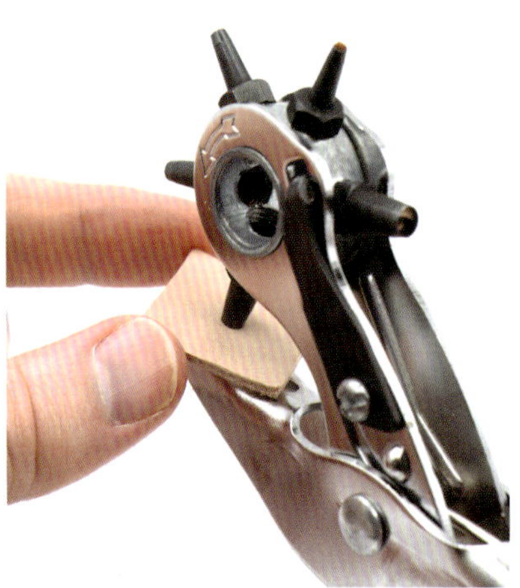

2. Push the eyelet through from the front side of the material.

3. Place the front of the eyelet down onto the groove in the anvil.

4. Line up the eyelet setting tool against the part of the eyelet sticking up through the hole. The tool should be held straight up.

5. Strike the setting tool with a mallet until the eyelet is tightly set and gripping the material.

Grommet setting:

1. Punch the hole for your grommet. The hole you punch should be just big enough to get the grommet front through. If you're using a large grommet, you may need to widen the punched hole with more punches.

2. Push the grommet front through the front side of the material.

3. Push the grommet backing down onto the grommet front piece until it lies against the material.

4. Place the front of the grommet down onto the groove in the anvil.

5. Line up the grommet setting tool against the part of the grommet sticking up through the hole. The tool should be held straight up.

6. Strike the setting tool with a mallet until the part of the grommet sticking up through the hole rolls down onto the grommet backing and the grommet is tightly set and gripping the material.

Snaps

The last piece of hammered hardware we'll cover is snaps. Snaps are a convenient attachment method involving a stud that fits snugly into a socket and holds together until pulled apart again. They're very easy to attach and detach, but the trade-off is that you can't use them in places with too much tension because they're designed to detach easily. Snaps are a little more complicated to set because they come in four pieces. They also come in multiple styles, setting methods, and sizes. Line 20 and Line 24 snaps are commonly used, and come in four parts: two parts for the socket, and two for the stud. Line 20 snaps are smaller and work well for thin and medium-weight leather up to 7 oz. (2.8mm) or so. Line 24 snaps are larger and work well at 8 oz. (3.2mm) or thicker.

To set the stud side of the snap:

1. Punch a hole where you want your stud. The hole you punch should be just big enough to get the post through.

2. Push the cap piece through the front side of the material where you want your stud.

3. Place the cap down on the anvil.

4. Fit the stud over the cap post and push down until it's snug.

5. Line up the snap setting tool against the cap post. The tool should be held straight up.

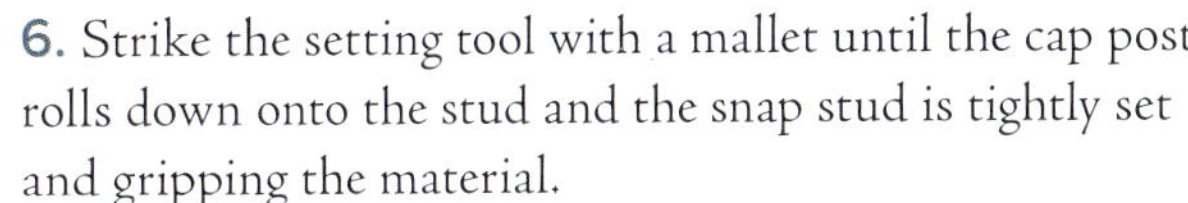

6. Strike the setting tool with a mallet until the cap post rolls down onto the stud and the snap stud is tightly set and gripping the material.

To set the socket side of the snap:

1. Punch a hole where you want your socket. The hole you punch should be just big enough to get the post through.

2. Push the backing piece through the back side of the material where you want your socket.

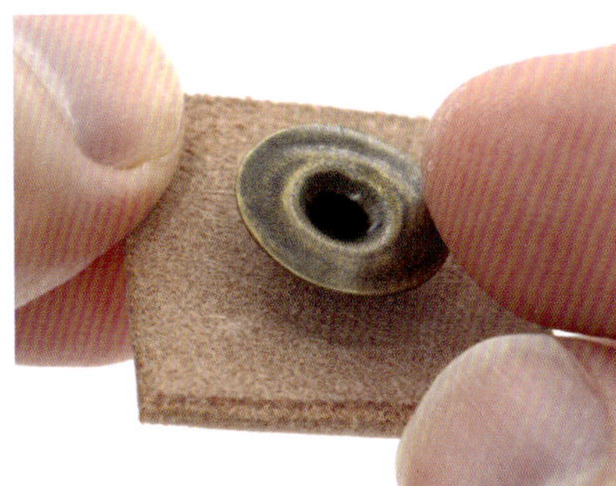

3. Place the backing piece down on your solid working surface.

4. Fit the socket over the backing post and push down until it's snug.

5. Line up the snap setting tool against the backing post. The tool should be held straight up.

6. Strike the setting tool with a mallet until the backing post rolls down onto the socket and the snap socket is tightly set and gripping the material.

Connecting Leather to Other Materials

Hammered hardware can also be used to connect leather with other materials. Depending on the material, different types of hardware work better.

Hammered hardware works especially well with very rigid materials such as metal, wood, or solid plastics. In these cases, the material is tough enough to handle any attachment type as long as you aren't overly aggressive when setting.

You can use hammered attachments with fabric as long as there isn't much tension or weight put on the fabric at the attachment points; otherwise, you risk the fabric fraying or tearing over time. Try to use hardware with a wide grip so that a small amount of fabric wear and tear doesn't allow the fabric to escape the hardware's grip. You can also add a small leather backer and sandwich the fabric between your main piece and the backer to add durability and reduce strain on the fabric.

It can also work for foams or thin thermoplastic, but for these types of materials, you really want to have the exact correct post length. If your post length is too short, you risk damaging the foam or plastic when setting. Test first with a scrap piece, especially if you're attaching to an already painted material! We don't recommend rolled set hardware (like snaps) because it's harder to get the set tight without pushing into the foam or plastic and damaging it.

From left to right, leather riveted to: fabric, foam, wood

SEW-ON HARDWARE

Earlier, we covered sewing leather together by hand. In this section, we'll combine that sewing know-how with hardware.

Zippers

Zippers are a staple in modern clothing, and they aren't uncommon in cosplay. Though you're more likely to need them when working with garment leather (page 130), you can absolutely use them with veg tan. With veg tan, you'll want to use more heavy-duty zippers, usually metal, unless you've got a specific reason not to. All-purpose zippers work, but they might not last very long. If you've worked with zippers before, the methodology is very similar. The more common method is to line up the zipper fabric under the edge of the leather, leave a small gap between the metal teeth and the leather so that the zipper pull tab can move freely up and down the teeth, and then sew the zipper fabric to the leather. Contact cement will often work as well, but it isn't as reliable and the constant pull on the zipper will wear it out quickly.

Hook-and-Loop Fastener

Though hook-and-loop fastener isn't technically hardware, we've included it here as a sew-on attachment option. Hook-and-loop fastener is a convenient way to keep pieces where you want them, especially in areas that aren't really seen and don't need as much decorative flair. Attaching the fastener is straightforward as well. You can punch holes and hand sew the outer edge of the hook-and-loop fastener directly to the leather, or if you want to save time you can stick it to the leather with contact cement. Because hook-and-loop fastener is consistently pulled apart and restuck, though, the contact cement won't last as long as it normally would. We don't recommend using the standard adhesive that comes on self-adhesive hook-and-loop fastener to attach to leather, as we've found this adhesive doesn't stick well to leather over time. Hook-and-loop fastener is also a great way to attach pretty much any other material to leather, as long as the fastener can be attached securely to that other material. This is especially useful if you want a nonpermanent attachment for transportation or wearability.

OTHER ATTACHMENTS

There are a number of options outside of hammered and sew-on hardware. Here are some common ones.

Buckles

Character designers love buckles. Luckily, they're pretty straightforward to install. Buckles come in a huge variety of designs, but the thing to keep in mind when shopping for buckles is that the size on the website or the packaging is the measurement of the inside of the buckle. In other words, it's the width of the belt or strap of leather that will go through the buckle.

The next consideration is whether you want to skive the leather to reduce its thickness before installing the buckle (see Skiving, page 34). Skiving allows the leather to bend more easily and reduces the thickness difference between where the buckle is installed and the rest of the belt. There are different schools of thought on skiving around the buckle, but in general if you have very thick leather you probably want to skive, whereas thinner leather doesn't need it. For medium-thickness leather (6–7 oz. [2.4–2.8mm]), you'll have to make your own judgment. We like to skive these widths for a smoother look, but that's not a hard rule. We also don't skive leather thinner than 5 oz. (2mm) to avoid weakening the leather at an attachment point.

There are two options when skiving for a buckle. First, and most common, is to skive from the end of the belt or strap back to where that end will fold back. This reduces the bulk along the entirety of the fold for a more consistent thickness overall. You want a nice gentle angle at the point where you start skiving down to your desired thickness so that it doesn't look jarring. The second option is to skive a rectangular channel right where the buckle will sit, just to reduce the extra bulk it's adding.

To install the buckle, follow these steps:

1. Punch a hole in the center of the belt or strap where you want the buckle to be. Make sure you leave enough leather to fold over! Often, people use an oblong punch for this hole so that the buckle is easier to maneuver and so that the leather fits tightly artound the bar of the buckle.

2. *Optional:* If you have a buckle set with a loop, slide that on now. Alternatively, attach your own leather loop by folding a strap of leather around the belt to make a loop and securing it with glue or rivets.

3. Put the end of the leather through the buckle, insert the buckle prong through the hole you punched in Step 1, and fold the end over.

4. Attach the folded-over end of the belt or strap back to the rest of the piece, securing the buckle. Usually this is done with rivets (page 98).

A buckle is only useful when paired with a strap end with sizing holes. For a belt, these are on the other end, but it could also be a completely separate strap. For sizing holes, simply use a hole punch with a size slightly bigger than your buckle prong to punch holes along the center of the belt or strap. The distance between these holes will vary based on your adjustment needs. The end of the strap is often rounded or tapered to a point. You can draw this freehand, use a compass, employ a French curve, or purchase templates or cutting tools that help you get a consistent shape for your tips. Some buckles come with a metal tip that you can install on the end with a tight fit and a little bit of glue.

Chicago Screws

There are a number of other rivet types we won't cover in this book, but we want to call out Chicago screws for their usefulness in cosplay. Chicago screws aren't hammered, but instead come as a head with a screw post housing and a post backing with a screw post. Instead of setting these rivets, you simply screw them down. This makes them removable, which has some neat uses like being able to replace pieces or disassemble your cosplay for travel. Make sure you get the right post length because the screw posts can't be compressed.

Conchos

Concho is a loose term for a circular decoration made of metal. Conchos are sold in a variety of shapes and sizes, with the two main types being screw-back conchos and slotted conchos. Screw-back conchos work exactly like Chicago screws, but they have a bigger head. Slotted conchos are tied on with lacing or straps that are fed through matching slots cut into the leather underneath the concho.

Extra TECHNIQUES

Now that you've learned the foundational skills for leatherworking, the doors to experimentation are opened wide! In this chapter, we explore some advanced techniques for integrating leather into your costuming.

Pukei-Pukei Armor Sets from *Monster Hunter Rise*

Cosplays by Matthew__Barry and Chloecat.Cosplay • Work-in-progress photos by Chloecat.Cosplay
Photo of Pukei-Pukei Armor Sets by helloimfran

Lining, Strengthening, and Doubling Layers

You may come across a project where you need to line your leather, strengthen a part of your project, or stack layers of leather but have a clean edge.

LINING LEATHER FOR AESTHETICS

Most leather projects don't necessarily need to be lined because the flesh side of chrome tan and veg tan can be smoothed through the burnishing and sealing processes, leaving you with a nice back to your piece. However, you can absolutely line your leather for an alternative, professional finish.

When lining your leather simply for looks, you'll want to pick the lining material and weight that works best for your project. You won't want to pick a lining that will add weight or additional thickness to your project, so aim for leathers that are supple and 1–3 oz. Using thin veg tan can create a congruent piece between outer and inner lining. Suede- and garment-grade leathers like pig and lambskin are great for lining as well, and they come in many colors!

NONSLIP LINING

Suede is great for lining because it has a soft texture and comes in a variety of weights and colors. Its best quality as a liner, though, is the fact it's nonslip. This makes it perfect for lining straps, belts, or anything that may want to twist or move around while being worn. The only downside is that it can transfer color with friction, so if you're wearing a white shirt and using a colored suede to line a piece, be aware that you may end up with some staining on your shirt.

A quick way to line your leather is by gluing. Apply contact cement to the flesh sides of your leather and your lining. Smooth from the center to the edges, pushing out any air bubbles and pressing the pieces together. You can use a seam roller, tailor's clap, or even a rolling pin to help if your piece is large. Trim off any excess lining.

At this point, you can either leave your lining and main leather with a crisp exposed edge, or you can enclose using methods like leather piping, or skiving and folding your main leather over. If you choose the latter, before you cut your leather pieces, you'll need to add seam allowance into your pattern for folding over the edge. If you choose to add piping, you can either purchase premade leather piping or create your own.

If you're lining a piece that has been wet formed, the process will be similar, except you can't lay your piece flat and use a roller. Cut your lining, apply glue to both pieces, and then carefully lay your lining into your main piece, smoothing from the middle to the edges, slowly working out any bubbles or creases with a bone folder before the glue dries. Sewing clips can help hold edges flush as you work.

Another way to line your leather is by sewing. The process is similar to gluing but instead, you can either glue your lining down and then sew (which is more for looks) or sew your lining on without gluing. This creates a lining that feels like those in bags: attached around the edges but free to move around in the middle. Be sure to choose whichever method works best for your project.

If you want a bag-type lining, you'll want to use clips to assist with holding your leather in place. You can use a water-soluble glue along your stitch line as that will afford some grip but is not as intense as contact cement.

NOT JUST FOR KIDS

Elmer's glue sticks are a water-soluble and budget-friendly option for a quick hold on leather that is not as permanent as contact cement. It's also easier to clean off hand-sewing needles and thread if you experience any buildup.

Making Leather Piping

To make leather piping, you'll need a rectangle of very thin leather. You can either purchase what's called a *piping strip* or cut your own out of a very thin veg tan or garment leather, depending on the project. The length is the amount of piping you need, and the width just needs to be enough to fold over and sew in, normally somewhere around 2″ (50mm).

Next, you need a core. You can use lots of stuff for this depending on the size and firmness you want, from round leather or plastic cording to softer filler like yarn. Once you've chosen your core, cut it to the length of your leather strip. Sometimes people will skive the ends so that the piping tapers at the edges when used. Measure extra carefully when you do this, because you'll have to make a whole new piece if it doesn't shrink away at just the right spot.

To assemble your piping:

1. Apply contact cement to the flesh side of the entire leather strip and leave to get tacky.

2. Once it's tacky, lay your core carefully down the center of the strip and press.

3. Fold the strip over and glue the flesh side together starting in the center and working your way out, resulting in a nice little length of piping.

LINING LEATHER FOR STRENGTH

You've found the absolutely perfect leather to make a set of pauldrons. The only downside is that it's not thick enough to hold the shape. No problem! You can line your leather with veg tan to provide the rigidity you need. Following the steps in the previous section, you can apply contact cement or stitching and combine these leathers together to make the perfect match.

Reminder: If you line your leather with veg tan, you'll need to condition (page 68) and seal it (page 72). You can tool, stamp, paint, or dye if you want, but at a minimum, a quick replenish of hydration and oils followed by a topcoat will have your veg tan looking great, even if it isn't the star of the show.

Lining with Furs: *While not recommended for most fur-on leather, sheepskin (page 15) is a common liner on wearable products. It's a great liner for both insulating and sweat-wicking, as wool is a natural barrier against the cold and is also antimicrobial, lessening odor retention.*

A thin veg tan can work as a great liner and allows for you to create a seamless transition between the inside and outside of your pieces—literally. After gluing two pieces of veg tan together, you can use your burnishing tools and compounds to blend the layers together to make it look as if there is only one layer of leather.

There are two keys to achieving this: clean-cut edges and patience. When cutting your main piece and your lining, cut them slightly bigger than you need and then glue them together. Using a sharp blade, cut your glued piece to size. Doing this when the outer and lining leathers are combined allows for less uneven edges or accidentally miscutting and trimming off too much. If you already have your main piece cut and you didn't add any extra allowances, cut the lining slightly larger and then trim as needed.

Now take your burnishing tool and burnishing agent of choice and work through the process found in Burnishing (page 69), taking time to repeat the process until the line between the layers is less apparent and looks like one edge.

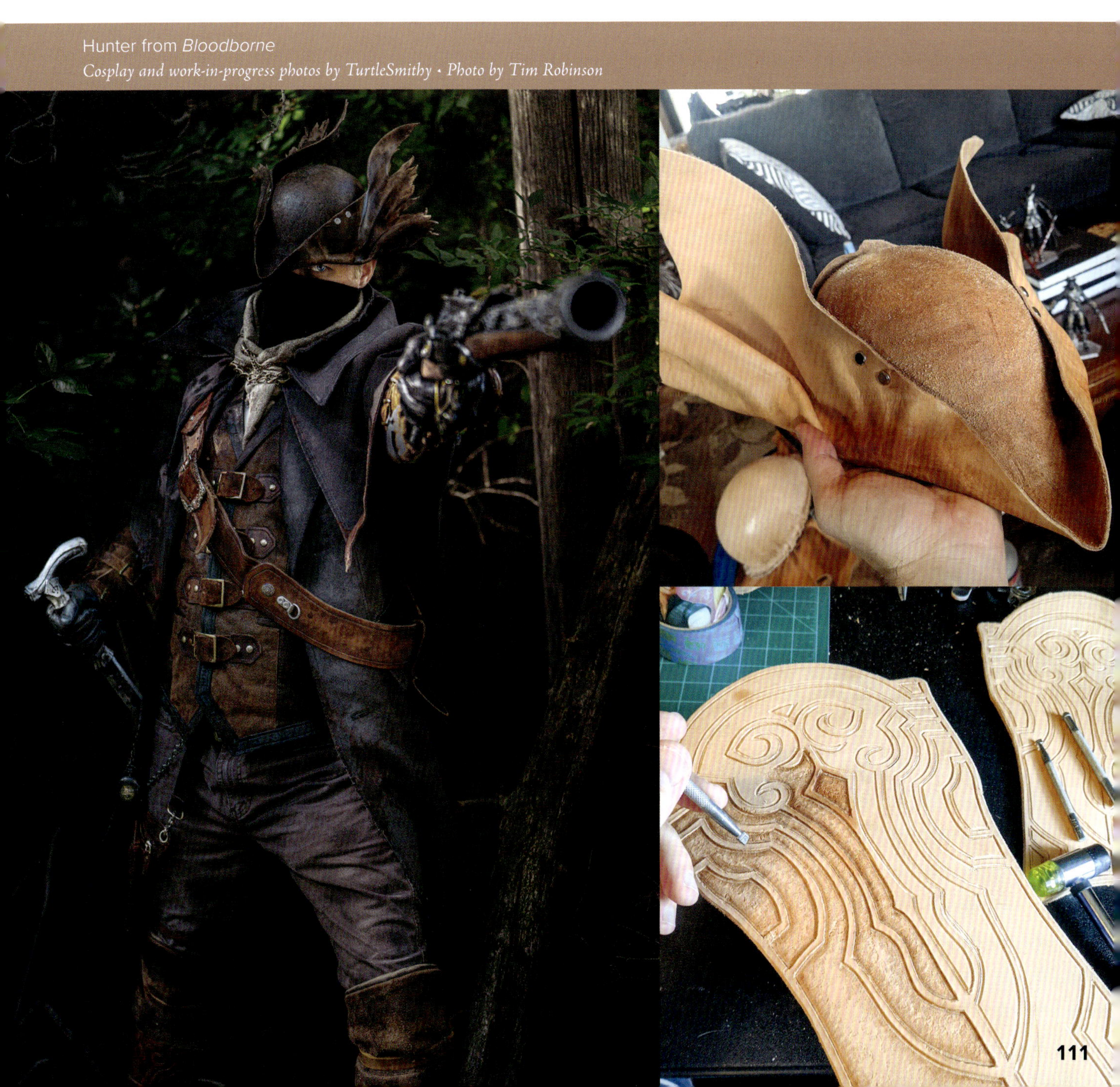

Hunter from *Bloodborne*

Cosplay and work-in-progress photos by TurtleSmithy • Photo by Tim Robinson

Wet Forming

An extremely useful property of veg tan leather is that it becomes more pliable when wet. Chrome tan doesn't have the same molding abilities as veg tan due to its tanning process, so we don't recommend it for wet forming.

Essentially, wet forming veg tan is the process of applying water to leather, shaping it, and then allowing it to dry. You can use this technique to fit-form armor pieces, shape thin leather over a base surface (known as *plug embossing*), or even ease a little more stretch from leather to help with 3-D curves.

TIP

Be careful when you need to make the grain curve inward instead of outward. Looser parts of the hide like the belly or leather that was dried out before wet forming can easily wrinkle as the topmost layers attempt to compress inward on that inside curve. Be gentle and condition your leather beforehand (see Leather Conditioning, page 68) to reduce the chances of this happening. If the wrinkles are minor, you might be able to smooth them with steam, but this method is hit-or-miss.

Most wet forming also involves heat. As your water gets hotter, the leather becomes easier to work and holds its shape more effectively once dry. However, if you go too hot (somewhere around 175°F/80°C), the leather will begin to shrink and thicken as it sits in the water. This is not reversible. As a rule of thumb, stick to the hottest temperature you can stand on your hands—after all, you'll be using your fingers to shape.

We recommend two basic techniques for heated wet forming. For hand molding, swiftly wet the grain side of the leather; then flip and wet the flesh side. Don't fully dunk! By not wetting the center layers, they provide stability while the wet outer layers become flexible to form shapes. If you try to do delicate molding on a piece of leather saturated with water, your details will lose their definition as you work because there's no dry core to hold the shape.

Your other option is to fully soak the leather. To get good results with this method, you need a way to hold your piece in its final shape while it dries, such as gently tying it to a mold or a cling-wrapped mannequin with strips of cloth.

Before soaking, wet the leather with room-temperature water so it doesn't shrivel when it hits the hot water; then submerge your leather in the hot water. More soaking time will yield a stiffer result up to a point, but too much time will again lead to shrinkage. Finally, pull it out, mold the piece into its final shape, and then set it up to dry. Historically, leather would be soaked in water hot enough to intentionally shrink and thicken it before being pressed into molds and allowed to dry and harden. Look up *cuir bouilli* if you're curious!

When using either method, if you need precise mold lines, use a craft knife or rotary tool to cut away troughs from the flesh side of the leather. By reducing bulk, you're not only allowing the leather to bend more sharply in those places but also encouraging it to follow your guidelines, leading to crisp and neat molding.

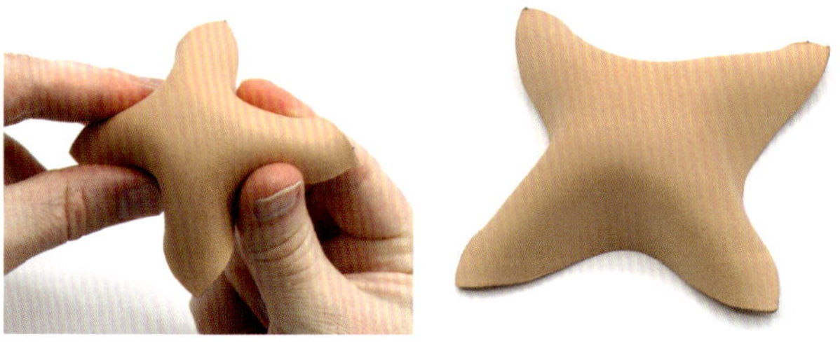

When you need your piece to stretch, mix a solution of two parts water, one part rubbing alcohol, and one part baby shampoo in a spray bottle. This solution will help loosen up the leather and give it a bit of stretch. After you apply it to the leather, you need to work **fast** because the leather will harden after the alcohol evaporates. You can also use this method to mold leather over an existing shape to create embossed patterns.

Leather Braiding

Braiding leather is a wonderful way to add a texture-filled component to your leather pieces and costumes. Just as braiding embroidery floss, fabric, or yarn, working with strips of lacing or cut veg tan/chrome tan opens up techniques from flat plaits to round plaits, button knots to belt weaving. There are detailed resources dedicated to just this leatherworking style, and if you like the examples we share, we encourage you to explore more!

When working with veg tan leather strips, it is important to condition the leather before attempting to braid it. It will be handled several times, bent, and tugged tightly during the braiding process and conditioning will keep the leather supple and lessen any warping that can occur from multiple retries of a pattern. If you're confident in your braiding, once your conditioner has been applied, wet your leather strips before braiding for maximum malleability. If you're using garment leather or suede lacing, there is no need to condition or wet your strips.

We suggest labeling your strands, especially if you're doing complex eight- or twelve-strand braids. It's easy to lose your place, and some patterns can become tricky the more strands are involved.

When you braid leather, the length of your strips will drastically decrease. You'll need more than you think! We have noted the approximate shrinkage we've experienced with each braid, but use your judgment and cut your strips longer if you're worried you may run out. Better to have extra than not have enough when doing an intricate pattern.

Burnish and dye your leather before you begin to braid. Once leather is braided, it is harder to reach all the edges and crevices, which can cause uneven dye jobs. If you're making a slit braid, burnish and dye after you've cut your slits to ensure the inner edges are also treated. We recommend sealing your leather after braiding has been finished.

THREE-STRAND TRICK BRAID

Approximate shrinkage is 5%–10% with medium-weight leather.

We'll start off with a little magic trick! This braid is a type of *slit braid*, and it's usually made with veg tan or chrome tan. Slit braids are cut from a single piece of leather and do not have any free-hanging lace ends like a common braid. Instead, the laces are separated only by straight, even cuts that do not extend through the top or bottom edges of the leather strap. These kinds of braids are great for straps, belts, wristcuffs, or appliqués on top of armor pieces.

1. To prepare your leather strap, first measure and mark your lines to create three equal laces; then cut them carefully with a box cutter or craft knife. Remember to leave uncut space at the top and bottom of your strap. Next, take a small round punch or stitching hole punch and use it at the top and bottom of each cut. This is not mandatory, but it does help stop your cut line from splitting any further as you work the braid. This is especially important if you're not leaving much uncut space at the top and bottom of your laces.

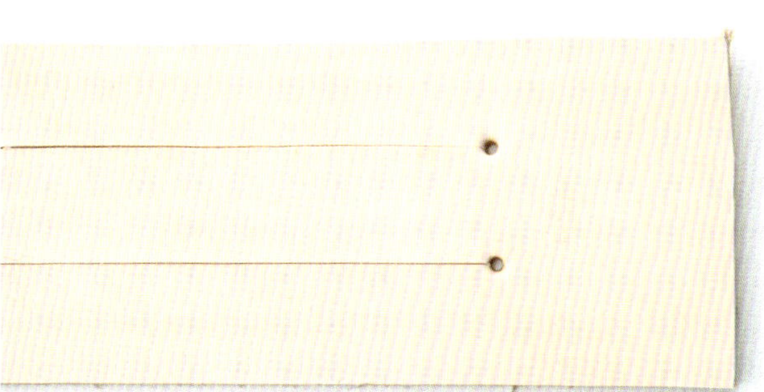

2. Condition your leather. For this braid, because of its finicky nature and the need to constantly reposition, we suggest wetting your leather.

3. Start with a traditional three-strand braid: Take the leftmost lace and place it over the center lace. Now take the rightmost lace and place that over the new center lace. Then take the current leftmost lace and place that over the new center lace. The pattern is always placing the alternating outermost lace over the lace currently in the center.

4. As you braid the top, the bottom will twist into a mirroring braid. This will need to be undone to make space for the top braid. To do this, take the entire bottom of your strip and, going from front to back, feed it through the opening between the leftmost lace and the center lace. Pull slack through, making sure the bottom is grain side up. Trust the process. It will look like a tangly mess.

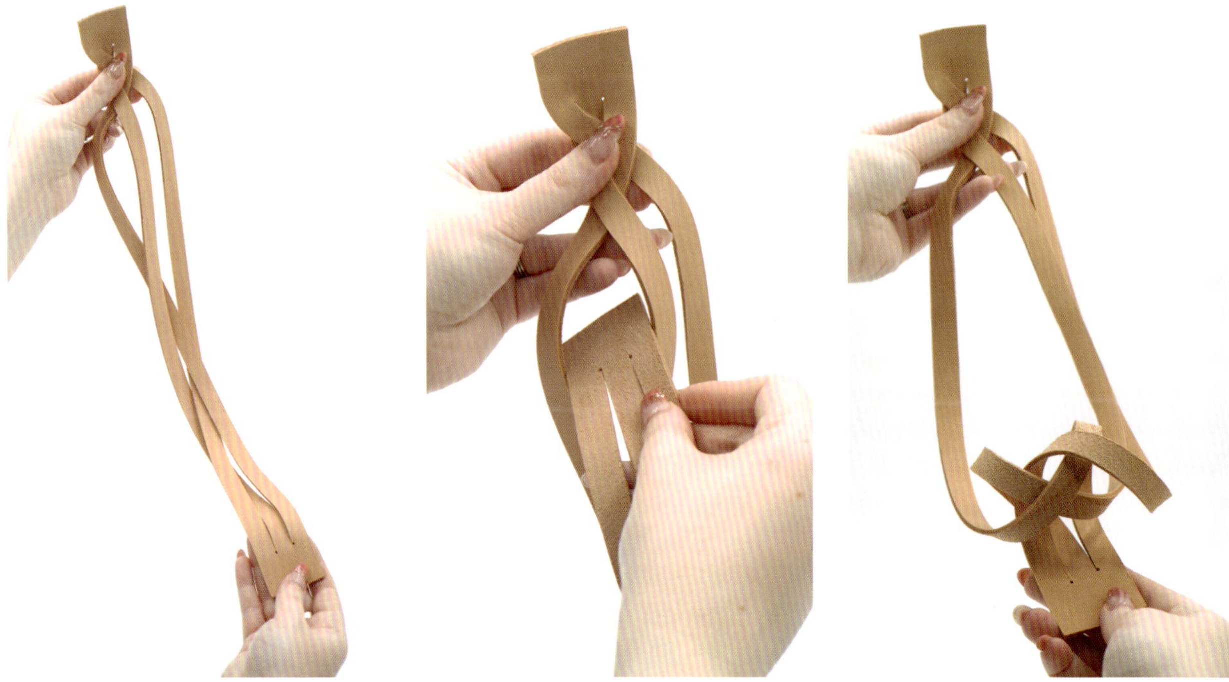

5. Take the left corner of the bottom and flip it through the opening between the center and rightmost laces. You may need to do some additional tweaking of the laces, but this should correct the twists and tangles.

6. Repeat Steps 3–5 until you don't have enough lace length to complete Step 3. You'll probably have space left at the end of your braid, but don't worry! Use it to flip your bottom through and straighten out the extra twists.

7. To even out the braid, loosen the braid and fine-tune the slack to evenly space each section.

FOUR-STRAND BRAID

Approximate shrinkage is 5%–10% with lacing and 25% with medium-weight leather.

A four-strand braid is second only to the three-strand braid. It's helpful in learning strand passes and tracking which strand you're working with. To better show the pattern of movement, our examples are loosely braided. Give the steps a try and then try again with more tension for a tighter braid.

1. Start by lashing together 4 strands of lace or cutting 4 strips of veg tan connected at the top. If you opt for veg tan, remember to use a small round punch or a stitching hole punch to punch the top of the cut line to stop it from splitting further. If you're new to braiding, we suggest labeling your strands **A, B, C,** and **D.**

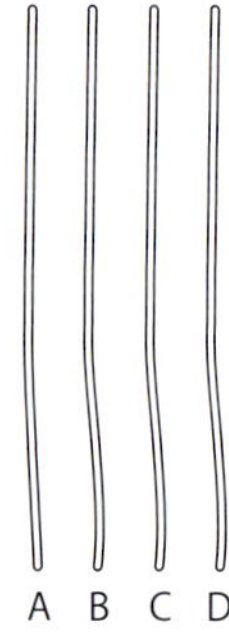

2. For the first pass, cross strand **C** over strand **B.**

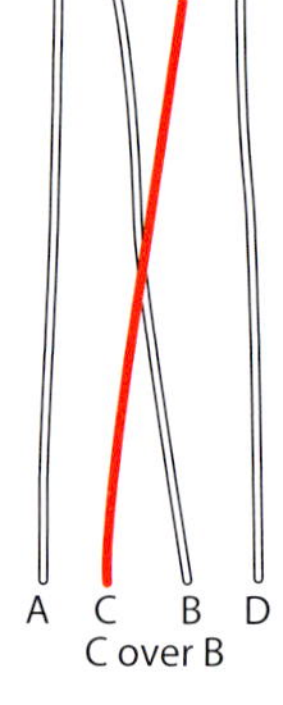

3. Move strand **D** to the left under strand **B.**

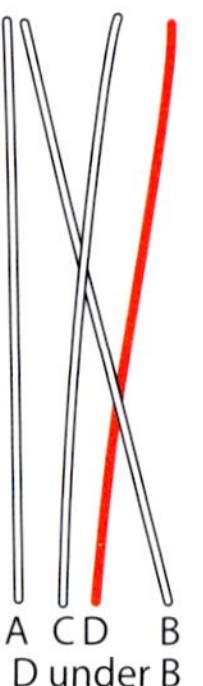

4. Move strand **A** to the right over strand **C** and under **D.**

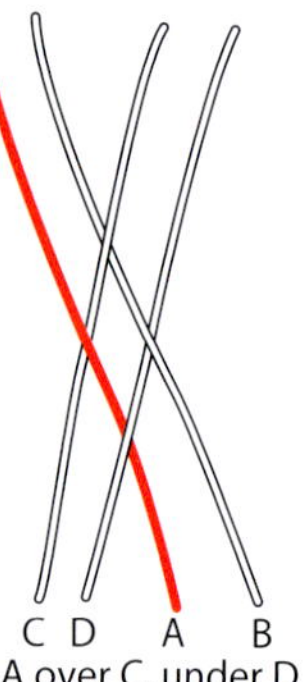

5. Now move strand **B** to the left under **A,** and move strand **C** to the right over strand **D** and under **B.**

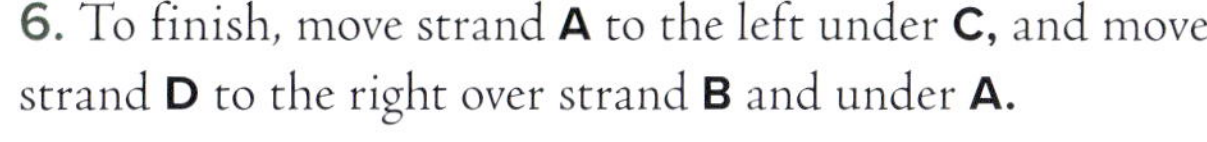

6. To finish, move strand **A** to the left under **C,** and move strand **D** to the right over strand **B** and under **A.**

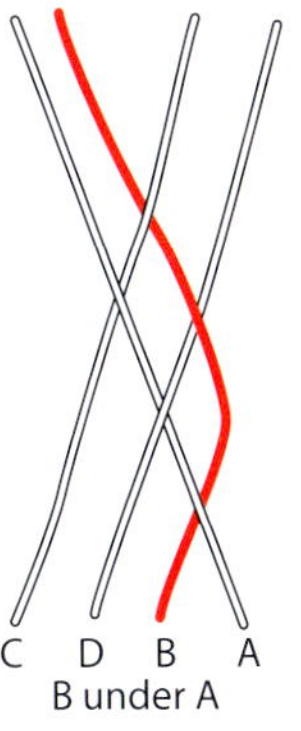

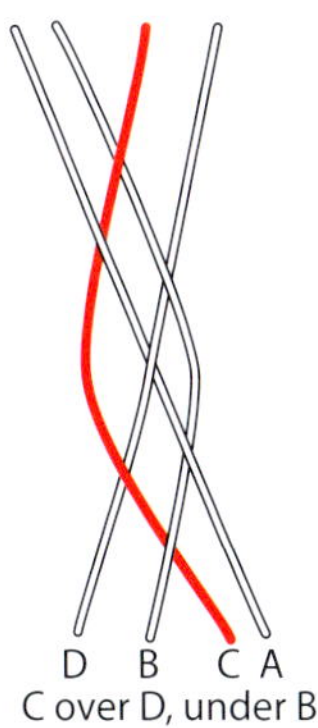

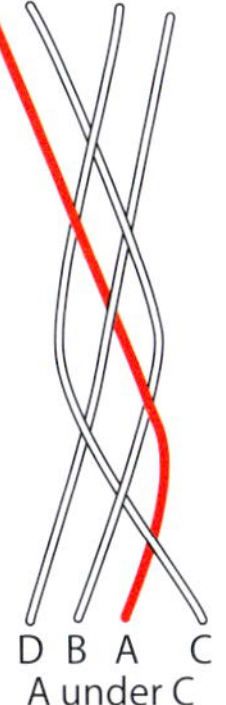

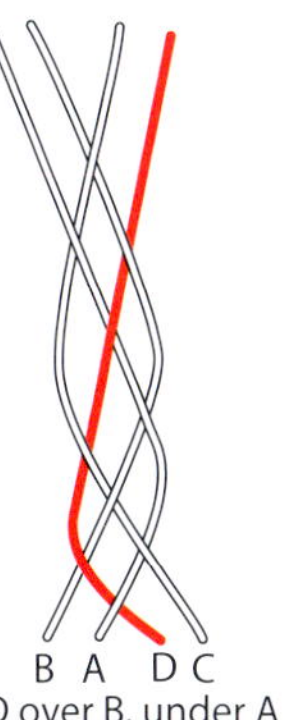

Another way to think about these passes once you move into Step 5 is that you're always taking the farthest strand in your right hand to the middle under the strand next to it. Then you're taking the farthest strand in your left hand to the middle over the strand next to it and then under the following strand. Repeat the process.

EIGHT-STRAND SQUARE BRAID

Approximate shrinkage is 15%–20% with lacing and 30%–35% with medium-weight leather.

This braid is also a type of flat braid, making it great for details on top of clothing or armor, but it can be manipulated at the end to be a 3-D shape. This braid will take a few tries to get the tension and spacing tidy, but stick with it. It's a rewarding braid to master!

1. Start by lashing together 8 strands of lace or cutting 8 strips of veg tan connected at the top. If you opt for veg tan, remember to use a small round punch or a stitching hole punch to punch the top of the cut line to stop it from splitting further.

2. Divide your strands into 4 on the right and 4 on the left. Number the strands **1–8** from left to right.

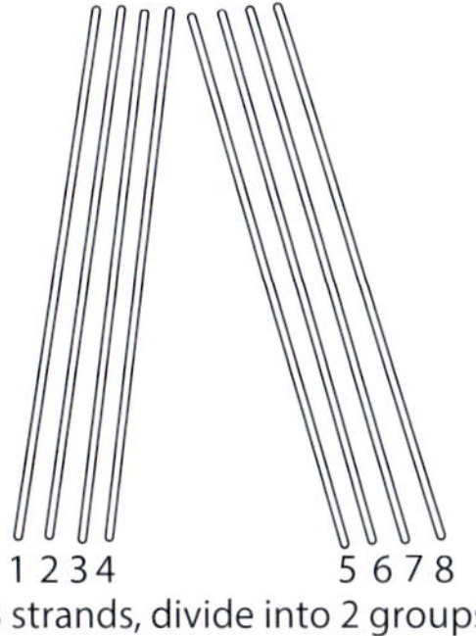

3. Bring the outermost right strand **8** to the middle by going under the 3 remaining right-side strands **7, 6,** and **5.**

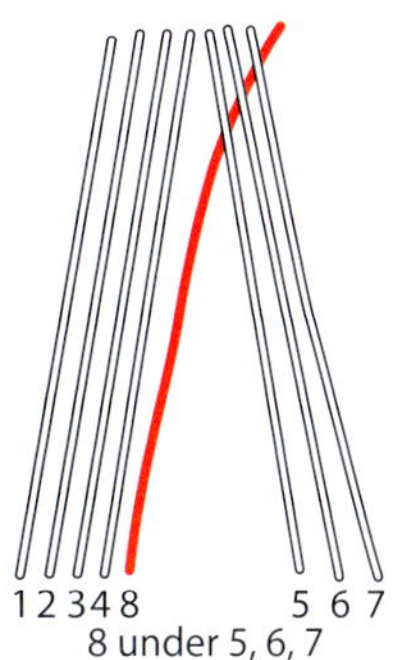

4. Bring the outermost left-hand strand **1** to the middle by going over the 3 remaining left-side strands **2, 3,** and then **4** and under **8.**

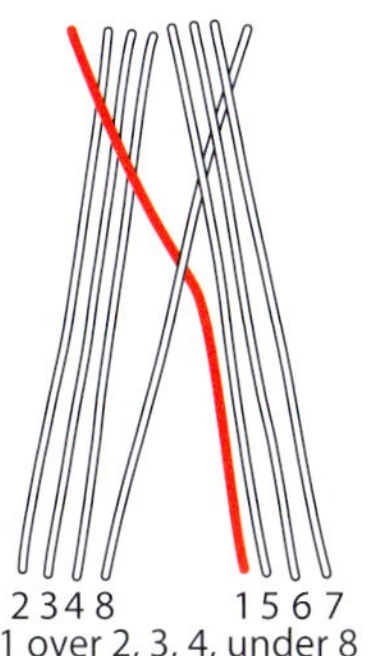

5. Next, take strand **7** to the center by passing it over strands **6, 5,** and **1.**

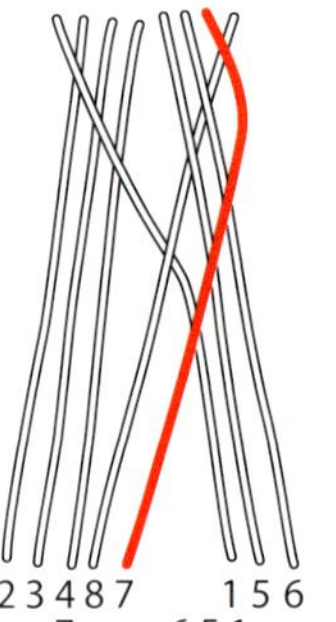

6. Now take strand **2** to the center by passing it under strands **3, 4,** and **8,** and then over **7.**

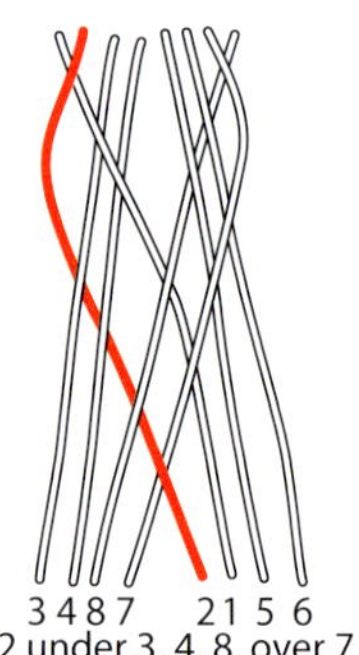

7. Take strand **6** to the center by passing it under **5, 1,** and **2.**

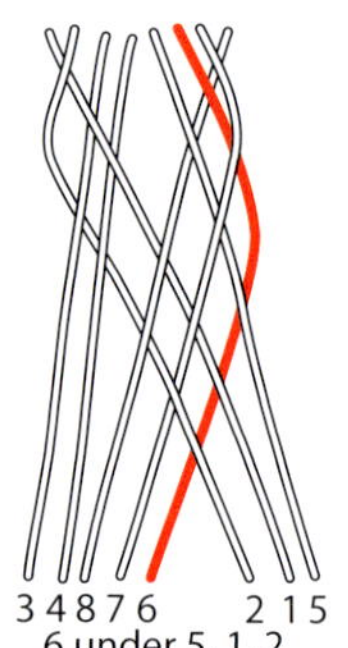

8. Next take strand **3** to the center by passing it over **4, 8,** and **7,** and then under **6.**

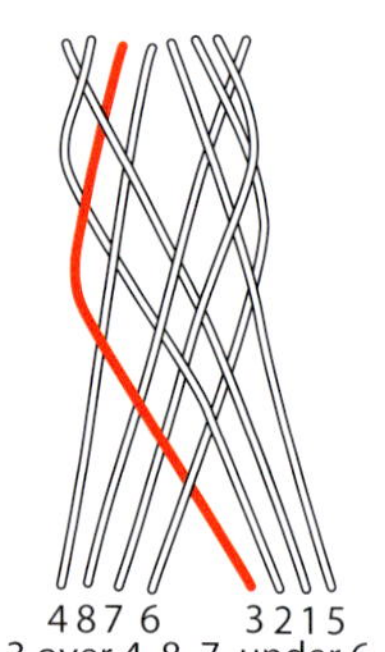

9. We're almost there! Take strand **5** to the center by passing it over **1, 2,** and **3.**

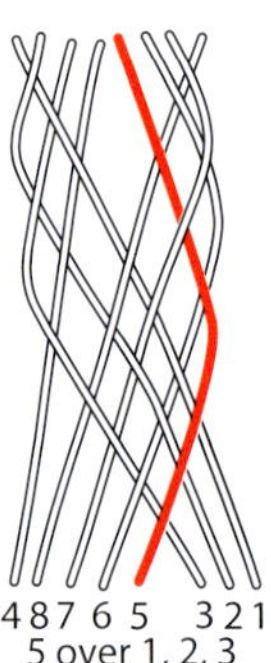

10. Last, take strand **4** to the center by passing under **8, 7,** and **6,** and then over **5.**

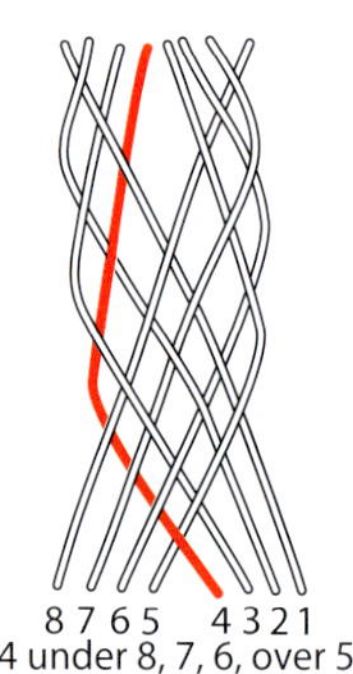

11. Repeat the pattern, paying special attention to Step 7.

12. If you want to make your square braid truly a square, once it's secured on the ends, push on the sides to inflate the weave. Tap each side gently with a mallet to help form the braid's sides into even planes.

Laced Edging

When you're adding a decorative trim to the edge of a piece, whether it's through one or more layers of leather, lace is a great way to both stitch it together and dress it up. We recommend using a stitching hole punch for this process because the bulk of lacing adds up quickly and it can be tricky to sew through chisel holes when working with multiple layers.

THREADING A LACING NEEDLE

Lacing needles are not like normal needles. Instead of threading through an eye, you pinch the lacing between the split ends of the needle like a clip.

1. To thread your needle, first prep your lace by using a craft knife to skive approximately ¼″–½″ (6.35–12.7mm) from one end to reduce the bulk.

2. Cut the skived end into a point using a craft knife.

3. Place that end in between the tweezer-like gap at the back of the needle.

4. To secure, use a plier to gently crimp down the needle end. In most lacing techniques, you won't tie a knot; instead, you'll loop your lace tails through your stitching.

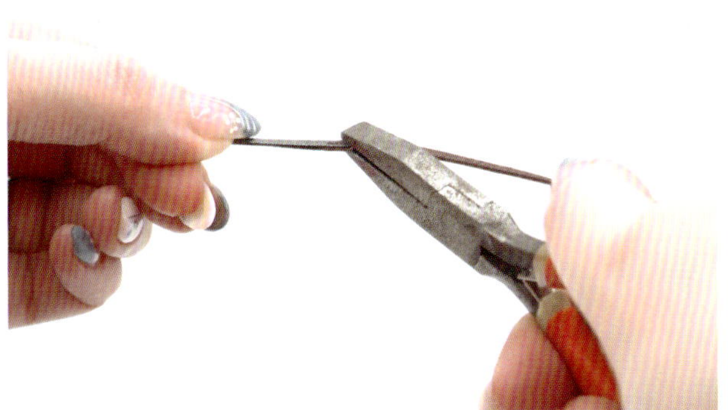

WHIPSTITCH

A nice and quick way to attach layers of stacked leather and give a dressy, finished edge is the whipstitch.

1. To start a whipstitch, prep a needle with a length of lace and begin by passing through the middle of the leather layers and out the second hole on 1 side. Leave a 2″–3″ (5–8cm) tail in between the leather layers.

2. Now loop your thread over the top of the piece and lace fully through the first set of stitching holes.

3. Loop your thread over the top of the leather again and stitch through the second set of stitching holes. Your lace should "roll" over the top edge of the leather, locking down the tail.

4. Repeat Step 3 for the next set of holes, looping over and stitching fully through the leather to the other side.

5. When you reach a corner, repeat the corner stitch, placing 1 loop on 1 side of the angle, and the second on the other side.

6. When you reach the end, stitch through the final set of holes as normal, but don't pull your slack too tight. Loop over and pass through the final hole again, but on the second pass, come back up between the leather layers on the inside between the first and second loops. Pull all your slack tight and then stitch under a few more loops before cutting off your lace length. Tuck in any length that may be sticking up between the leather.

Distressing and Weathering

Veg tan leather can genuinely take a beating. No, really, it can! Throw it on the ground, run sandpaper across it, gash it with a rotary tool, or even run over it with your car! The tanning process makes leather resilient, so go ahead and be a little rough.

Leather Armor Set from *Monster Hunter World: Iceborne*
Cosplay by Matthew__Barry • Photos by Chloecat.Cosplay

HOP TO IT!

One of our favorite distressing techniques happens at the very beginning of a project. When we know we want our finished piece to have a naturally pebbled or beat-up look, once we cut the piece, we take it outside and find some small rocks or a neat pattern in the concrete. We then wet the leather thoroughly, place it grain side down where we want the texture to transfer, and jump on it! You can also use a mallet or maul and hit it with medium force, or press with a rolling pin as shown here. But jumping is pretty fun!

After a couple steady jumps (steady is the key—you don't want to slide or push in a direction as that can skew your design), check to see how your leather has imprinted and if you want more texture. You can also mix and match by combining natural texturing with tooling to emphasize parts of the design.

THE SANDS OF TIME

Sandpaper is also a useful weathering tool! While sanding isn't always recommended after dyeing because it can remove color, you can create a unique texture by sanding away at the grain side, or using a rotary tool to do precision sanding with different types of bits. Purposefully wrinkling your leather and then using high-grit sandpaper to sand the ridges can create added layers of depth. This technique is great for leather that has braved the harsh elements, survived an apocalypse, or tussled with a mighty foe!

SUN "TANNING"

Using sunlight to UV age your leather is a great way to naturally fade dyes, and by far the easiest! All you have to do is put your leather in the sun, or part sun/shade, and watch as it leeches away your new dye job. Be sure to condition your leather to prevent cracking during rounds of sunbathing! If it's hot out, leave your leather in the sun only for short periods of time, or it can become too dry and will be damaged.

TAN LINES

If you don't rotate your leather while it's in the sun, you may experience tan lines. Remember, leather is skin! So be sure to go out and turn it if you don't want harsh shadows and highlights.

Another trick to using the sun to your advantage is stencils. Cover areas with a UV-protective cloth or, if the temperatures aren't too hot, painter's tape. Once your leather begins to show sun-fade, expose the covered areas and you'll see the contrast.

STRATEGIC TOOLING

You can distress leather using your tooling tools (page 39). Random strikes with bevelers, undercut bevelers, and shaders work quite well. We also like the look of a group of tooling strikes from the same angle in an area. Another option is to use a backgrounder or texture stamp to selectively texture parts or even most of a piece. This option looks cleaner but still weathered. You can also use sharp tools to scratch the leather to simulate a scratch from claws. Really it's all up to your imagination and how much you're willing to beat up your creation.

WEATHERING WITH DYES AND PAINTS

You can weather your leather (say that five times fast!) with dyes and paints during the dyeing step.

An easy way to create a worn look is to apply your dye more heavily in some places than others. When buffing in your dye, press harder and deepen the color of the dye to create a unique marbled effect that mimics wear. To deepen the illusion, you can apply dye or paint with a paintbrush to accentuate shadows and highlights.

While not highly recommended, deglazer can remove dye in areas, simulating UV damage.

BONE-DRY BRUSH

Drybrushing is a great technique for applying highlights. Use a dry brush with a small amount of paint to color an edge or highlight a raised section. For example, if your leather is dyed with a saddle brown, try dry brushing dark brown paint around rivet holes and lighter tan on raised areas.

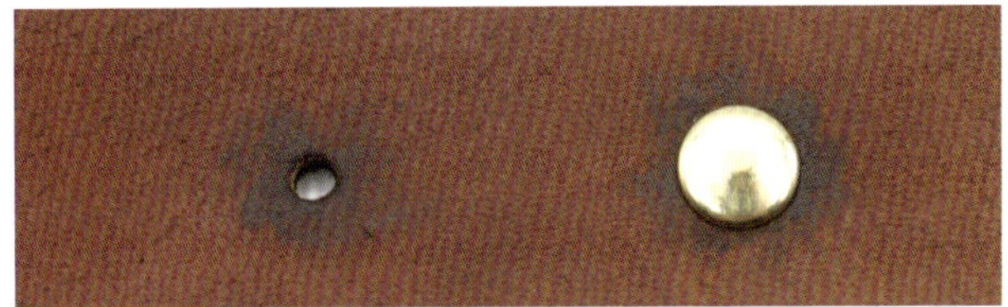

FROM THE ART SUPPLY STORE AND YOUR KITCHEN

Grime is the name of the game when adding 3-D textures on top of leather. Using household spices is a fun way to recreate muddy smears, rusty corners, or sandy pebbling. If you've textured on foam or in painting miniatures, you may see some crossover here and have several ideas already churning!

Dig into your kitchen cabinets and check out the spices you may have on hand. Mixing spices such as cumin or paprika, and even coffee grounds, with a clear-drying, heavy-body gel medium or gel leather sealant will yield a paste that looks like mold, dirt, or rust. The mixture base is up to your discretion, but we recommend using enough medium or gel to ensure that your spices are coated and don't flake or rub off.

From left to right: Coffee grounds, cumin, paprika, coriander

This technique is not restricted to spices. You can mix leather paints with gel sealants or mediums and use a stipple brush to create a buildup for layers of textures. You can use a clear-drying, heavy-body gel medium to create water droplet effects on pieces for a dewy look or even dive deep and get a glass bead gel or pumice gel to re-create pebbling or sand. Be sure to follow the use and safety instructions when using art supplies, and do a test!

Heavy body gel medium

Glass bead gel

Pumice gel

Glass bead gel, some mixed with dyes

Antiquing

Want your newly made project to look vintage? Or want to bring out your tooling but keep the natural hues of your veg tan? Antiquing is a fun way to add depth without spending an exorbitant amount of time painting or aging it naturally! Much like how oil paint can be applied and then wiped away to give a project an aged look, antiquing gel, paste, and stain (all oil-based products) will give the same effect.

Be sure to condition or oil your leather before antiquing to keep it well hydrated and in good condition!

DIGGING THAT GROOVE

If you want to create dark grooving details or stitching lines, you can make them after dyeing or painting. A standard edge beveler or French bevel can skive off the grain, leaving the fibers exposed for a different color. Once the antiquing medium meets this exposed leather, it will become saturated and take on the antiquing color. Be sure to seal your leather around these sections to ward off any overspill of color.

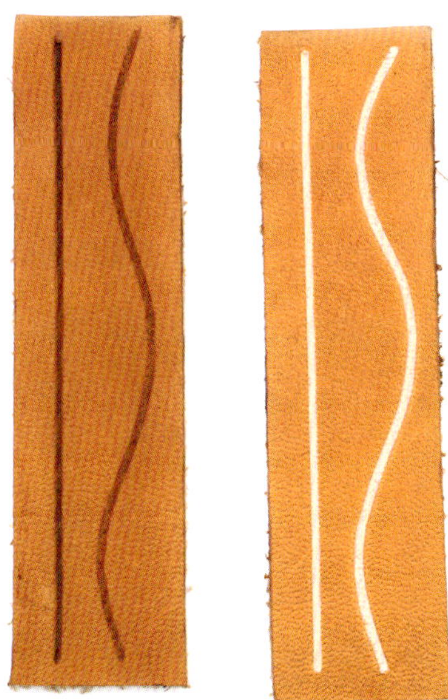

The left example was grooved and then antiqued with antiquing stain. The right example was antiqued with antiquing stain and then grooved.

ANTIQUING GEL

Antiquing gel can be used as your dyeing method or added after dyeing and painting your leather. Do not seal your leather before applying the gel, or it won't stick. Once applied, the gel is wiped away, leaving behind a thin but saturated layer of stain to age your colors and create contrast on tooled or stamped designs. Antiquing gel will usually come out lighter on heavily tooled areas due to the leather being burnished, which causes the pores to be more closed up than on the flat surfaces of your leather piece. In cut or stamped areas, it can come out quite dark. Always test a leather scrap or a part of your piece that is not noticeable because the gel may turn out darker than you anticipate.

Mix-and-Match Mistakes: *Avoid mixing brands from this point onward—water and oil-based won't want to mix, and some solvent-based products will react to each other. If you choose to work with Eco-Flo products or Fiebing's, it's safest to stick with their line of products until you're finished, especially if you're new to this process. After a few tries, if you want to mix and match, make samples and test your results. Keep a swatch log or take notes on the back of the test pieces for future reference.*

How to Apply Antiquing Gel

Antiquing gel is easy to apply, so even new leather workers can create pieces with depth of design and creativity. It is one of our favorite techniques on tooled leather. Antiquing paste is applied with this same method.

1. To apply antiquing gel, first put on gloves. Use a cloth rag to apply the antiquing gel. Be generous in the amount of gel you put on your cloth and work in circular motions, applying medium pressure to work the gel evenly into the piece. This stage is the "trust the process" step, as your project will look messy. The next step is where the magic happens.

2. Allow the gel to set for 1–2 minutes. Take a clean rag or recycled T-shirt cut into small squares and wipe away the gel, removing more in areas you want lighter. It may take several passes, but you should begin to see less excess wiping off as you continue to buff. Using a fresh rag will remove more gel. Don't leave globs of gel behind—they can lead to streaking when sealing your piece. For our example, we took away as much as we could on the flat surfaces and left the tooled areas darker. Buff away any streaks that happened during the wiping process.

Wiping off antiquing gel. Clean off antiquing paste the same way as antiquing gel.

3. Allow your piece to dry overnight for 1–2 nights depending on the size of the piece and the humidity level. The more humid the air, the longer the drying time. If you can't tell if your piece is dry, take a cloth or a small rag square and lightly pass it over the antiqued areas. If you pull up more gel, your piece needs more drying time. Buff away any streaks that may have happened during the checking process.

4. When your piece is fully dry, apply sealant (see Sealing, page 72).

ANTIQUING PASTE

Antiquing paste functions and is applied similarly to antiquing gel. Antiquing paste works better for a couple other really cool techniques, though.

Antique Color Mixing

Costumes for fictional characters love to throw curveballs at real-life physics, but sometimes also real-life color schemes! If you need to create a specialty color for your antiquing, you can, and the process is easy with antiquing paste.

Start by using a neutral antiquing paste. Paste works well because it is a product with high body and is easy to control during mixing and application. In our example, we've used Fiebing's neutral antique finish.

To achieve a custom color, add leather paint to your paste. While the mix ratio isn't set in stone, the final consistency should be even in color, look like a smooth icing, and it should easily spread over your project.

Just like that, you have the ability to make any color you want. You can mix leather paints prior to mixing with the antiquing paste for even more possibilities!

Resist Painting

Resist painting is the act of applying a resist agent, such as Feibing's Pro Resist, prior to antiquing to create a permanent barrier that lessens the effects of antiquing stains, pastes, and gels. Apply two to three coats with a brush onto the areas where you want your antiquing agent to have less effect. Putting resist on areas with lighter painted colors or the highest points of tooled designs creates depth on a piece, leaving those areas looking highlighted after buffing away any excess antiquing agent.

Pro Resist can be used with any antiquing agent, but we've found that it works most effectively when paired with antiquing paste.

AGAINST THE FLOW

If you want to antique parts of your piece but you don't want your painted parts antiqued **at all,** *instead of traditional resist painting, change up the order of your steps!*

1. *Condition your leather.*
2. *Antique your leather.*
3. *Ensure all antiquing gel, paste, or stain has completely dried.*
4. *Paint your details with leather paints.*
5. *Seal your leather with a topcoat.*

This allows you to still have the antiquing details that can make tooling really pop,while at the same time having vibrant colors with no darkening due to the antiquing medium.

ANTIQUING STAIN

Antiquing gels and pastes have a thicker texture and sit on top of leather fibers, but antiquing stain is liquid and sinks into the leather just like a leather dye. Antiquing stain is applied in much the same way as leather dye.

Though resist agents don't stop antiquing stain from affecting the piece (see Resist Painting, page 127), you can still use them to control how strongly the stain colors different areas. In our example, we left the edges unsealed with no protection against the antiquing stain, and they dyed the darkest. For the center, we applied two coats of Eco-Flo sealant before staining and it stained slightly lighter. On the design, we used Eco-Flo's resist agent before staining and it was overall the least affected.

How to Apply Antiquing Stain

1. Apply sealant or resist to any desired areas and let dry.
2. Use a sponge or wool dauber to evenly spread the antiquing stain. Allow the stain to sit for a moment but do not let it dry.

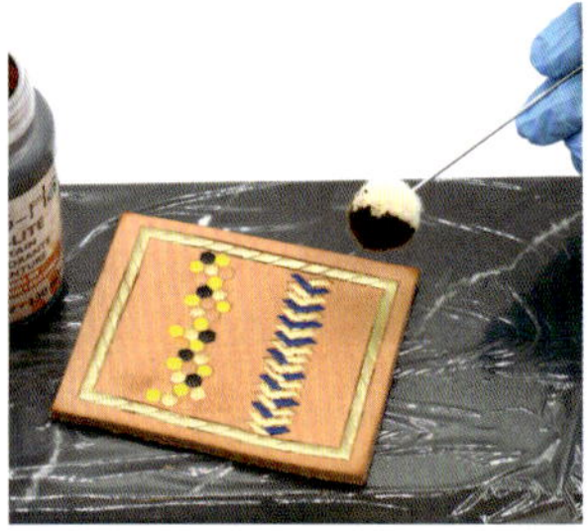

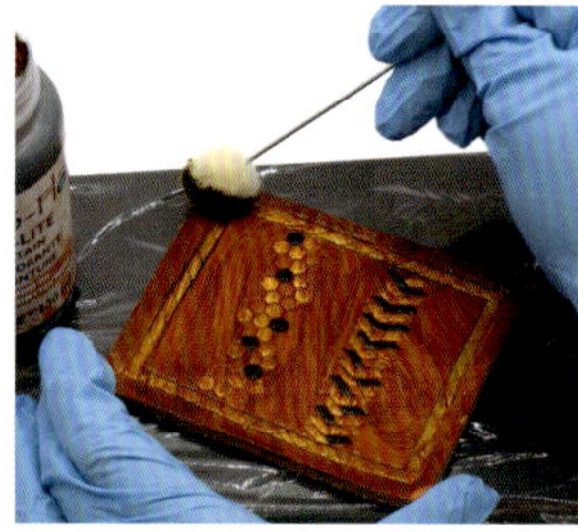

3. Take a clean rag and wipe away the stain, buffing away any streaks. This may take several passes to clean, but you should see less excess wiping off as you work. Using a fresh rag will remove more stain. If your rag is big enough, switch to a clean area when one spot becomes dirtied.
4. Allow the piece to dry fully; then apply a finishing seal (see Sealing, page 72).

KEEPING IT CLEAN

Antiquing agents are messy! Sometimes a mess is unavoidable and okay if you're lining your pieces or the inside is a well-kept secret. If the inside of a project will be seen, we usually cover it with painter's tape or, if the piece is flat, stick it down with painter's tape to our workspace so it doesn't slide around during the antiquing process. We also try to be careful during the cleanup and drying phases so we don't accidentally get any gel, stain, or paste on the flesh side of the leather.

ANTIQUING WITH OIL PAINT

Another way to antique leather is by using oil paints. If you choose to use oil paints, do not do so on pieces that need to flex after the application. The finishing sealant used in this technique is a decoupage sealant, made with a varnish or lacquer, which causes the leather to become rigid. It's great for durability, but it'll be inflexible after curing. If bent, the sealant and paint will crack.

This is one of our favorite techniques to age painted leather because the decoupage sealant acts as a barrier between the acrylic and oil-based paints, eliminating the guesswork of whether your dye/paint, antique, and finisher all work together. Some decoupage sealants are water-based products, and we haven't had adverse reactions with the oil paint as long as it's dry before application. It goes against all odds and allows for even more unique leather crafting!

We especially like this method for thin cut line designs and details on leather, like scales or hex patterns. Again, if the piece needs to flex, stick with leather-specific antiquing products.

For application, once all dyeing and painting is completely dry on your piece, apply two coats of your decoupage sealant, allowing it to fully dry between layers. This will create the initial barrier between your dye/paint and the oil.

Wear gloves when working with oil paints and use a chip brush or large flat brush to apply an even layer of paint over the surface to be antiqued. Push down into the cut lines or designs so the oil paint rests in the crevices. Just as with the leather-specific antiquing medium, this will look messy and you'll need to work quickly.

Remove the excess oil paint with a clean rag. As the rag dirties, move to a clean section of the rag or grab a new one so you can remove more oil paint. Your artistic vision comes into play with how much weathering you want. Think about where dirt and shadows would be on your costume: seams, bottom edges, and around rivets and grommets. You can always add more oil paint back onto a section and wipe away again if you take away too much initially. Clean up the excess oil until you have your desired look.

Oil paint takes time to dry. Sometimes it takes days. Patience is key. Don't put it under a fan or in a hotter place—this will dry out the base leather and can cause chemical reactions within the oil paint, causing seeping oil or incorrect curing. Places with more oil paint will take longer to dry than shallower areas of application, so test multiple spots with a clean rag or a gloved finger for dryness. There are a few products containing alkyd resins such as Zel-kin or Liquin that can be mixed directly with the oil paint before application to speed up curing times.

Once your oil paint is dry, apply two or three even coats of decoupage sealant.

MAKE YOUR CHOICE

For leather projects that don't need to be flexible we enjoy using oil paint as an antiquing method. However, it is **only** for non-flex pieces due to the use of decoupage sealant between the base and the oil paint. If you need your piece to be flexible try antiquing gel, but if you find yourself struggling with antiquing gel, then antiquing stain may be more your speed. We use antiquing paste primarily when we need to color mix or do some specific resist painting.

From left to right: Antiquing gel, antiquing paste, antiquing stain (and leather paint)

Garment LEATHER

Wearing leather is as old as leatherworking itself. What was once donned for survival or functionality has been given new life as artisan clothing and high-end accessories. Because they can be treated like fabrics due to their weight and malleability, garment leathers add another layer of potential to cosplay!

Garment leather can be crafted with many common sewing tools you may already own. Unlike veg tan, which leans into the skill sets shared with foam and thermoplastics, garment leather is more aligned with general sewing knowledge in many ways.

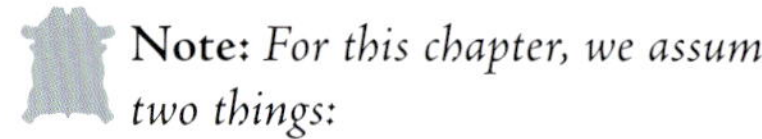

Note: *For this chapter, we assume two things:*

1. You have beginner to intermediate sewing skills. We won't cover general sewing basics or garment fitting.

2. You'll sew garment leather on your standard domestic sewing machine. We won't include sewing on industrial machines.

Vash the Stampede from *Trigun*
Cosplay and photos by Jacqueline Collins

Tools: Gadgets for Garments

Some tools for garment leather overlap with those used for veg tan. Others you'll only need if you're working with garment-weight leather.

ESSENTIALS

Domestic sewing machine: For machine sewing garment leather and lightweight veg tan leather. Must be able to handle heavyweight fabrics such as denim, pleather, and vinyl. *Note:* Due to motor strength, not every domestic machine can handle leather.

Leather/denim/microtex needles: These are specialty machine needles that can sew through garment leather.

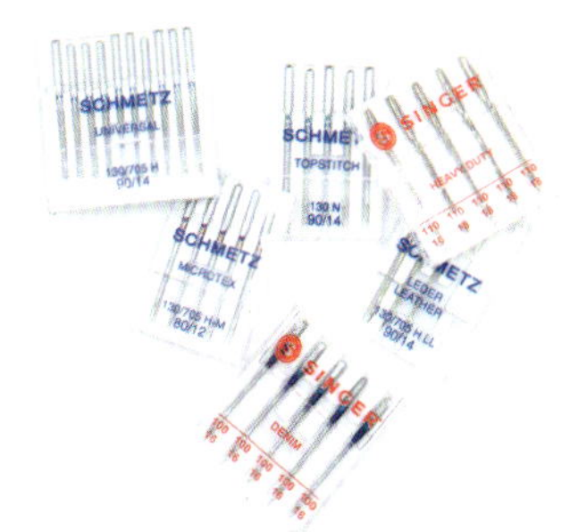

Sewing/quilting clips: Use these to hold pieces together while sewing instead of pins.

Heavy-duty/topstitch thread: Specific threads used for sewing leather by machine.

Ruler: For measuring seam allowance and creating straight lines.

Tailor's chalk or marking pen: For marking patterns and alteration notes on leather's flesh side. *Note:* Some pens are permanent, so use with care. Do not use heat-erasable markers—you should not use heat.

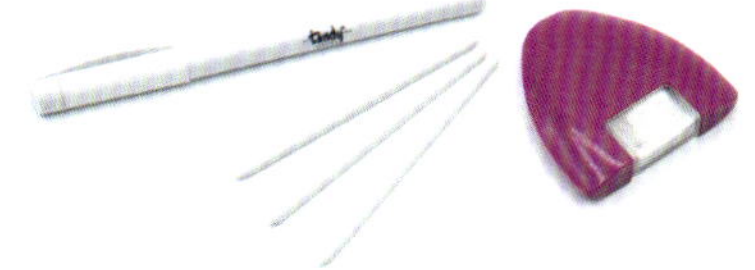

Hand-sewing needles/leather hand-sewing needles and thimble: Used when you can't use your machine or need to attach certain hardware.

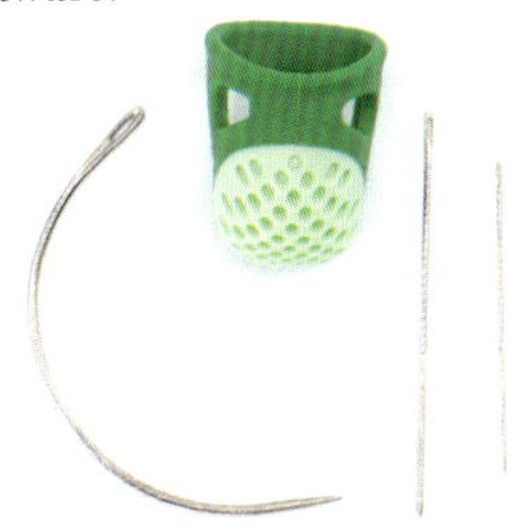

Specialty sewing machine feet: Designed to assist with sewing leather or "sticky" fabrics. There are many types that are specific to your machine's brand. Some common types are Teflon and roller feet.

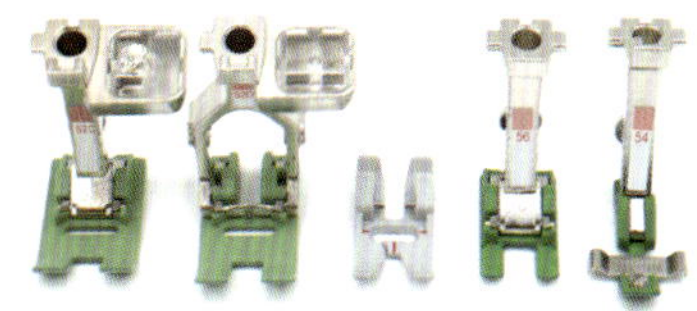

Shears: Used for cutting garment leather and should be regularly sharpened for best results, especially if cutting heavier-weight garment leathers.

OPTIONAL

Seam folder: Used to crisp folds and flatten seams. Can be made of bone, synthetic bone, plastic, wood, or metal.

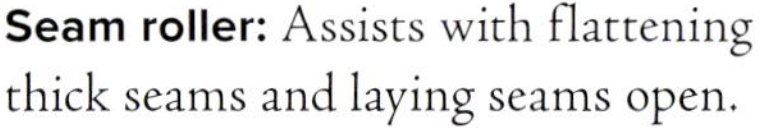

Seam roller: Assists with flattening thick seams and laying seams open.

Seam gauge: Small ruler used for measuring seam allowance.

Tailor's clap: Often made of wood, claps assist in adding weight to a pressed seam for additional crispness.

Standard- or button-weight threads: These threads can be used when hand sewing finishes or hardware onto leather and work best if paired with beeswax.

Water-soluble glue/leather sewing glue: For gluing seam allowances down. Water-soluble glue can be used alone or combined with topstitching.

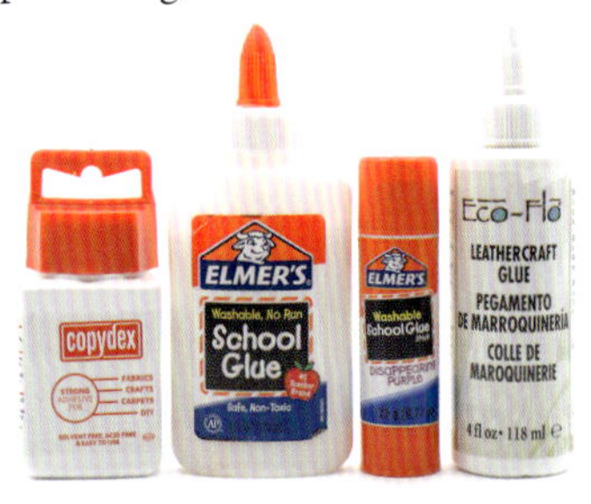

French curve: Used for measuring and creating smooth curves when pattern drafting.

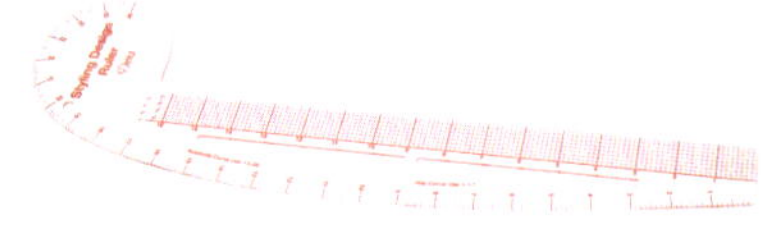

Basting spray: Used to hold appliqués or lining in place. Basting spray is temporary and should be sprayed with care. Not recommended for suede because it can stain the nap.

Repositionable tape: Semipermanent tape that can last multiple repositions and is used to hold pieces together for layered placement, such as appliqués, or to hold seams down for topstitching. Should not be used in lieu of a permanent attachment.

Repositionable tape and permanent tape

Rotary cutter: An alternative to using shears for cutting out garment leather pieces. Most efficient for long cuts, cutting fringe, or sloping curves.

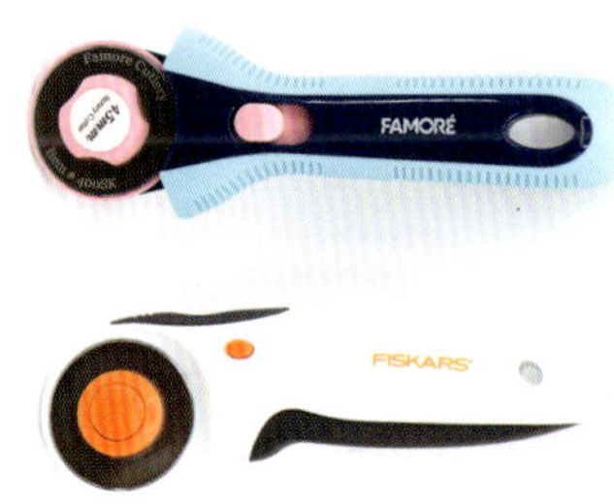

Pattern weights: Helpful to keep pattern pieces in place while tracing or cutting.

Seam jumper: Used to assist your sewing machine's foot over lapped seams to mitigate skipped stitches and broken needles.

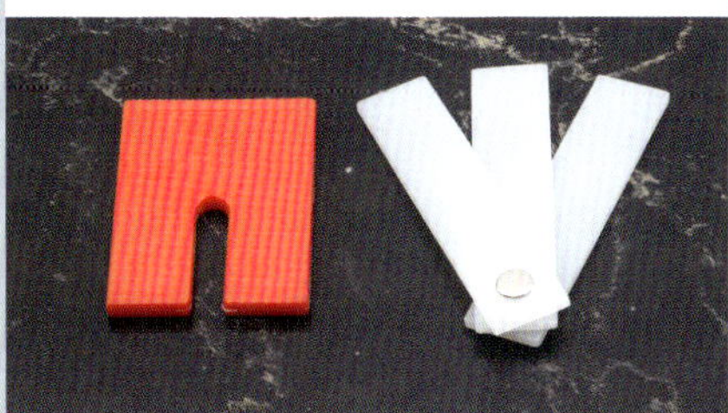

Interfacing: Paired with flimsier garment leather to provide more structure. Also can provide stability to pieces with too much stretch.

Transferring and Cutting

When patterning, a rule of thumb is to always pattern your mock-ups in a fabric or material that is similar to the final project. In the case of veg tan, we discussed using paper or foam. For garment leathers, we recommend finding a fabric with little stretch that is similar in weight and drape to your leather. We will not be covering pattern creation here but will provide some tips on how to transfer your pattern to garment leather.

TRANSFERRING PATTERNS FOR GARMENT LEATHER

When thinking about transferring your mock-up, first study the leather you're going to use. Is it ultra thin? How is the drape? Will it be able to make darts or tucks? With this information, selecting a fabric for doing your mock-up will be easier. We suggest twills or comparable fabrics and caution away from using muslin unless the garment is loose-fitting. The reason behind this is that muslin has more stretch than most garment leathers. Having a perfect mock-up and a too-small final piece out of an expensive material is the worst feeling.

Balthier from *Final Fantasy XII*
Cosplay by wigsmall of Wig-Wig Cosplay • Photo by Anthony H. Nguyen Photography

On the left is a mock-up made with twill. Right is the completed piece of layered garment leather.

Once you've chosen your mock-up fabric and successfully drafted your pattern pieces, place them on your garment leather, flesh side facing up. Here's your reminder to mirror your pattern pieces (see Seeing Double?, page 28)!

Be sure to check the grain side for any markings and avoid placing weight-bearing seams near the edges of the hide because that is where the hide will be noticeably thinner. To use as much of the hide as possible, try to arrange pattern pieces so the seam allowances are in less desirable areas.

To transfer your pattern pieces, you have a couple options:

- A white or black **fine-point marking pen** is permanent, but it makes sharp lines that are easy to follow when cutting. If you're looking for an erasable option, keep away from heat-soluble pens. Garment leather and your iron don't always play nice together. Some gel pens work well and come off with soap and water. Always test a scrap before tracing your pieces.
- **Tailor's chalk** or a **chalking pen** works well on the flesh side of leather, and usually better on darker colored hides. While not our favorite tracing tool, it will always completely come out of the leather without much more than a good dusting.

To keep your pattern in place:

- **Pattern weights** come in handy, but if you don't have any, then glass cups, coffee mugs, or paint bottles work great in a DIY pinch. Anything that can provide weight to a pattern piece and hold it steady on the leather without leaving a mark passes the test.
- **Repositionable tape** or **painter's tape** leaves behind little to no residue and is gentle on the flesh side of the leather. Look for a repositionable tape that is double-sided for best application. Many leather suppliers carry specific tapes for patterning, as well as permanent attachment. Be sure to read the label to confirm you're purchasing the correct one to avoid any future heartache!

When placing your pattern pieces, we suggest working down or across the hide—in other words, lengthwise or girthwise—and not placing pieces that require fit at different angles. This is much like how you'd place and cut pattern pieces out of fabric with the sense of traditional grain line in mind. If cutting pants or sleeves, try to cut them from similar parts of the hide to mitigate differences in thickness and stretch. If the piece is loose-fitting or decorative, you have a little more freedom in your placement and can cut with less waste created.

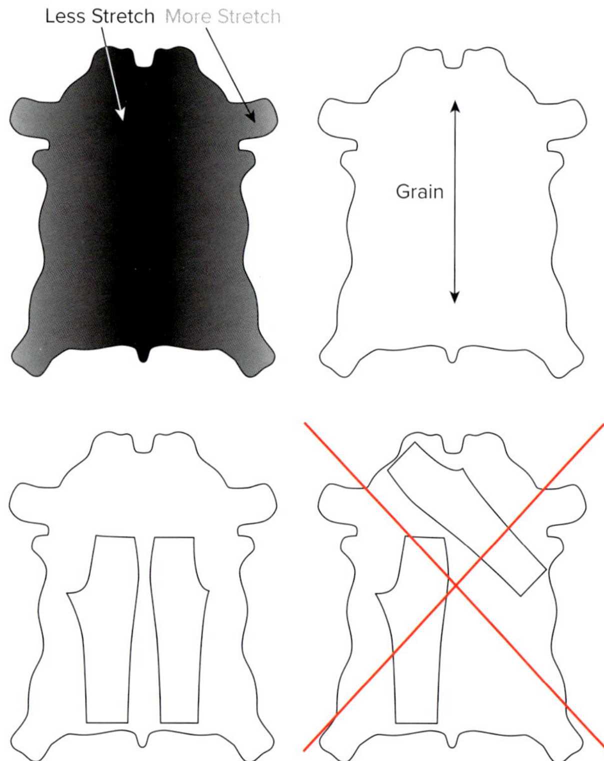

For embossed or printed leathers that need to be pattern-matched on your pieces, place your patterns on the grain side and carefully trace. For garment leathers that have a nap, such as deerskin suede, be sure to cut pieces in the same direction, just as you would with velvet or furs.

A stark difference between fabric and leather pattern placement is **to avoid cutting pattern pieces on the fold.** Stacked leather layers are prone to shifting under the pressure of a blade, leading to drifting cutting lines. To make sure you're getting accurate cuts, place each pattern piece flat on a single layer of leather.

CUTTING OUT GARMENT LEATHER

When your pattern pieces are placed or transferred onto your leather and ready to cut out, you may feel the urge to grab your fabric shears. With hides like lamb, standard fabric shears will have no issues. However, when you start cutting goat or pig, or even a ton of lamb, your shears may not cut as sharply after a short while. Leather dulls blades quickly! The best way to work around this is to have a shear sharpener or invest in a couple higher-grade shears to use only on leather. Shears that have a serrated blade also do well when cutting garment-grade leather. Avoid using a dull shear. Not only will it hurt your hand, but the dragging of the blade will be noticeable with each cut.

If you're a fan of rotary cutters, we have good news: Depending on the thickness of your leather, a rotary blade should pass through quite well. They can make quick work of cutting strips for fringe or handmade lacing, and make cutting larger pieces a breeze. Test your rotary blade on a scrap to see if it can pass through without resistance before attempting to cut into your hide.

Grain, Grain, Grain

You may be scratching your head wondering how the word *grain* can have so many different meanings in one craft. To assist, here are the ways we use grain in the context of leather:

Grain side: Referenced in opposition to the flesh side of leather. In veg tan, this is the tooling side. In garment leather, this is the right side of the leather, just like the right side of a fabric.

Textural grain: Referencing the texture or pattern of the leather itself. This can be denser or looser across the hide. Influenced by both the original location on the animal and the tanning process.

Directional grain: Referencing the horizontal (girthwise) and vertical (lengthwise) layout of the hide. Influenced by proximity to the spine, this is similar but not identical to grain line in fabric.

The main thing to remember with garment-grade leather is that the denser directional grain will follow the spine from the shoulders to the tail. The farther away you travel from that line, the more varied the leather thickness, stability, and textural grain will become.

So Sharp Shears!

When choosing to purchase a higher-grade shear, you really are investing in your wrist and hand health, as well as saving time. We highly recommend taking a look at companies that specialize in scissors. You'll find that many of them have customer testimonials, a foundation in customer satisfaction, and offer lifetime warranties. We're partial to the shears and rotary cutters made by Famoré!

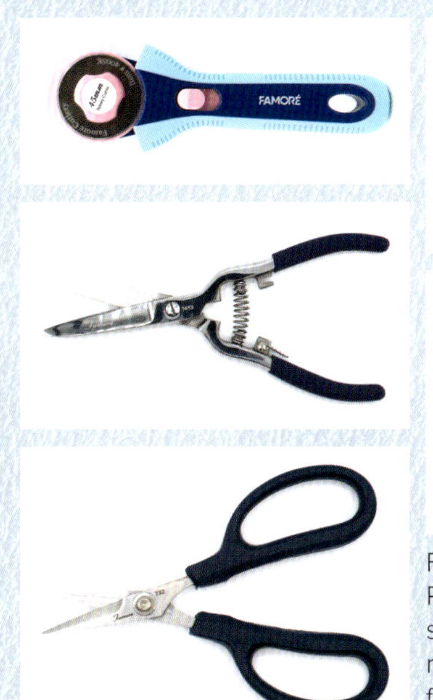

Famoré features from left to right: Rotary handle with blade, heavy-duty straight serrated snip, comfort handle razor-edge scissors, Jr. razor-edge fabric shear, heavy-duty razor-edge fabric shear

Sewing Garment Leather

Thankfully, with a few exceptions, sewing knowledge is transferable to garment leather. In this section, we'll share the tips and tricks we've learned over the years to make your journey into garment leather one of fair winds and smooth sewing.

SPECIALTY NEEDLES

We don't recommend sewing garment leather with a standard universal needle unless you're sewing paper-thin garment leather. Denser garment leathers require a little more push to get the needle through, and universal needles don't pack enough power to get through leather consistently without occasional skipping stitches or broken needles. Below are the needles we've found work best.

Leather needles for sewing machines are available at sewing centers and fabric stores in a variety of brands. Two things are noticeable when you compare a leather needle to a standard universal needle: the size of the eye and the tip. The eye of leather needles is large, allowing for thicker threads and more wiggle room for the thread when sewing, which reduces friction and possible tension snags (and the resultant broken needles). The tips of these needles are specially crafted to puncture leather using a small knife-like blade, allowing it to pass through even lightweight veg tan.

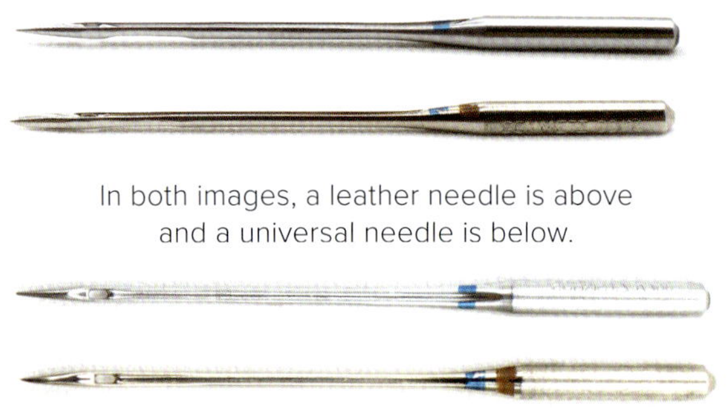

In both images, a leather needle is above and a universal needle is below.

If your stitches are skipping, change your needle, because leather needles, like shears, dull faster due to the friction of the leather. If your leather is folding under the pressure of the leather needle (it's too soft or thin), try switching over to the alternate needle types below or back to your universal needle.

Denim needles are another option for sewing garment-grade leather. Although they're missing the knife point, their durability when paired with a machine with a strong motor will get the job done. They leave slightly smaller holes than a leather needle, which can be a bonus if you're working with thinner garment leathers.

Microtex needles also can work in lieu of leather needles. Slim and sharp, these needles are designed for precision work through tough fabrics and can sew through garment leathers, but they do struggle with lightweight veg tan because they lack the knife-like blade of a leather needle. Being the closest to the universal in stitch hole size, microtex needles are a great option for extremely thin hides.

Organ needles, which are known for their sharpness, also allow for leather sewing. They share many similarities with microtex needles and have a larger eye hole, perfect for sewing through dense materials. If you're having a hard time threading your microtex needle with the thread type you chose, try switching over to an organ needle. Just be sure that you're using the sharp version and not a ballpoint.

KNOW YOUR NEEDLE SIZE

Sewing machine needles are labeled with two numbers. The first number is the European size, and the second is the American size. The smaller the number, the thinner the needle. Garment leather varies in thickness, but you'll consistently use a size 90(14) to 110(18) needle. All the needles mentioned above fall somewhere in that range or, in the case of universals, offer needles within that range. Some lightweight suedes can be sewn with needles as small as 70(10), but using a 90(14) is fine.

Needle Size

70/10	Lightweight suede
80/12	Midweight suede
90/14	Denim, twill, leather, suede
100/16	Canvas, leather, suede
110/18	Canvas, leather, heavyweight suede
120/19	Canvas, leather, heavyweight suede

When sewing leather, no matter the needle, backstitching is not required. In fact, if you backstitch, you're adding more holes into your leather and weakening your stitch line. There is added danger in backstitching when using a leather needle because you could accidentally stitch through a previous hole and nick the thread, either cutting or weakening it. Forgo backstitching and instead remove your piece from your machine, leaving tails long enough to tie. Thread the tail of your top thread through a standard hand-sewing needle and thread it back through the previous hole to the bottom. Unthread your needle; then tie approximately three knots with both threads. Trim off the tails and dab with a water-soluble leather glue for added security.

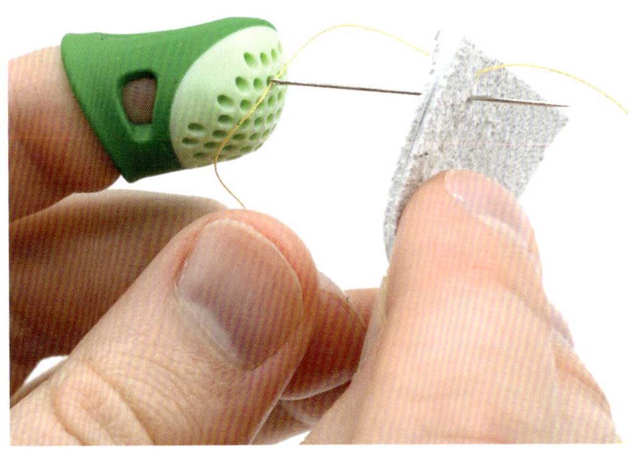

WHAT THREAD TO USE

Several kinds of thread work well for garment leather sewing. However, standard all-purpose polyester thread may not cut it on thick seams or leathers with nap. Due to the height of the nap, the thread can appear to sink into the leather and look too tight.

Heavy-duty and topstitching threads, which are noticeably thicker, provide the correct weight and durability for the longevity of the seam. These types of threads are great if you're sewing gloves or pants, items that undergo constant stretching and relaxing of seams.

Heavy-duty (top), topstitching (bottom)

Some sewing machines can be fussy about having heavier threads in the bobbin (we have a machine like this). If you need to use standard all-purpose thread in the bobbin and a heavy-duty thread for your top thread, that's fine, but know that you may need to dial in your machine's tension and stitch length with a little more care. Always test on a swatch before jumping straight into your project.

SPECIALTY SEWING MACHINE FEET

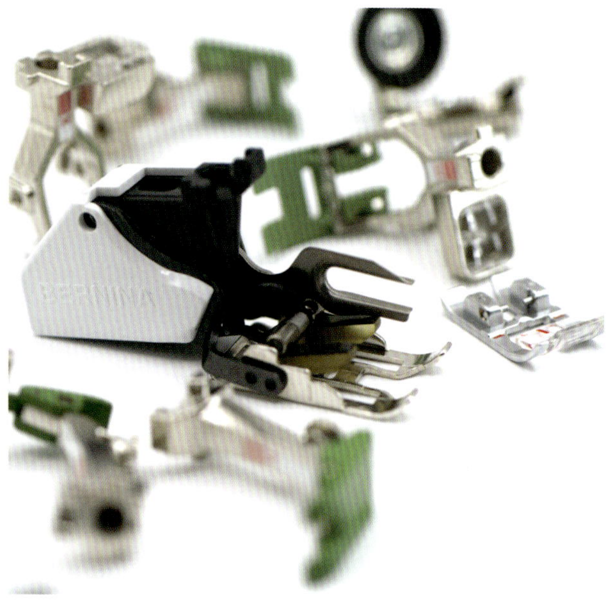

Because garment leather is "sticky," meaning it likes to cling to standard plastic and metal machine feet, specialty feet and accessories can make it less of a hassle.

For best results, use a foot with a coated, usually Teflon, sole. Most *nonstick feet* mirror their standard counterparts and work exactly the same. Some nonstick feet come with a wider opening around the needle, perfect for topstitching or sewing lapped seams on garment leather. The only downside of nonstick feet is that most are opaque. If you're used to sewing with a clear foot, not being able to see your material once it passes under the foot could take some getting used to.

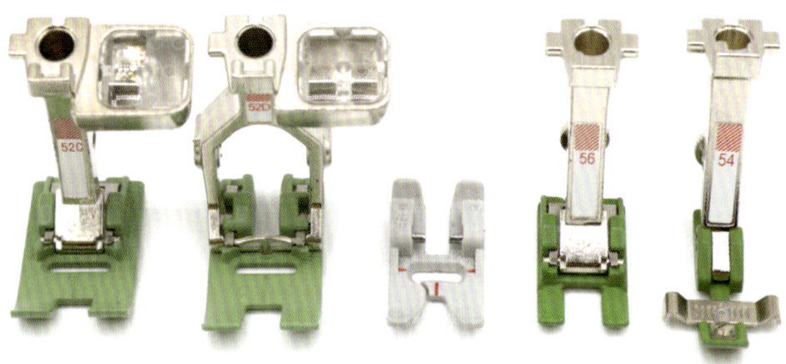

If you don't have access to nonstick machine feet, see if your machine is compatible with a roller wheel or walking foot. These types of feet assist the feed dogs and help regulate the movement of the top layer of leather while they pull through the bottom layer. *Roller feet* come in a few different types. One we like is the roller wheel, because this can be used in addition to the foot already on the machine and has great maneuverability. If paired with a clear foot, you'll still have good visibility. Some roller feet are an entire foot with a wheel like a rolling pin in the middle that helps move the leather while under the foot. Be careful to check how pronounced the gripping texture on the wheel is, though—it may leave imprints on your leather's grain side while stitching. A *walking foot* can also assist in moving leather through your machine. Some domestic sewing machines have a built-in walking foot, which comes in handy when paired with a nonstick foot or roller wheel. Doubling up on tools that assist feeding leather through your machine only makes the job easier!

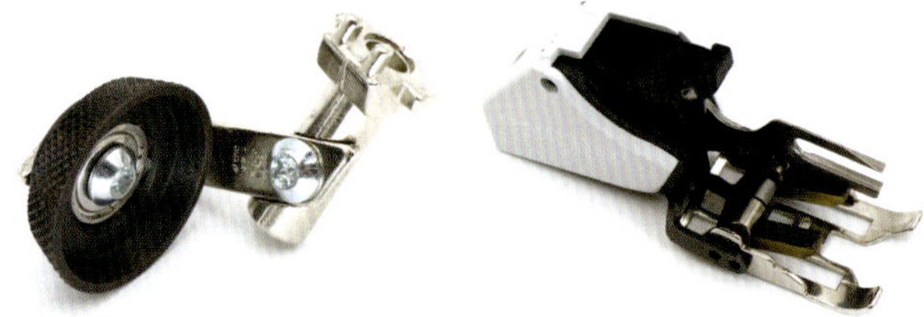

Usually all you need to change out is your sewing foot and needle, and you should be set to sew, but if you're still experiencing some drag, try a few of these alternatives or add them to your current setup.

One hack that many have found helpful is sandwiching your leather between tissue paper. By doing this, you can skip using a nonstick foot and you may be able to sew without any additional aids because your leather isn't coming in contact with the needle plate, another sticking point on some machines. However, when you need to remove the tissue paper, you may snag your stitch and pull its tension, causing irregular stitch lengths or stretching of stitch holes, leading to loose stitches. You also can't see your leather clearly while sewing, so if you're doing any topstitching lines, you may drift from your seamline.

Along with tissue paper, painter's tape strategically placed along your needle plate and on the leather where you're sewing sometimes works, but again, removing the tape from the leather after stitching has a high chance of pulling your stitches and ruining your hard work. Plus, covering your needle plate in tape also covers the measurement guides on most machines.

If you're interested in trying out any of these homebrew solutions to combat sticking garment leather, we suggest trying them on a scrap.

BEWARE PINPRICKS!

While pins are helpful when sewing most fabrics, they're the opposite when working with garment leather. This is due to the fact that each pinprick will leave a tiny hole and, over time, that hole can stretch and weaken the leather around it. To hold your leather pieces together while sewing, we recommend sewing clips. Note that some clips have ridges and will leave an imprint on your leather. If your clips have ridges, don't worry! You can carefully place them in seam allowances or put felt or a leather scrap between them and your pieces. On larger pieces, we've used binder clips wrapped in suede or canvas scraps.

GLUE IT TOGETHER!

In more fiddly places where clips or pins won't go, use glue. You'll want to use a glue that can be removed easily and completely, because it's only temporarily holding your pieces together. Look for water-soluble glues or basting sprays—your machine will thank you! Contact cement and other solvent-based glues are best used for seam finishes not requiring any additional sewing because they'll gum up your needle and lead to all sorts of machine issues. Note that the grain side of leather usually doesn't take glue as well as the flesh side, which works in your benefit for temporary adhesion.

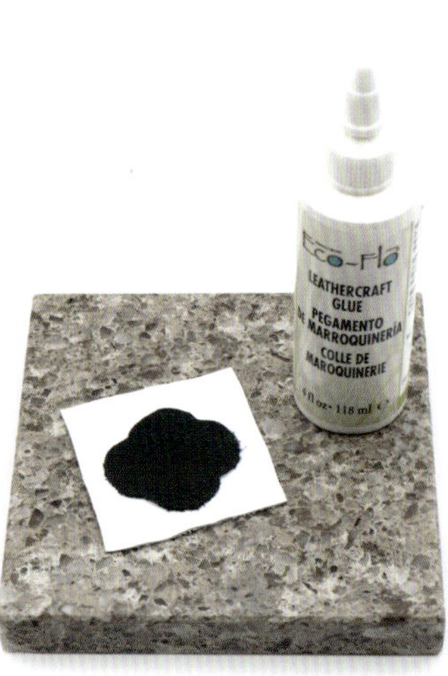

STITCH LENGTH

A longer stitch length is better with garment leather. In fact, 4mm is common across several machine brand recommendations. Every time you make a stitch in leather, you're poking a hole into the hide. The more holes, and the closer together, the weaker it becomes along the stitch line, similar to perforation.

With lengthened stitches, you're also allowing your leather more space to move between each stitch, which helps on curves, like *armscyes* (armholes) and collars. Leather has natural ease and may not require as much clipping as fabric, but tight turns will require some notching and, if necessary, additional reinforcement such as interfacing to reduce stretching or tearing.

Top: 4mm stitch length
Bottom: 2.5mm stitch length

LEATHER SEAMS: FLATTENING AND FINISHING

Now that you've sewn a few pieces together, you might be curious about what to do with the seam allowance. Unlike fabric, leather should not be pressed with an iron. With garment leather, there are a couple of options for keeping seam allowances tacked down.

Jaheira from *Baldur's Gate 3*
Cosplay by Owl & Coffee • Photo by Wild Momo Photography

If you need your seams to lay flat but you don't need them to be tacked down, we recommend a seam roller or folder. Open the seam with your fingers and slide the roller or folder along the seam. Repeat a couple of times.

If you don't have these tools, your mallet will work just as well. Open the seam allowance with your fingers, press open with the heel of your hand, and then tap your seam allowance with the mallet for a few passes. Be sure to do this on a hard surface with minimal to no texture, because it can transfer onto the grain side. We recommend doing this on a cutting mat or the marble slab you may have from tooling veg tan.

Although the seam won't stay perfectly flat, you'll see the allowance relaxing to the sides. You can further assist this by placing pattern weights or a tailor's clap on the seam for a few minutes. The additional weight will help train the seam to lay open.

To keep seam allowances down, gluing is the most common method. Water-soluble glues are used in areas that may be lined or may be paired with topstitching. Most water-based glues are safer for your sewing machine and won't gum up your needle as much as a solvent-based glues. Solvent-based glues are a more permanent answer to seam allowances. If you're using a glue like contact cement, remember to wear personal protective equipment and work in a well-ventilated area.

After flattening your seam allowance with a mallet, roller, or folder, carefully apply your glue in a thin coat on both the flesh side of the piece and the flesh side of the seam allowance, covering evenly. Solvent-based glues need resting time to become tacky, but water-based glues can be pressed down right away. Apply pressure while the glue sets.

Note: *If you're gluing lining onto a curved piece, place your lining and smooth from the center to the edges, keeping the base item curved. To keep your project curved while the glue dries, tie it around a similarly shaped item using cotton strips or yarn. This helps reduce excess lining that will pucker or bunch on a curved surface. In sewing, this is similar to rolling the lining when making bodices.*

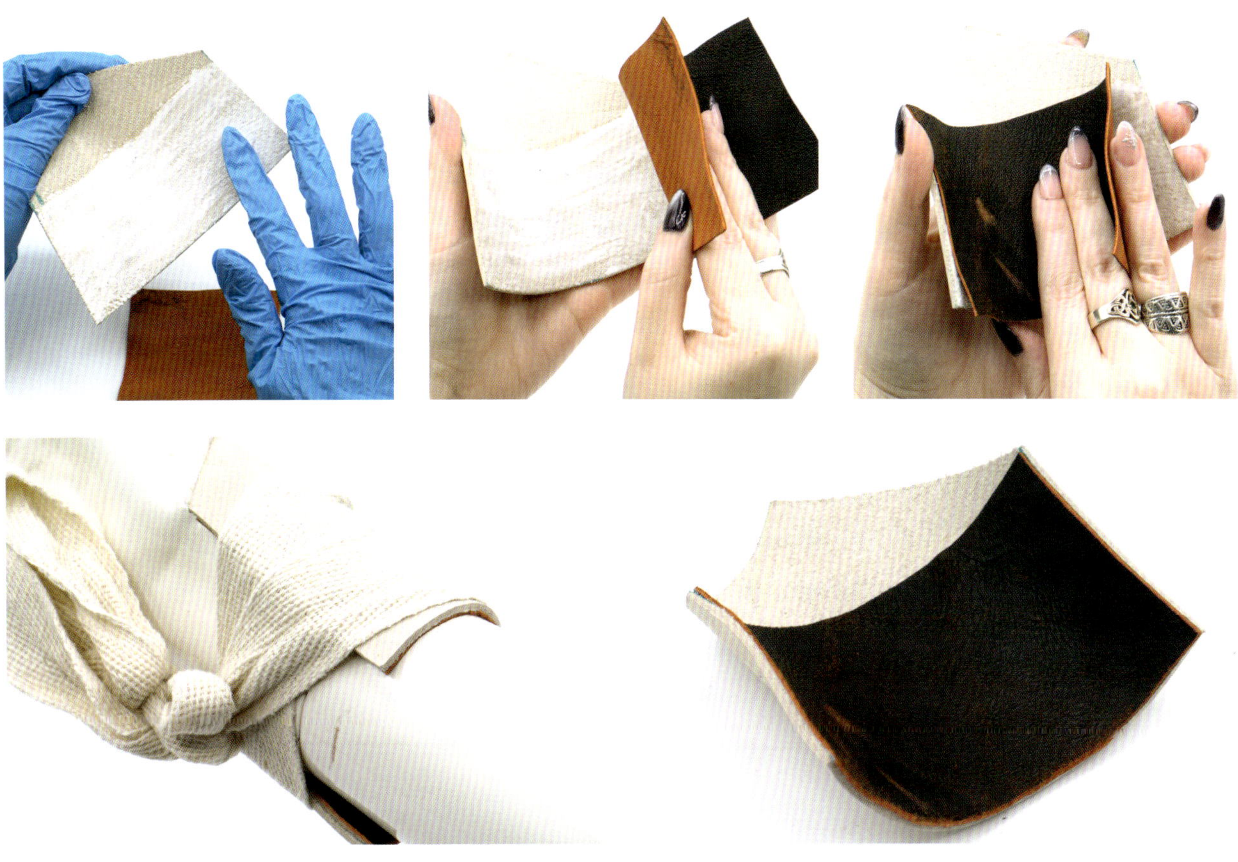

If you need to permanently glue the grain side of leather to either the grain side or the flesh side of another piece (which is common when stacking leathers or adding appliqués), most glues will have a tough time making a strong connection due to the coating on the grain side. To get a good stick, rough up the grain side you're applying glue to with sandpaper or carefully swab the area with deglazer. Deglazer will take off any topcoating and allow the pores to accept the glue, but it may also ruin the dye job of the area. Apply with care and always wear personal protective equipment when using deglazer.

Topstitching

Much like fabric, garment leather looks great with a topstitch! After sewing and doing an initial pass to flatten your seam, stitch about ⅛" (3mm) from each side of your seam. We recommend stitching starting from the same point instead of sewing down one side then back up the other. Doing the latter can cause unnecessary tension or warping of the seam.

After stitching your seam allowance down, you can trim it closer to the stitches to reduce bulk. This helps if you're going to have another seam intersect with this one or you're lining the piece. Trimming your seams at different lengths after securing them down is a process known as *seam grading*, and it helps create a slope, rather than a cliff, so bulkier seams can lay flatter.

The left side of the seam is not seam graded. The right side is seam graded.

IRONING AND STEAMING GARMENT LEATHER

When it comes to heat, there are two rules of thumb that really set garment leather apart from veg tan:

- Never apply heat directly to the grain side of garment leather.
- Never steam garment leather.

Introducing heat and moisture can cause shrinkage, wrinkling, and reactivation of paints you may have added, or even of glues and chemicals from the tanning process. If you must use heat, apply it only to the flesh side of the leather with a pressing cloth, with no steam or water in your iron. If you have suede with a nap, before pressing with an iron, place it grain side to grain side with another piece of suede or a soft cloth so the texture isn't flattened under the weight of the iron.

These rules can cause a bit of head-scratching when it comes to adding interfacing to garment leather. Adding sew-in interfacing can be done by holding it in place with water-soluble glues or clips. We usually don't stitch in our interfacing and opt for glue to avoid adding holes. Some leatherworkers will use fusible interfacing and hit their leather with a hot iron for a pass or two, but we hesitate to do that because many leathers react differently to extreme heating, even if it's only for a moment. If you want to try this out, we recommend testing a lightweight fusible interfacing on a swatch before moving to your final piece.

Use a Seam Jumper!

As you sew, you'll no doubt encounter a thick seam of multiple leather layers that your presser foot may not be able to glide over, causing jamming or skipped stitches. Even with seam grading, bulky seams are sometimes unavoidable. A neat tool to help with leveling out the seam and your presser foot is a seam jumper. Commonly used in sewing jeans or denim goods, this tool also works great with leather sewing!

1. Sew up to the bulky seam and, with your needle down, lift your presser foot. Insert the seam jumper under your presser foot from the back with the notch facing the seam, and lower your foot. The back of your presser foot should now be sitting on the jumper and be even with the bulky seam.

2. Slowly stitch forward, manually turning the hand wheel to walk the needle over the seam if needed.

3. Once you're through the seam with your needle, stop with the needle down, raise your presser foot again, and remove the jumper. Insert the jumper from the front with the notch facing the seam. The front of your presser foot should be on the jumper and the back of your presser foot should be on the bulky seam.

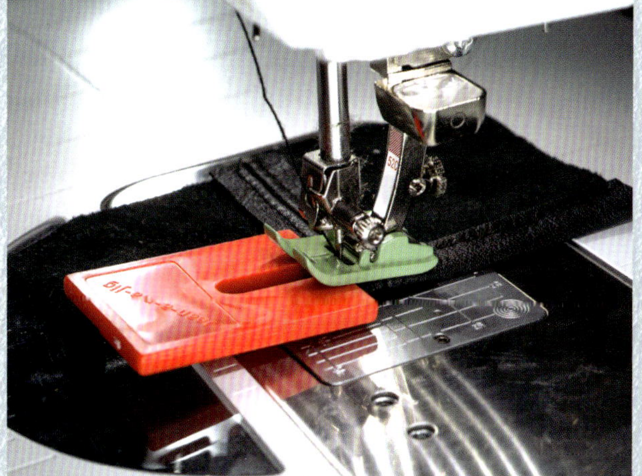

4. Walk your needle forward a few stitches, being careful not to sew into the jumper, until the back of the presser foot is off the seam and onto the jumper.

5. Stop, needle down, and raise the foot.

6. Remove the jumper, and lower the foot. Continue sewing as normal.

If you don't have a plastic jumper tool, you can fold several layers of denim or canvas and use that as a stand-in.

HAND-SEWING TIPS

Sometimes, stitching on the outside is just as important as sewing on the inside to complete the overall look. Characters may have an edgestitch that is a specific pattern or need beads added to the lapel of a coat. Hand stitching on garment leather shares the majority of its techniques with fabric hand sewing, from stitches to stabilizer, with only a few notable differences.

Glover's, Curved, and Standard Needles

You don't need to use a special needle on garment leather if you're adding embellishments. A standard sharp hand-sewing needle will do the trick, but the finer, the better because each prick will become a hole that will weaken the leather. If you're doing heavy beading or embroidery, pair your leather with stabilizer or create your embellishment as an appliqué that can be stitched on.

Glover's needles are used for all sorts of garment leather hand sewing, not just on gloves. Named for the glove makers who originally used them, this needle is specially designed to pierce through leather, much like a machine leather needle. While not always necessary for lighter weights of garment leather, they're useful when hand sewing thicker hides.

Curved needles lend nicely to tricky areas that require more bend than a straight needle can give without breaking. As in hand sewing veg tan, curved needles are good to have in your collection in a variety of sizes.

Sewing Seams Inside versus Outside

There are times where a seam may be too small or awkwardly placed to put through a machine, like a glove *fourchette* (the strip of fabric that gives depth to the finger piece on gusseted gloves). The thinner the leather, the more chance the weight of a motorized needle will push it beneath a needle plate and cause the leather and the needle to get stuck. A solution is to sew by hand! Not just for adding embellishments, hand stitching leather with a standard needle or a glover's needle can make quick work of tiny or bulky seams that your machine can't. Many fabric hand stitching techniques also apply to stitching garment leather, such as a blanket stitch, running stitch, and more.

One way that leather hand stitching differs from fabric is that you can put your seam allowance on the outside or overlap your seams and stitch them because leather doesn't fray. Your stitches will be visible with these techniques, so take your time! Two stitches known traditionally in garment leather sewing are the pique and prix. A *pique stitch* is one in which seam allowances are placed on top of each other and stitched with a stab stitch or a running stitch; this reduces bulk and omits the need for gluing or trimming seam allowances. A *prix stitch* is a tiny whipstitch over the edges of the leather for seams ⅛" (3mm) or smaller, mostly used on gloves so you have no seams on the inside taking up space.

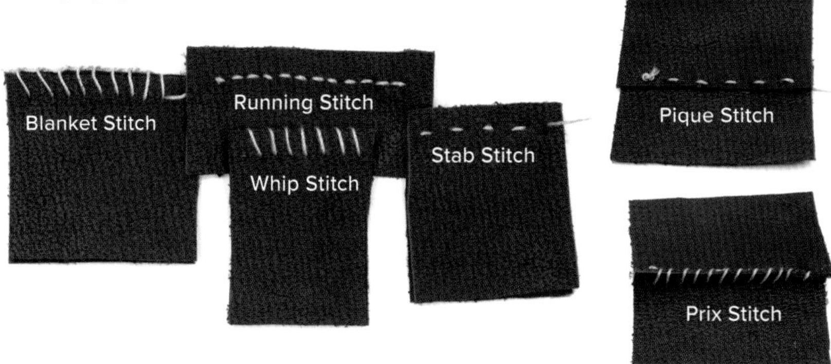

Beeswax on Thread

Adding beeswax is only needed when hand sewing. Do not wax thread used in your sewing machine.

As when sewing thicker leather, thread used on garment leather should be waxed because it can undergo a fair amount of friction. This helps the thread glide more easily through leather. Waxing all-purpose polyester or heavy-duty thread is simple: Just take a chunk of beeswax, place the end of your thread length on the wax, anchor with your finger, and pull forward, holding the thread against the wax. To make quick work of waxing, cut a divot into your beeswax to act as a channel. You may need to reapply beeswax every so often, so keep it nearby.

Adding Embroidery, Beading, and Embellishments

Adding fanciful decorations is really the highlight of any project. It means you're almost done with your piece and you get to wear it soon!

Stabilizers are key to safe and secure embellishments and reduce the strain on your leather. Think of it like hanging a picture on the wall: The stabilizer is like hitting a stud. It anchors while also providing additional strength to share the weight and tension of the embellishments.

Leave-in stabilizer is most commonly used for lined leather. Leave-in stabilizer is tightly woven and works as a strength layer when added to leather, holding stitches securely and not allowing the stitch holes to stretch. This is great for embroidery, beading, or bracing heavier appliqués.

Wash-away stabilizer is water soluble and good for pieces that are not lined. Instead of submerging in water to remove the stabilizer, cut away excess stabilizer so it's only around your stitches, and then carefully dab away with a warm damp cloth until the stabilizer releases from the stitches and can easily be removed by hand or with a tweezer. Don't force any stabilizer to release from a stitch, as you could accidentally pull your thread tension or stretch a stitch hole, making beading loose or embroidery floss gape.

Tearaway stabilizer is another type of commonly used stabilizer, but it isn't ideal because the force of removing the stabilizer can easily tug your stitches and cause the issues mentioned previously. If you choose to use tearaway be sure to have tweezers handy to carefully remove any small bits of stabilizer left in your stitches.

From left to right: tear-away, leave-in, and wash-away stabilizers

When hooping garment leather for machine or hand embroidery, it's important not to overtighten your hoop. This can cause markings known as *hoop burn* to mar the leather due to the friction. If using a hand embroidery hoop, we recommend not tightening the leather to be drum tight—just tighten enough so that the material doesn't sag. If you're doing machine embroidery, float your material rather than hooping it. Because the material is placed on top of the hoop, held down by basting spray, stitches, or magnets, it won't undergo the friction that causes hoop burn.

Adding Hardware to Garment Leather

Hardware on garment leather is generally the same as hardware on veg tan. The major difference is that garment leather is thinner and has some stretch. Because of this, you need to be more cautious with how and where you attach your hardware. For example, lacing without eyelets or grommets will stretch the leather over time (even with eyelets and grommets, you may see some stretching), as will buckles, snaps, and other attachments in places with tension or weight bearing. You should also lean toward circular punches in garment leather instead of slices and cut lines to reduce the likelihood of tears. When using very thin garment leathers, be careful with how tightly you set your hardware, as you could puncture or slice through it if you set too tightly. If possible, back your garment leather with another layer of leather, fabric, or interfacing to help stabilize.

That said, as long as there isn't a lot of tension, you can feel free to put hardware on garment leather using the techniques from Hardware (page 97).

Painting and Sealing Garment Leather

Similar to hardware application, using paints and sealants on garment leather is like painting on veg tan. For inspiration and how-tos, check out Painting Leather (page 64) and Sealing (page 72).

When painting on garment leather, acrylic leather paints are favored for their opacity, vibrancy, and flexibility. We recommend painting in thin layers to avoid buildup along the edges of your painted area. Mix and create custom colors to achieve those perfect matches to your character's outfit. If covering large areas, evenly apply the paint, taking care to minimize brushstrokes or use an airbrush.

To seal acrylic leather paints, we've found that Angelus Acrylic Finisher provides great coverage and longevity, and it doesn't interfere with the drape or movement of garment leather. It comes in finishes like matte, satin, and high gloss, which allows for some fun mixing of final looks. Sealants like Eco-Flo Shene also work on garment leather, as does Fiebing's Resolene.

Practice PROJECTS

Now that we've talked through a book's worth of techniques, here are a few foundational veg tan projects to get started on. Grab your hide (you knew this pun was coming) and start building invaluable experience!

Tifa Lockhart from *Final Fantasy VII*
Cosplay and photos by Gillian Conahan

BELT

Belts are the most common piece in character designs that can be translated to leather, and making one on your own is a great first project.

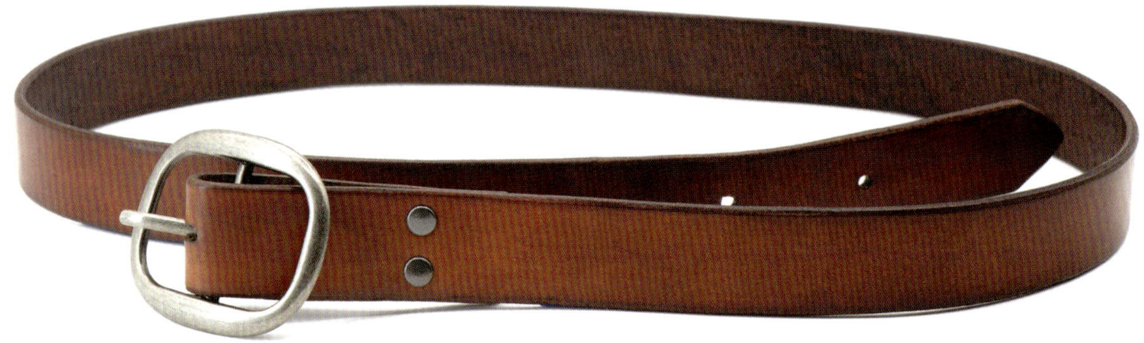

Supplies

A belt blank, or 1″ (2.5cm) × your waist plus 11″ (28cm) of heavyweight veg tan, at least 7 oz.

- Measuring tape or yardstick
- Marking tool
- Bladed cutting tool
- Cutting mat
- Hole punch
- Edging tool
- Burnishing agent
- Burnishing tool
- Disposable gloves
- 2 sponges
- Leather dye
- Leather sealer
- Buckle: 1″ (25mm)
- Mallet
- 2 rivets
- Rivet setter

Instructions

1. Using a belt you own, measure its length and add 3″ (7.6cm). If you don't have a belt, measure your waist or where you would like the belt to sit, and add 11″ (28cm).

2. On your leather, draw a rectangle on the flesh side with a length equal to the length you found in Step 1 and a width of 1″ (2.5cm). Cut out your shape.

3. Trim one end of the belt into a rounded point.

4. Starting 2.5″ (6.4cm) from the tip of your point, mark five spots along the center of your belt's width, each 1.5″ (3.8cm) apart. Use your hole punch to punch holes at each of your marks. Use the hole punch size that is just big enough to fit the tongue of your buckle.

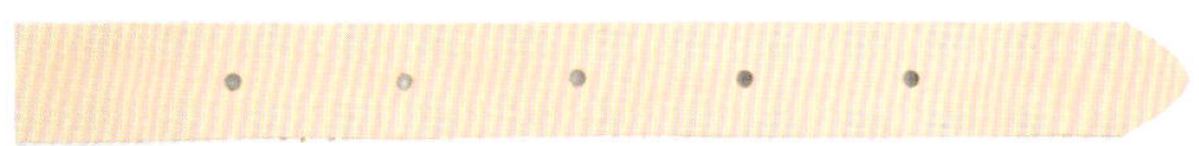

5. On the other end of the belt, mark two spots ¾″ (18mm) from the end and ¼″ (6mm) from each edge. Use your hole punch to punch holes at each of your marks. Use the hole punch size that is just barely big enough for the posts of your rivets.

6. Starting 3″ (7.6cm) from the same end, mark an oblong hole for the buckle's tongue along the center of your belt's width. Use your hole punch to punch out your oblong hole. Using a cutting tool or sandpaper, clean uyp the edges. If you have an oblong punch, just use that instead.

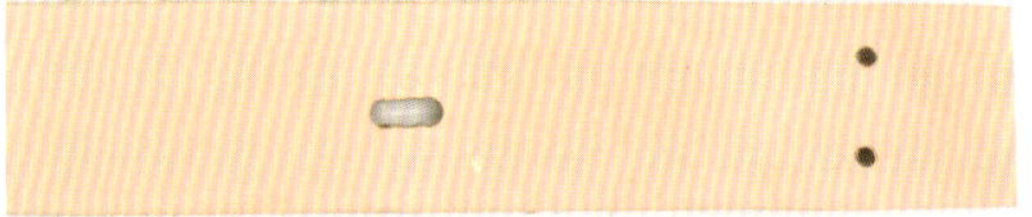

7. Use your edging tool to bevel the edges of both the grain side and the flesh side of the belt (see Edge Beveling, page 36).

8. Use your burnishing tool and burnishing agent to slick the edges and flesh side of the belt (see Burnishing, page 69).

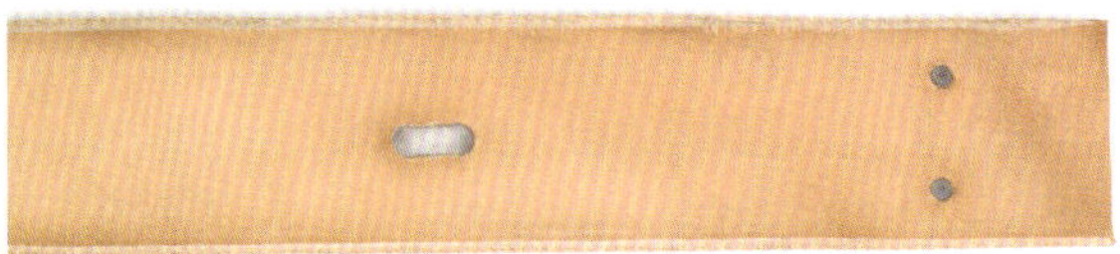

9. Follow the process in Dyeing and Painting (page 54) to add some color! Allow to dry and repeat as needed for desired color saturation.

10. Once the leather has dried and you're satisfied with the color, put your gloves on and use a second sponge with leather sealant and seal the leather (see Sealing, page 72).

11. After the leather is dry, loop your buckle onto the belt so that the tongue is sticking through the oval hole from the flesh side to the grain side (see Buckles, page 106).

12. Bend your square end down around your buckle so that it lays flesh side to flesh side; then mark 2 spots through the holes you made in Step 5. Punch holes where you marked; then set your rivets through the holes (see Rivets, page 98).

Customization Ideas

Now you can modify and add to these basic steps to replicate belts from all sorts of costumes!

To make this belt, we added tooling between Steps 3 and 4 (see Tooling, page 43). To mirror our design, we first made a paper pattern (see Tooling Designs, page 44). Between steps 6 and 7 we skived the leather around the buckle area for better folding. Between Steps 9 and 10, we added antiquing gel for more color contrast (see Antiquing, page 125), and we used an alternative buckle type on Step 11 instead of a standard one.

This example required a lot of patterning work, (see Patterning, page 20) to get the main belt silhouette, and then more sketching to get the shapes and angles right. That effort took the place of Steps 1 and 2. Between Steps 10 and 11, we added gluing and rivet assembly of all the component parts of the belt (see Gluing, page 93, and Hardware, page 97).

Gale Dekarios' belt from *Baldur's Gate 3*

As an added option, you can add a belt loop (or keeper) so your belt end doesn't stick out!

POUCH

A pouch doesn't look out of place on most fantasy designs, but a cell phone does! It's nice to have a place to carry a phone or wallet while at conventions, so give this project a try, and you can proudly proclaim your cosplay has pockets ... er, pouches!

Supplies

- 12" × 18" (30.5 × 45.7cm) medium-weight veg tan, approximately 4–5 oz.
- Pouch template
- Printer
- Paper
- Scissors
- Tape
- Marking tool
- Bladed cutting tool
- Cutting mat
- *Optional:* Stitch groover
- Stitching chisels or stitching hole punch
- Mallet
- Edging tool
- Burnishing agent
- Burnishing tool
- Disposable gloves
- 2 sponges
- Leather dye
- Leather sealer
- Leather sewing needle
- Waxed thread
- Hole punch
- Line 20 snap
- Line 20 snap setter

Accessing Patterns

To access the pattern through the QR code, open the camera app on your phone, aim the camera at the QR code, and click the link that pops up on the screen. Print the templates directly from the browser window or download the pattern. To print at home, print the letter-size pages, selecting 100 percent size on the printer. Use dashed/dotted lines to trim, layer, and tape together pages as needed. To print at a copy shop, save the full-size pages to a thumb drive or email them to your local copy shop for printing.

For complete instructions, go to: tinyurl.com/11641-patterns-download

Instructions

1. Print the pouch template and follow the instructions to assemble the template.

2. Trace the pattern pieces on the flesh side of your leather. Cut out the pieces.

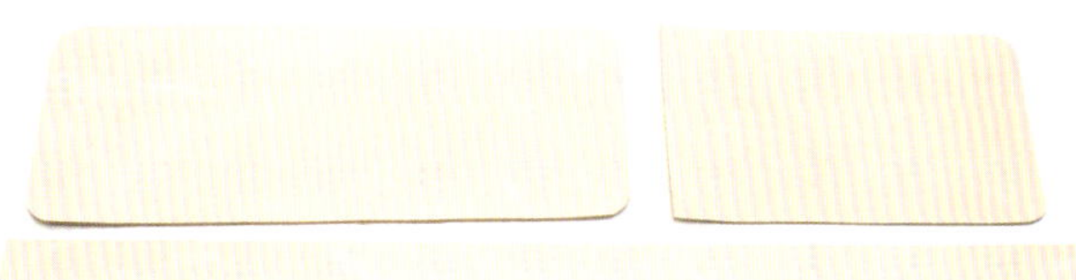

3. Either tape the pattern pieces to the flesh side of your leather or use a stitch groover to lightly mark a guideline at the correct distance in from the leather's edge. Using stitching chisels or a stitching hole punch, punch holes at an equal distance along all marked edges of the pattern pieces (see Stitch Grooving, page 78).

4. Use your edging tool to bevel only the grain-side edges of the pouch front and pouch back (see Edge Beveling, page 36).

5. Use your burnishing tool and burnishing agent to slick the edges of the pouch front and pouch back, as well as the short edges of the pouch side (see Burnishing, page 69).

6. Follow the process in Dyeing and Painting (page 54), to add some color! Allow to dry and repeat as needed for desired color saturation.

7. Once the leather has dried and you're satisfied with the color, put your gloves on and use a second sponge with leather sealant and seal the leather (see Sealing, page 72).

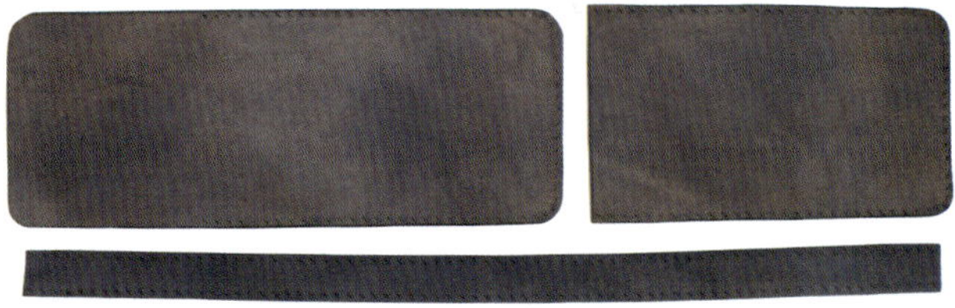

8. After the leather is dry, stitch your pieces together using a cross-stitch (page 89).

9. Punch a hole in the center of the width and 1″ (2.5cm) from the top edge of the pouch back piece. Fold the pouch back piece over the front and decide how far you'd like them to overlap. Mark and punch a matching hole in the pouch front piece.

10. Set your snap using those holes (see Snaps, page 102).

Customization Ideas

This pouch pattern gives you a starting point when patterning pouches for your own cosplay. Here are two pouches we made by adjusting the pattern's shape and size.

For this pouch, we added width to the front and back pieces, which added length to the side piece. We also put two tentacles on the side piece to hold the snaps against the top instead of the top snapping down to the front, modifying Steps 10 and 11. Between Steps 3 and 4, we added our thematic tooling (page 43) and wet formed (page 111) the back piece to fold over the top. We inserted two steps between Steps 7 and 8—one to add the wave texture mentioned in From the Art Supply Store and Your Kitchen (page 123), and one for painting onto the tooling (see Painting Leather, page 64). For Step 9, we instead marked and punched two holes at the top of the tentacles, and then matching holes on the back piece while folded over. We then set two snaps in Step 10.

In this example, we rounded the shape and adjusted the side to match. Between Steps 5 and 6, we added just a little bit of tooling (see Tooling, page 43) and a lot of weathering using the technique in Hop to It (page 122). In Step 7, we used two dye colors on different areas of the pouch. Between Step 8 and 9, we put a running stitch (page 84) on the top flap of the pouch and glued in a rectangle of fringe made from green lambskin.

Jagras Armor Set's pouch from *Monster Hunter: World*

As a further option, you can cut and sew the optional belt loop pieces from the pattern to the back of your pouch so you can easily wear it on your belt!

BRACER

Bracers are used often in character designs, even on characters who aren't wearing additional leather armor. They're also our recommended way to get started in armor making so you can look and feel epic!

Supplies

- 18" × 18" (45.7 × 45.7cm) medium-weight or heavyweight veg tan, less if you have a smaller forearm
- Paper bracer pattern made using instructions from Flat Drafting (page 26)
- Marking tool
- Bladed cutting tool
- Cutting mat
- Hole punch
- Edging tool
- Burnishing agent
- Burnishing tool
- Disposable gloves
- 2 sponges
- Leather dye
- Leather sealer
- Mallet
- 8 grommets
- Grommet setter
- Leather lacing

Instructions

1. With your paper pattern created, trace it onto the flesh side of your leather. Cut out your bracer.

Note: *If you're making a bracer for each arm, be sure to flip your pattern so you mirror any designs, making a right-hand bracer and a left-hand bracer.*

2. From each corner, measure ⅜″ (1cm) down and ⅜″ (1cm) in from the edge and mark the flesh side of the leather. Now put 2 more marks at equal distances down the sides of your bracer. These marks should also be ⅜″ (1cm) from the edge. Punch large holes for your grommets centered on each of these marks. You may need to make multiple punches to make them big enough. If needed, clean up uneven holes with a craft knife or sandpaper.

3. Use your edging tool to bevel the edges of both the grain side and the flesh side of the bracer (see Edge Beveling, page 36).

4. Use your burnishing tool and burnishing agent to slick the edges of the bracer (see Burnishing, page 69).

5. Follow the process in Dyeing and Painting (page 54) to add some color! Allow to dry and repeat as needed for desired color saturation.

6. Once the leather has dried and you're satisfied with the color, put your gloves on and use a second sponge with leather sealant to seal the leather (see Sealing, page 72).

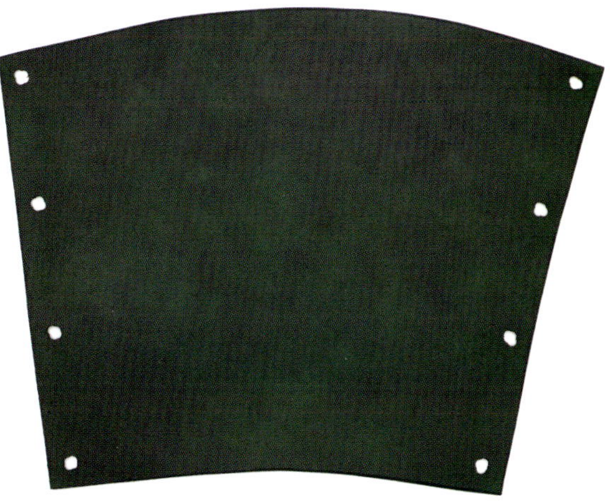

7. Set your 8 grommets in the holes (see Eyelets and Grommets, page 100).

8. Thread lace through the grommets to tighten your bracer.

Customization Ideas

Bracer patterns are good practice for pattern modification because they're all one piece and laced together, creating some freedom in sizing. Let your creative brain roll!

For this example, we switched up the bracer shape, making it less boxy. We also added some subtle tooling (page 43) between Steps 3 and 4. As part of Step 5, we added extra layers of a darker brown with a paintbrush to certain parts of the tooling and the edges to bring out the design (see Edgy Color Choice, page 59). We also punched much smaller holes in Step 2 and skipped Step 7, opting for a more natural look and lacing directly through the leather.

This one was extra complicated! We cut up two paper bracer patterns, slicing in different directions, to create the pattern for the weave. We skipped Steps 2, 7, and 8, instead adding rivets at Step 7 to keep the weave together (see Hammered Hardware, page 98) and using a wider wrist opening so that the bracer can be slipped on instead of laced. Then we wrapped the top and bottom with a thin strip of leather and sewed it down (see Hand Sewing, page 78).

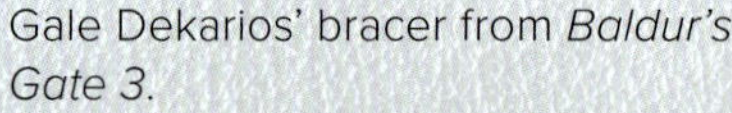

Gale Dekarios' bracer from *Baldur's Gate 3*.

If you have a gap in the bottom of your bracer, try adding a panel underneath the lacing that prevents your arm from showing!

About the AUTHORS

Wig-Wig Cosplay is an award-winning competitive cosplay duo out of Minneapolis, Minnesota. Alan and Janella, known as WigTall and wigsmall by fellow congoers, have been cosplaying together since 2012 and have enjoyed traveling the world with costumes in tow. In 2019, they were the Team USA representatives for the International Cosplay League in Madrid, Spain, where they won first place in the duo category (a first for the United States)! They are best known for their combination of leatherworking skills and entertaining performances. Alongside competing, they have been invited to conventions as guests, featured as speakers in online courses and podcasts, and printed in magazines for their work. When not wearing their "Saturday finest" on the convention floor, these two can be found assisting cosplay departments and hosting panels.

Photo by Court Matthies/cremebrulee.cos

Photo by Charlie M./O2.Supply

Growing up around leatherworkers, Janella was introduced to the craft via Old West reenactment, which became the gateway to costuming and eventually cosplaying. Every once in a while, she will step out of her craft room, usually covered in paint, and enjoy buying a new board game to add to the collection or write a chapter on her fantasy novel passion project. Rivaling her love of cosplay is her enjoyment of Japanese role-playing games (JRPGs), K-pop, and cats!

Through medieval reenactment and live-action role-playing, Alan began dabbling in leather projects and caught the crafting bug, which led him into the wonderful world of cosplay. When not tooling away the evening at the workbench, he can be found playing games—any kind: tabletop, miniatures, board, or video! Put a game in front of him, and he'll be excited to try it out (but usually after he has been asked to read the rules and teach everyone else).

And a special member of Wig-Wig Cosplay is their cat, Peppy. There from the beginning of the "Wig-Wig" name, she's the calico quality control for each mock-up tried on and leather hide rolled out on the floor.

For more content from Alan and Janella, follow their social media:

Instagram: @wigwigcosplay
Facebook: /wigwigcosplay

Cosplayer's Ultimate Guide to Eva Foam *Fabulous Cosplay Footwear* *Creative Cosplay*

Fabulous Cosplay Footwear

The Art of Extreme Wig Styling

The Art of Extreme Wig Styling

Creative Cosplay *The Art of Extreme Wig Styling* *The Cosplay Book of Ballgowns*

FanPowered PRESS

Developed with our cosplay authors, FanPowered Press evokes how C&T's authors inspire and expand crafting topics by presenting innovative methods and ideas. We hope to inspire you to jump into something new and get outside of your comfort zone!

Want more creative content? Visit us online at **ctpub.com**